Praise for Duncan Wall's

The ORDINARY *Acrobat*

"Wall's technical descriptions of what happens on a trapeze, or even of how a somersault is turned, make you look afresh at what had previously seemed obvious. And that may be the greatest trick of all."

—*The Wall Street Journal*

"Wall is a charming guide. . . . His appreciation of the circus is deepened by his understanding of its long and distinct history."

—*The New Republic*

"Blending cultural history with biography, memoir and travelogue, Wall's carefully balanced book is, in itself, a successful tightrope traverse."

—*Kirkus Reviews*

"If ever you have the urge to run away and join the circus, you can save yourself the trip and still have the thrill of it all by reading *The Ordinary Acrobat*. Duncan Wall's adventures as a novitiate in a Parisian circus school are wonderfully entertaining. A beautifully written account of life past and present under the big top."

—Eric Lax, author of *Woody Allen: A Biography*

"*The Ordinary Acrobat* is an i[...]nd historically—into the captivat[...]."

-[...]*ge:*

Culture[...]*op*

D1113463

"Wall [does] an admirable job of pursuing [...]ysteries and endlessly winding paths. . . . It isn't a conventional memoir, but the circus isn't a conventional subject, either."

—NPR

"An exquisite exposition. . . . Proving himself even more adroit verbally than physically, Wall offers a revelatory love letter to the simultaneously ancient and contemporary art of acrobatics, the circus and its denizens."
—*Library Journal*

"In this enchanting memoir sprinkled with historical anecdotes, Wall pulls the reader into the world of circus, past and present. . . . His captivating journey of discovery may lead others to consider running away to join one."
—*Publishers Weekly*

"Wall is intoxicated and obsessed with the circus. . . . It's infectious."
—Biographile

Duncan Wall

The ORDINARY Acrobat

Duncan Wall studied as a Fulbright scholar at France's École Nationale des Arts du Cirque de Rosny-sous-Bois. He was the founder and co-artistic director of the Candidatos, an acclaimed clown-theater company, and currently serves as the National Director of Circus Now, an organization dedicated to promoting contemporary circus performance and participation. He lives in Montreal, where he teaches circus history and criticism at the École Nationale de Cirque, Canada's national circus school.

The ORDINARY *Acrobat*

A Journey into the Wondrous World of the Circus, Past and Present

DUNCAN WALL

Vintage Books
A Division of Random House LLC
New York

FIRST VINTAGE BOOKS EDITION, NOVEMBER 2013

Copyright © 2013 by Duncan Wall

All rights reserved. Published in the United States by Vintage Books, a division of Random House LLC, a Penguin Random House Company, New York, and in Canada by Random House of Canada Limited, Toronto. Originally published in hardcover in the United States by Alfred A. Knopf, a division of Random House LLC, New York, in 2013.

Vintage and colophon are registered trademarks of Random House LLC

The Library of Congress has cataloged the Knopf edition as follows:
Wall, Duncan.
The ordinary acrobat : a journey into the wondrous world of the circus, past and present / Duncan Wall.
p. cm.
Includes index.
1. Wall, Duncan. 2. Acrobats—Biography. 3. Circus performers—Biography.
4. Circus—History. I. Title.
GV1811.W16A3 2013
796.47'6092—dc22
[B] 2012038250

Vintage ISBN: 978-0-307-47226-7

Author photograph © Sarah Fishbein
Book design by Cassandra J. Pappas

www.vintagebooks.com

Printed in the United States of America
10 9 8 7 6 5 4 3 2 1

To my family

For me the circus is at its best before it has been put together. It is at its best at certain moments when it comes to a point, as through a burning glass, in the activity and destiny of a single performer out of so many. One ring is always bigger than three. One rider, one aerialist is always greater than six. In short, a man has to catch the circus unawares to experience its full impact and share its gaudy dream.

—E. B. WHITE, "The Ring of Time"

Contents

The ORDINARY Acrobat

1

Circophiles

GROWING UP, I had no connection to the circus. My ancestors weren't acrobats or wire-walkers; I'm aware of no Gypsy blood.

I was born in Milwaukee, Wisconsin. My mother and father both came from the Midwest, from Ohio and Iowa, respectively. After meeting in Chicago, as a pair of corporate accountants working three floors apart, they retreated to the suburbs, first of Milwaukee, then of Saint Louis, where I received the blessing of an upper-middle-class childhood. I attended a good public high school, where I captained the soccer team and edited the yearbook. When I didn't have practice or a meeting, I liked to lie on the couch and watch *Saved by the Bell* with my sister. On the weekends, I met up with my friend Sean, and we cruised around in his Nissan. If we scored some beer or met up with some girls—well, that was a pretty big night.

And the circus? It was around, of course, but I don't remember thinking about it, or even really noticing it. I saw one show in the sports arena downtown. What sticks with me most about the experience is the atmosphere. Built in the late sixties, the arena was battered and unattractive, and I can remember walking across the enormous asphalt parking lot with my father, hand in hand, past the rows of cars and the soot-stained trucks. Inside, we climbed the concrete stairs to our seats, which peered down on the three rings from a great distance. I remember watching the show with a mixture of confusion and boredom. The overweight acrobats wore out-of-style sequins. The tigers looked sluggish and distracted. Their trainer, a stocky man dressed like Indiana Jones, snapped his whip indiscriminately.

My father clearly had a soft spot for the circus—he had insisted that we come. I didn't really understand why. I had video games with motion-capture graphics. I had blockbuster movies that filled screens as tall as my house. I had been to Space Camp and Disneyland. *That* was entertainment. The circus felt like some previous generation's idea of fun, a tradition almost, like the Pledge of Allegiance, or the sweater my parents forced me to wear to church on Sundays—something you did not because you wanted to but because that's what people had always done. The world had moved on, I felt, and left the circus behind.

And in these judgments I wasn't entirely wrong. As I later learned, I first encountered the circus at a historical low point. Founded by a British cavalier in 1768, the art, a combination of popular physical forms, had spread around the world like a virus. In less than fifty years, it infected every continent but Antarctica. During the nineteenth century, the circus was arguably the world's most popular entertainment, as popular as cinema today. Circus performers were revered as celebrities. The biggest shows were famous brands, as familiar as Disney and MTV are now.

This golden period lasted through World War II, after which, plagued by economic hardships, such as the oil crisis of 1973, and the rise in mass media, the circus fell into precipitous decline. Troupes plunged into bankruptcy. Those that survived did so by slashing costs, importing acts from abroad, and trading their tents for arenas. By the late sixties, the art was a shell of its former self. "The great days of the European circus are over," Jack C. Bottheim, a prominent member of Holland's Friends of the Circus, wrote in 1967. Even die-hard fans wondered how long it would survive. They expected the circus to limp along, scrounging by on nostalgia and manufactured pride, until the day when—like vaudeville, like pantomime, like the wandering minstrels of the Middle Ages—it would either pass quietly from the world or exist thereafter as a sort of museum entertainment, a reminder of how strange and simple the world had been.

But then, just when nobody expected it, the freefall came to a halt. During the seventies, the old circuses regained their footing. In France, a circus run by Alexis Gruss, Jr., an equestrian from one of the oldest families, was named the country's national circus. In America, Ringling Bros. and Barnum & Bailey Circus saw attendance rise by upward of 12 percent a year.

At the same time, a new type of circus emerged. I first encountered this new form while studying in Paris during college. I was enrolled in a special program for American students, and as part of our curriculum the program directors escorted us on a series of "cultural excursions," chaperoned visits to local highlights we might have missed in our rush to the newest Irish-style pub. These were tasteful visits, designed to expand our understanding of France and its culture. We saw Molière at the Comédie-Française. We went to the Louvre and the Musée d'Orsay. You can imagine, then, our surprise when the program's *directrice*, Madame Sasha, came bustling into the school's lobby one afternoon with a handful of flyers for the circus.

"The *circus*?" a girl from Ohio sneered. "Is that, like, some kind of a joke?"

Madame Sasha flashed an educator's smile. *"Non, ce n'est pas une blague."* She arranged the flyers into a neat stack on a wooden table. "But it's not a regular circus. *C'est un cirque moderne*."

I can still hear the words: *C'est un cirque moderne*. "It's a modern circus." The term intrigued me. The circus as I knew it seemed almost willfully *unmodern*, its resistance to change even part of its charm: the world changes, people change, but the circus stays the same. I took a flyer from the stack and examined it. The picture on the front was blurry and artfully composed. It was of a man in a white tank top and black pants, performing what looked like a break-dancing maneuver, his palms pressed against the floor, one leg shot out in front of him. A dozen white cubes littered the ground around him. It looked more like an advertisement for a band or a contemporary dance show than for a circus.

Curious, the following Friday I followed the directions on the flyer to Parc de la Villette, a concrete compound of museums and playgrounds at the city's northern edge. It was dusk when I arrived. An orange haze had spread across the horizon, casting an eerie glow on the autumn evening.

After picking up the flyer, I remembered an experience from several years before. I was studying in my dorm room one night, when I received a call from a friend, an actor, urging me to turn on the Bravo channel. I did, and there discovered a pair of acrobats, a buff man and an even buffer woman, both painted head to toe in silver and bathed in a shimmering aqueous light. The man held the woman above him, and he was manipulating her through a series of impossible positions—holding her above him in a handstand on his hands, balancing her inverted on his shoulders. "It's Cirque du Soleil," my friend whispered breathlessly. "It means 'Circus of the' something-or-other."

The show had been amazing, unlike anything I had ever seen, but I'd somehow forgotten about it. Remembering it now, I wondered: Was that the sort of show I was in for? Was that a *nouveau cirque*?

After ten minutes of walking, I arrived at the site. A pair of tents pushed up from the horizon. Neither looked anything like the stereotypical circus tents in my imagination. One was tall and white, and surprisingly sleek, like an enormous witch's hat designed by IKEA, with vinyl sidewalls that sloped cleanly skyward. The second was smaller but equally stylish. Nestled against the first, its flap was tied back, spilling a wash of buttery light and tango music onto the cobblestone sidewalk.

I bought a ticket and went inside, where the surprise continued. Across an open floor, black café tables alternated with red velvet couches illuminated by white Christmas lights tastefully festooned where the sidewalls met the roof. What appeared to be a photography exhibit decorated the walls, black-and-white photographs of thighs and horse haunches. I made my way to the back, where a bar was selling various artisan *tartes*, espresso, and imported beer.

I bought a Heineken and roamed around. I couldn't figure out what to make of the scene. The space reminded me of the lobby of a hip urban hotel. Where were the clamoring hordes of children? Where were the carnival barkers, the cotton candy? The crowd here was almost prototypically Parisian. There were lots of thin black ties and meticulously weathered jeans. Nobody looked younger than twenty or older than fifty. It felt like the crowd you might see at an art gallery opening. And yet we all stood chatting in a tent, on a dirt floor, waiting to see a circus.

The lights flickered. I felt a breath of air tickle the back of my neck.

"*Excusez*," a voice said behind me. A woman in a black top hat and crimson tie stood at the tent's rear entrance. She had folded back the flap and was smiling and waving us into the night, toward the other tent.

THOUGH YOU MIGHT NOT know it, there is a genre of literature known as the circus memoir. It dates back hundreds of years, covers a range of forms, and usually adheres to a number of conventions. In a good circus memoir it is customary for the author to begin with a flashback to his first childhood exposure to the art and his ensuing obsession. In *Learning to Fly*, for instance, Sam Keen waxes on about that "mythic day" when "the flying man soared into the center of my imagination." In *Ringmaster!*, Kristopher Antekeier's account of his year as a ringmaster with Ringling Bros. and Barnum & Bailey Circus, he writes, "I remember staring at the empty field that had been the site of the Clyde Beatty–Cole Brothers circus, unable to contain my sadness that it was now gone."

Since I experienced no childhood circus magic, I'll present no such vision. Still, I understand and appreciate the sentiment the authors describe—the blood rush of big feeling, the swelling sense of fantastical possibility, the awareness of your mental aperture ticking open a notch. It's almost exactly what I experienced in Paris.

How to describe the show? All of the usual acts were there: the juggler, the strongman, the acrobats. But the tone was totally different. The juggler had a Mohawk. The acrobats were unshaven and dressed in ratty black suits with the cuffs rolled up. They flipped and danced and spun and fought, like actors in a kind of physical drama. At one point a microphone emerged and one of them began singing Simon and Garfunkel's "The Sound of Silence" in a halting, screeching voice. Shortly thereafter, a juggler strutted onto the stage, juggling five oranges and reciting what sounded like poetry but turned out to be Proust. " 'Many years had elapsed during which nothing of Combray,' " he declaimed as he smashed the oranges into a pulp against his forehead.

I watched, stupefied. I was young, but I thought of myself as an educated theatergoer. I was studying theater in college. I had seen dozens of shows, including avant-garde work in New York and Chicago. But I had never seen a show like this. It was easily the most theatrical thing I had ever seen—physical, tough, intelligent. I left feeling as if I had discovered a new type of theater—a new type of art, even. Yes, it was vaguely related to Cirque du Soleil, but only distantly. There was nothing sexy about the show. The movements were part of a poetic, cohesive whole. It was visceral, real, and admirably raw.

Afterward, lingering in the lobby, watching the flushed and exhausted performers mingle with the crowd, I found myself wondering about them. Who were they? How had they created such a compelling, curious show?

When I got home that night, I researched the company on the Internet. It turned out that they weren't unique, but part of a movement, what French critics called *"nouveau cirque,"* or "new circus."* Born in the seventies, the genre had reinvented the circus by stripping the art of the codes of old. The new circuses got rid of the animals and emphasized human talents. They "theatricalized" the form by incorporating character and plot. Instead of vast arenas, they played in intimate settings—in theaters and single-ring tents.

Cirque du Soleil was the big example of the genre in America, but there were hundreds, possibly thousands, of others around the world. Paris, I learned, was a mecca for the form. In a given weekend you could see three and sometimes upward of five different shows.

Pariscope, the local entertainment guide, dedicated a separate section to circus listings: *"Le Cirque,"* sandwiched between *"Le Théâtre"* and *"La Danse."* The Parisian dailies—*Le Monde, Le Figaro, Libération*—published circus reviews.

And so I started attending other "new circuses." Some were artsy and smart like my first show. Others were more "classical," with horses and ringmasters in red riding jackets. I didn't like every show, but on the whole my fascination with the form continued to build. By March I was attending multiple shows a week. Often I waited around after the shows to chat with the performers. I came to understand that there was a world of intelligent, artistically minded young people who were passionate about the circus, who took it seriously. It was inspiring.

* Scholars have a plethora of names for the movement: the new circus, the new-style circus, the contemporary circus, the circus of creation, the other circus. I'll use "modern circus" as the blanket term for anything after 1968.

As circus historian Antony Hippisley Coxe once wrote, "The circus is a disease which it is very difficult to eradicate." The most famous cases are of course the performers. As circus folk are fond of saying, every family starts somewhere, with somebody who decides to "run away," a doctor who absconds with acrobats, a duchess who falls in love with an equestrian. But the performers aren't the only circus victims. The circus annals are full of stories of fans who had their lives seized by the art. Stuart Thayer, an insurance agent in America, retired early from his job to conduct a sort of personal circus pilgrimage, driving up and down the Eastern Seaboard, scouring local libraries for arcane circus records. Howard Tibbals, another American, built a fifty-thousand-piece scale replica of a 1920s circus in his basement, a model that included eight miniature tents, seven thousand folding chairs, and five hundred hand-carved animals.*

In America such circus addicts are known as "gawks"; in the days of the old traveling circuses they would flood to the lot at dawn to "gawk" at the circus as it unloaded from the train. The French call them *"circophiles."* What engenders such rabid dedication remains a subject of debate. Most writers allude to the art's appeal in vague, even mystical, language. William Lyon Phelps, a longtime circus lover, once referred to the "centripetal force" of the ring. In *Circus: A World History*, Rupert Croft-Cooke and Peter Cotes devote a chapter to the "cult of the circus," which they describe as "the intangible *something* that gets into your bloodstream forever and exercises an authority upon its victim that you are unwilling to part with." Of the specific theories, most attribute the art's gravity to how it functioned. In the old days, the argument goes, the traveling circuses were naturally and irresistibly exotic, living fairy tales of freaks and heroes that swooped into town one night and vanished the next. This exoticism was exaggerated by the circus families, who, subject to suspicion and often scorn, kept the world at a distance. "They are more explicitly detached than almost any other class of people," Morris Markey wrote of the families for *The New Yorker* in 1927. But the distance imbued their lives with an air of excitement. As Markey notes, the romance of their itinerant existence—"no false and shoddy thing"—made us "ache with the imprisonment of our unadventurous lives."

I mention these old reports as an indication of how much the circus

* Today the model is housed at the Ringling Estate's Tibbals Learning Center in Florida.

has changed. In Paris, I experienced little of the exotic wonder and even less of the distance. Yes, there was a scene of sorts. There was a style (bohemian chic), an age range (twenty to fifty), and even what you might call an ethos (group over self). There were names you were expected to know (Archaos, Zingaro) and ideas that prevailed (the importance of creative play). But there was nothing detached about any of it. The performers were open, even welcoming. Most of them had grown up in "regular" families, and, as adults, they lived "regular" lives. They rented apartments in Paris and drove their kids to school. For fun, they attended movies and art gallery openings. In fact, their normality was probably what attracted me most: the modern circus life was a life I recognized. What intrigued me was the combination of qualities it endowed.

By May, with my return to America approaching, my circophilia had reached a plateau. I was still going to shows, but with less regularity, and I anticipated that the fascination would end with my study abroad, that the "new circus" would be, forever after, a quirky French treat, something to look forward to if I ever came back, like the booksellers on the Seine or *pain au chocolat.* Then, one muggy afternoon, a discovery changed my plans.

PERUSING THE *PARISCOPE*, I stumbled onto a listing for a trapeze workshop. I had never swung on a trapeze, had never even considered trying, but the workshop was free and directed specifically at amateurs.

And so, the following Saturday, I caught the RER, Paris's regional train, to one of Paris's eastern suburbs. The workshop was held in an old factory, and I arrived feeling anxious. People deal with nervousness in all sorts of ways: I tend to babble, and that day I was babbling a lot. First, I babbled to the other amateurs as we wiggled into our harnesses under the shadow of a giant net. Next, I babbled to the ox of a man holding the bottom of a precariously thin wire ladder. The big man showed me how to climb the ladder and then dispatched me up to the perch, a table-sized platform bolted to the ceiling, where I babbled even more uncontrollably to the pair of startled stocky acrobats assigned to help me fly.

The acrobats were from Sweden and Portugal. I told them about my recent interest in the circus, and all the kind circus people I'd met in Paris, and how heartbroken I was to be leaving. They were nice, and nodded amicably as they prepped the bar for me, but something must have gotten lost in translation, because the acrobats missed a critical point: they somehow mistakenly understood I had flown on a trapeze before. And so, instead of strapping my harness into the safety ropes—the way they had done for every other amateur—they let me fly "open," without ropes. Obviously I should have noticed it myself, but I was too busy babbling, and it was only after I had gripped the bar, hopped off the platform, and rushed into the open air that my perilous circumstances dawned on me.

An unfortunate scene ensued. Once I realized the potential danger of my situation, my body seized into a fist, every muscle clamping simultaneously in fear. Voices sprang to life around me, voices shouting instructions. From below: *"Bouge pas! Bouge pas!"* Don't move! Don't move! From behind: "Speak English! Speak English!" In the end, the coach below and the acrobats behind managed to talk me down, but only after my swing had drifted to a stop, so that I hung, limply, ridiculously, like a dead fish on a string.

Back on the ground, my brain buzzing with unfamiliar chemicals, I paced in delirious circles. It was the single most traumatic experience of my adult life. But I had survived! And it was invigorating.

After a few minutes, I fled outside for some air. More pacing ensued, until I noticed a young woman, small and svelte, with short, spiky hair. I recognized her immediately. Before the workshop, while I had been wrestling with my harness, she had scurried up the ladder with the ease of a jungle monkey climbing a vine and breezed out over the net with pointed-toe perfection. She was obviously a professional, and she watched me now, leaning against the bike rack, with an amused curiosity, as if I were a squirrel trying to bury a nut in the sidewalk.

Propelled perhaps by the chemical cloud in my brain, I decided to talk to her. I asked where she'd learned to swing so gracefully.

"The National School," she replied.

It was the first I'd heard of the place. I asked her if it was indeed a state-subsidized circus school. She nodded, puffing on her cigarette in that cool, casual way they must teach in French kindergartens.

"*En fait*, we're all students there," she said, waving a hand in the direction of the hall.

The words seeped into my brain. The ox, the Swede, the Portuguese acrobat—they were all students at a professional circus school, on their way to becoming circus performers. I grunted in admiration, and then, for reasons I still don't entirely understand, I asked, "What about me?"

The girl looked at me skeptically. I could feel my heart thumping in my chest.

"You want to be in the circus?"

I feigned nonchalance. "Is that an option?"

She shrugged and took another long forties-film-star pull on her cigarette. "I don't see why not," she said finally. "The National School has an entrance exam. You might not get in, but there are plenty of other schools. I'm sure somebody would take you. It's not like the circus is some secret club anymore."

The rest was logistics. Back in America, I started scheming ways to return to Paris and its circus scene. That summer, with my senior year approaching, I received an e-mail from my college about the Fulbright fellowship, a government program for projects abroad. I applied with a proposal to study the contemporary circus in France, and, six months later, received word: I would be attending circus school in Paris the following fall.

Later, during my circus sojourn and afterward, people would occasionally ask me if I had run away with the circus. It never felt that way. Nothing could have felt more natural. I was young and unencumbered. I found something that inspired me and profited from an opportunity to explore it.

Which is maybe the biggest indication of just how much the circus has changed. Not only can you be born outside the circus, you don't even need to work that hard to get in. You can decide, in a capricious, curious way that it might have something to offer, and because the circus is open, because anybody can take pleasure from it, you can go explore it. As people in the business today like to say, the circus has a place for everyone.

"You know that's hilarious, right?" a friend said. My bag lay half packed on the bed. I had called to tell him about my upcoming adventure.

"Why's that?" I said.

"To be honest, I didn't even know you liked the circus."

I laughed. "Yeah, neither did I."

2

State of the Art

FOR GOING ON FORTY YEARS NOW, the government of France has funded a National School for the Circus Arts. Most people don't know this fact about France, and lots of puns spring to mind when they hear it. Americans especially enjoy it, since the circus occupies roughly the same artistic echelon in America as synchronized swimming or pot-holder-making. "How do you pick the class clown?" they frequently ask. "Boy, it must be hard to juggle all those classes!"

Not surprisingly, the attitude toward circus education is different in France. The government allocates €9 million a year to the circus, an amount equivalent to their support of the Palestinian Authority. The money is earmarked for a variety of functions—troupes, festivals, and other special events—but the largest chunk, roughly 40 percent, goes to support the National School, the crown jewel of their circus educational system and one of the most prestigious circus training grounds in the world.

As in most American universities, the curriculum at the National School takes four years to complete. The first two years occur at the École Nationale des Arts du Cirque de Rosny-sous-Bois, where I would be studying. The rest are hosted at a bigger facility, the Centre National des Arts du Cirque, located in Châlons-en-Champagne, a village ninety miles east of the capital. Technically, the schools exist as separate institutions with distinct budgets, directors, and facilities, but practically, they function as a single track, and admission is highly competitive. Each year more than three hundred circus hopefuls apply. Fifteen students are picked to attend—an acceptance rate lower than most Ivy League schools. The students come from all over the world—from Brazil, Holland, Finland, Sweden, England, Switzerland, Italy, Spain, Portugal, Argentina, Japan, Chile, Germany, the United States, China, and a dozen other countries. What attracts them varies. Many praise the unique curriculum, the renowned staff. The free tuition is a plus, as are the fringe benefits. It's not uncommon for a student to find a lifelong performance partner or even a spouse while training at the school. France also has munificent cultural policies, making it a good place to start a company after you graduate. If you want to organize a show, for instance, the government will seed you the money and the school will often provide a space to train. Being an elite institution, the National School has networking tentacles that reach across the continent and around the world. There is, so to speak, no better springboard.

Not that any of this mattered to me when I enrolled. My interest in the circus was personal—I wanted a taste of the circus life—but it was mostly intellectual. I wanted to understand how and why the art had changed, and why it had become so popular in France specifically. Although the movement was international, with companies and schools from the Arctic to Australia, the French had played an exceptional role in its development. Many of the early "new circus" companies were French, including what many consider the first, Le Cirque Bonjour, founded in 1971. In 1974, Annie Fratellini and Alexis Gruss, Jr., a pair of descendants from famous French circus families, had created the first western circus schools in Paris. Beginning in 1981, the French state even began subsidizing circus companies, the way it subsidized theater and dance companies. It initiated infrastructural support for the industry in the form of professional networks and a series of "circus poles" around the country, venues specializing in circus shows.

This attention isn't completely surprising. As I would come to find out, the French have always had an impassioned relationship with the circus. Italian filmmaker Federico Fellini once commented that Paris was "the city that made the circus an art," and, during the Belle Époque, Paris was to the circus as Vienna was to opera, or as New York was later to jazz, with elegant, aristocratic shows featuring ballerinas on horseback and acrobats in bow ties.

Still, the current enthusiasm seems unprecedented. In 2003, the year of my investigation, the country, which is slightly smaller than Texas, had more than four hundred circus companies, 85 percent of which were founded in the last twenty years. The French Federation of Circus Schools included more than 150 institutions, extending from the Alps to the English Channel. In 2002, the government even went so far as to declare a "Year of the Circus," during which the circus portion of the federal budget rose to €10.5 million, with additional aid for circus companies, schools, publications, and theaters, as well as a bevy of special events (e.g., "The Cinema Goes to the Circus," three days of circus-film projections). A headline for *Libération,* the Parisian daily, said it all: *"Vive le cirque!"*

How had the French helped spark this theatrical revolution? What place did this new form have in Europe's contemporary artistic landscape? How did the French performers perceive their work?

Such were my questions when I embarked. I thought they amounted to an artistic study—an examination of the renaissance of a theatrical form. Later I realized that my study would be as much cultural as artistic, that the circus spoke volumes about what it meant to *be* French. I didn't realize this when I landed, but there were intimations of it early on—even on my very first day.

After a night of fitful circus dreams, I reported for a morning meeting with Anny Goyer, the director of the École Nationale des Arts du Cirque de Rosny-sous-Bois. At first or even second glance, Anny hardly seemed like the sort of woman to be directing a circus school. Small and birdlike, she wore a schoolmarmish dress suit and a serious expression.

We met in her office, a cluttered room in a metallic trailer in Rosny-sous-Bois. The trailers, Anny explained as we installed ourselves, were temporary. A few years before, the school's tent, a marvel of Italian engineering and the pride of the neighborhood, had been ravaged by what some called the "storm of the century," which had blown through Paris on Christmas Eve of 1999. Since then, the school had been working to find a replacement, but the work was slow, the bureaucracy thorny. In the meantime, Anny said, classes were being held in a cultural compound across town, in a suburb called Noisiel. "If you have any trouble finding it, just ask around," she said, printing out a map.

She also printed out a copy of my classes. I was enrolled in what Anny referred to as the school's "preparatory program." It was a bit of an experiment. The goal was to prepare the students for the school's competitive entrance exam, which would take place the following spring. As such, my classes would focus on the three disciplines covered on the test: acrobatics, dance, and acting.

Anny and I had exchanged a few e-mails before my arrival. I knew the broad outline of the classes and had been excited. I imagined the experience joyfully, like some sort of summer camp for adults. But that was dreaming about the curriculum from afar. Now that I had the schedule in front of me, with the details printed in ink, I felt a surge of nervousness whip through me as the reality of my situation hit me for the first time. According to the schedule, I would be studying tumbling for three hours per day. I didn't really even know what tumbling was. Handstands? Back flips? I had never even *tried* tumbling. Down below, there was a course labeled "Trampoline." Of course, I had friends who had trampolines in high school. But I had never been on one, and even studiously avoided them for a period, after meeting a once aspiring doctor who had shattered his spine when he bounced off a trampoline at his high school graduation party.

And that wasn't the worst of it. At the bottom of the page, below the regular curriculum, there was a list of other classes, including the *Trapèze volant,* the "flying trapeze." At the sight of the words, I felt my heart kick.

"This here . . ." I gestured to the words. "I'll be doing the trapeze?"

Anny registered my hesitation. It wasn't a part of the regular curriculum, she explained. It was an adult amateur class that the school offered at night. I was of course invited, even encouraged to attend. "I know the trapeze can be scary in the beginning, but after you get the hang of it, there's really nothing better." It was, Anny added, how she'd been sucked into the circus herself.

I told her I would think about it.

Earlier I said that I sensed that the circus was accessible, and this is true. Nevertheless, looking back on this first meeting with Anny, reflecting on the sheer anxiety that the circus managed to incite in me, it occurs to me how wrapped up my feelings were in my perceptions at the time. On a purely physiological level, learning to fly on the trapeze is no great feat, at least no more complex than any number of physical activities, such as learning to swim, for example. And yet the trapeze *sounds* so much more difficult because of our mental context for the activity, because of everything the trapeze connotes—wagons bumping over country roads, clowns dozing on piles of straw, big-shouldered women waving from the backs of elephants. And, in spite of my explorations, I was still affected by those connotations. Even after my arrival in France, the art remained a magical question mark. Would I really learn to turn a back flip? Would I really fly on the trapeze? It all still seemed so impossible, not physically, but as an idea, because I romanticized that idea. It made up, as the writer Edward Hoagland once noted, part of the "furniture of [my] mind."

When we had finished chatting, Anny took me on a tour of the grounds, which, for the time being, consisted of a few metal trailers and an empty concrete slab. In the "library," a trailer cluttered with books, she assembled for me a sizable stack of contemporary circus information—brochures, newspaper articles, the school's student guide.

Back at the main trailer, Frédéric Leguay, the school's programming director, was waiting. Like Anny, he had a professional, almost professorial air, with dark hair, stylish horn-rimmed glasses, and a black V-neck sweater.

Reading the look on my face, perhaps, he asked me how I was feeling.

My French had declined with my nerves, and so I decided not to go into details, but instead gestured to the packet of information that Anny had given me and commented on the impressive amount of circus scholarship in France.

"Ah bon?" Frédéric replied. "It's different in America?"

I nodded. "Yeah, we're a little behind. All anyone talks about in America is Cirque du Soleil."

Immediately I saw Frédéric wince. He shot a look to Anny, who had raised herself on her toes, like a cat bristling under attack.

"Attention!" she said, waving a pedagogical finger. "Cirque du Soleil is fine, but that's not at all what we do here."

"It's not?" I said.

She shook her head adamantly. "What we do, it's not just *divertissement*"—not just entertainment. "It's . . ." She hesitated.

"Art?" Frédéric suggested.

Anny smiled. *"Exactement!"*

I promised to keep that in mind.

3

Ring

AT SOME POINT during my first week I noticed that Paris is shaped like a circus ring. Inside is *le centre ville,* the Paris of postcards, with its monuments and warrens of cobbled streets. Outside is *la banlieue,* the suburbs, gazing into the city with curiosity and sometimes envy. From my apartment in the center I made the transition almost daily to the school in the suburbs—inside the ring and out.

My days started at seven, with a hot shower, followed by a breakfast and a stretch on my shag rug in the sun. I tried to be out the door by nine. Paris at nine feels like New York at seven—dim, sluggish, and serene. It was autumn, and though the air had turned cold, the locals still huddled on the café terraces, smoking and sipping espressos from porcelain cups. I took my own espresso at a little café called L'Annex, a quaint, one-room place run by a jovial Moroccan named Omar.

Omar was fascinated by the circus. He had seen his first show as a boy, when a group of bear-toting Russians had pitched a tent in his mountain town. They had stayed a single night, almost forty years ago, but the troupe had so marked Omar, so defined the circus in his head, that he talked about the experience like it was yesterday, with a jovial look, as if he was describing his first kiss. Needless to say, Omar loved that I was in circus school. "So how are my lions today?" he would say, leaning his elbow on the corner of his bar. "Are they being fed?"

I would come to find out that this kind of thing wasn't uncommon. In fact, one of the first noteworthy aspects of my time in France was witnessing the effect the circus had on other people. Everybody had a reaction. They almost always smiled and asked me to repeat myself ("The circus?"). Often they would launch into stories of their own experiences, even if those experiences were only tangentially related. In a bar on Rue Oberkampf, I met a Spanish woman who had trained as an equestrian as a girl and felt the need to educate me on the finer points of horsemanship. My neighbor, a jolly father who worked at some sort of insurance company, told me about a friend of his from college who kept a cheetah on a leash. ("He used to bring the cheetah into restaurants. The cat would curl up under the table.")

Still, Omar was a particular case. For months, I tried explaining that the circus had changed, that my courses didn't include animal husbandry, but he couldn't resist making the same joke every morning. "So how are my lions today? Are they being fed?" It was as if the magical myth in his head was more real, more powerful, than whatever reality I had to offer.

From Omar's, I caught the RER, Paris's regional train, east to Noisiel, a suburb forty minutes outside of the city. As Anny had said, the classes were being held in a cultural compound called the Ferme du Buisson. In a former life, the site, which consisted of several large buildings surrounded by a high brick wall, had served as a chocolate factory, and it retained an industrial feel. You entered the compound through an enormous iron gate. The buildings themselves were imposing and windowless. Most had been converted into cultural venues, including a theater and a cinema, but the school occupied what had once been the factory's main floor, a cavernous hall affectionately known as the Grande Halle, or the Great Hall.

Regal name notwithstanding, there was nothing special about the space. The walls were exposed brick. The floor was concrete, covered by a thin industrial carpet. Gymnastic equipment littered the ground, including mats of various shapes and sizes and a pair of Olympic-caliber trampolines. I even remember feeling a wash of disappointment when I saw the facility for the first time. As part of my pre-arrival fantasies, I had imagined the school as an eccentric, jubilant place, Willy Wonka's factory crossed with an Olympic training center. Instead it looked like a boxing hall or a prison yard. The steel bars were rusted on the weight bench, the pads worn smooth. The spring-loaded floor was a narrow runway, a set of pads bolted onto squeaky springs.

And yet, as I discovered that first week, my fantasies weren't entirely out of line, either. There was a worn intimacy to the hall that felt natural, authentic to the work being done there. On busy days, the place crackled with an energy that I had never experienced. Heaving open the hall's rusted steel door one morning that first week, I found myself facing a scene of almost clichéd circus action. In front of me, a pair of women stood next to each other on their hands, gossiping. Nearby, a pair of jugglers were whipping around a rainbow of clubs, while two more acrobats—shirtless and muscular—thundered down the runway. Loud, accordion-rich music blared from a weathered boom box near the door.

I stood at the threshold for a moment and watched the scene. I was reminded of "The Ring of Time," an essay by E. B. White, the great *New Yorker* writer. In the essay, White recounts his experience visiting a circus, where he observed a young female equestrian in training. "For me," White writes, inspired by the girl, "the circus is at its best before it has been put together. . . . Under the bright lights of the finished show, a performer need only reflect the electric candle power that is directed upon him; but in the dark and dirty old training rings and in the makeshift cages, whatever light is generated, whatever excitement, whatever beauty, must come from original sources—from internal fires of professional hunger and delight, from the exuberance and gravity of youth. It is the difference between planetary light and the combustion of stars."

I had only vaguely understood what White had meant. Now, absorbing the scene, I felt that I knew better, and I felt lucky to have discovered it.

I ARRIVED IN PARIS with vague hopes of being thought of as a student rather than a scholar, a circus hopeful like the others in my program. If asked, I would of course tell the truth, but I honestly thought it wouldn't come up. Although I wasn't an acrobat, I was reasonably athletic—I had excelled at sports as a kid and done some rock-climbing in college. And it was, after all, a "preparatory" program. It would take me less than a class to figure out how hopelessly naïve I was.

Arriving to class early, I spent a few minutes milling around with the other students, making small talk. There were only three of them: Maud, Fanny, and Boris. All were French, all about twenty or so. None were particularly impressive physically. Fanny might have stepped out of a Woodstock poster. Her hair was knotted into dreadlocks, and she wore a ragged wool sweater and a pair of cutoff sweatpants, both of which looked voluminous on her tiny frame. Only slightly taller and thinner, Maud flaunted a tongue ring and a panoply of ear piercings. Boris had broad shoulders and a chiseled jaw, but even he didn't seem particularly athletic, more like a soldier than an acrobat. In my white Adidas T-shirt and black track pants, I was feeling confident.

After a few minutes, Luc, our paunchy acrobatics professor, arrived. He introduced himself and announced our goal for the day: we would begin with a "reference test," a simulation of the school's entrance exam, to gauge our progress over the year. But first, he said, we should take a few minutes to stretch before we got started.

Whereupon I hit my first snag. As I lay there on the ground, arms and legs pitched to the side, the hall lights sparking in my eyes, it occurred to me that I had no idea how an acrobat might stretch. My primary sport while growing up had been soccer, and soccer players don't worry much about their arms or their necks.

As a temporary solution, I imagined a relief pitcher stretching in a bullpen. I waggled my arm like a dead fish. I pulled my biceps across my chest and gave my arm a good tug. When I had extinguished this line of possibility, I stole a glance over at my cohorts for inspiration. All three of them were gyrating vigorously on the ground, as if engaged in a group Pilates class.

Maud was bouncing her nose toward her knees. Boris had rolled over backward, as if trying to catch a whiff of his crotch, and was alternately popping his legs skyward, then lowering them and squeezing his thighs against his chest. Nearest to me, Fanny lay sprawled on her back, sweeping her legs confidently from side to side—right over left, left over right. The cuff of her pants made a percussive swishing against the carpet. *Swish, swish. Swish, swish.*

I decided to give it a shot. Unfolding, as if to make a snow angel, I opened my arms and legs as wide as I could, gave a sigh to expel the air from my lungs, and twisted swiftly at the waist, so that my right leg swept across my left.

Immediately, a series of deeply unhealthy cracking sounds cascaded up my spine—*pop, pop, pop, pop, pop!* I had never heard my body make such sounds before. Out of the corner of my eye, I saw Fanny lift her head off the carpet. She eyed me, concerned. "Was that your body?"

I looked at her blankly and shrugged as if I didn't know what she was talking about. She scrutinized me and then went back to sweeping her legs. I rolled over for some more arm stretches.

It was my first sense that I was out of my league. It would only get worse.

"All right, who wants to go first?"

Stretching complete, Luc had summoned us to the spring-loaded runway, where he lounged on a black cube, a clipboard on his knee. Our "reference test," he had explained, would consist of a series of acrobatic movements, from basic to difficult. We would have three shots at each. Luc would score each movement: 0 was for not attempting, 5 for perfect. We would start with a basic somersault. "C'mon," he coaxed again, "somebody has to start." Maud emerged from our pack.

I had chatted a bit with her before class. She was dainty, with blond hair styled in a pixie cut, a button nose, and green eyes that sparked energetically. She seemed kind and a bit shy. Recounting her experience working as a mascot at Disneyland Paris, she had rolled her eyes, covered her mouth, and laughed an endearing, airy laugh.

But as Maud assumed her position at the head of the runway, there was a demonstrable shift in her demeanor. While Luc repeated the instructions—three somersaults per pass—she bounced on her toes and jiggled her arms like a sprinter prepping to settle into the blocks. Gone was tender Maud, the Disneyland Daisy. In her stead was someone darker and fiercer. Toeing the line, she gave a soldierly nod and exhaled sharply, almost snorting. Then she sprang.

It was a spring to behold. With her chin tucked, her toes pointed, and her whole frame taut, Maud arched through the air. Curling just before she hit the ground, she rolled and emerged on her feet, finishing with a little hop, her hands in the air. She paused only momentarily before pouncing again through a second somersault, then a third, each as flawless as the first, like a porpoise cutting waves.

I felt myself shudder. This wasn't rumpus room; it was Romanian. In the course of her young life, Maud had probably performed hundreds if not thousands of somersaults. To calm myself, I looked to the other students. They seemed unimpressed. Boris had bent over for some toe touches. Fanny was unraveling a loose seam on her sweatpants.

"Next!" called Luc sluggishly.

Over the last forty years, circus education has exploded in France. Today there are more than 150 circus institutions sprinkled around the country, from the Alps to the Mediterranean. Unofficially, the schools have structured themselves into an informal pyramid, like the system for athletics in America. At the bottom are the recreational schools, open to kids and amateur adults interested in practicing the circus for fitness or fun. Next are the circus high schools, where the students study academics in the morning and circus in the afternoon. One level up from these are also preparatory programs, which serve as feeder institutions for the professional curriculum at the National School, the aspiration of every young acrobat.

Practically, this pyramid means that a student who enrolls in a preparatory program comes equipped with a tool kit of circus experience. Most have been studying the circus for years, sometimes every day. The students in my program were no exception. As Luc ticked down his chart of moves—cartwheels, handstands, back handsprings—I watched in awe and horror as they performed each with technical proficiency. I didn't even attempt most of the moves, afraid of hurting myself. The moves I did attempt often ended in embarrassment. Trying to kick into a handstand, I ended up bucking like a mule. For the tests of flexibility, Luc told us to do the splits and then measured the distance between our hips and the ground. For the others, it was inches. For me it was a foot.

It was the first in a long series of lessons about skill and physical capability. Before coming to the school, I had assumed that my athletic ability would be transferable, that people who excel at one sport—soccer, in my case—excel at others. But acrobatics is in a different league. There's no analogue in everyday life. It's a whole-body activity that requires coordination, flexibility, strength, agility, and endurance. It engages different muscle groups and different mental capacities.

It's also maddeningly precise. Before starting my training, for example, I assumed that I knew how to do a handstand. From a standing position, I thought, you pitch onto your hands, arch your back, and let your feet dangle over your head, so that your body looks like a question mark. This was how I had seen people handstand my whole life, on playgrounds and beaches and in photographs (e.g., Robert Doisneau's *Les Frères*). And from a practical perspective, the technique made sense: arching your back widens your center of gravity, which makes your handstand easier to hold.

Unfortunately, such practicalities mattered little in the circus:

"What is *that*?"

I had kicked up into my image of a handstand—back arched, legs dangling above my head—when Luc's voice came booming across the hall. I levered down and found him glaring at me across a pile of mats, scolding me with a look of disappointment and disgust, like I was a dog who had messed his carpet.

He shook his Muppet hair. *"C'est pas bon, ça."* That's no good. "That's not how it works here."

A circus handstand, I learned, isn't flimsy; it's solid—an exclamation point, not a question mark. It looks like a tower of muscle, or as another instructor of mine said, "a human bar." Aesthetically, a straight handstand looks better. The lines are clean. The performer projects control, a holy circus quality. It's also better for your body, because the position puts less pressure on the spine. And once you get the hang of it, it's easier to hold. By bolting your body over a single point, you eliminate all the "searching" for balance, all the tips and sways.

Unfortunately, you have to get the hang of it first. And in my case, I would have to learn every move from scratch, even the basics, which took time because the patterns were so ingrained. I learned this working on my somersault.

Properly executed—as by Maud—a somersault is smooth and basically silent. Diving into the move, you curl your back in such a way that your entire spine, from your shoulders to your tailbone, makes constant, rolling contact with the ground. But of course this is easier said than done. Even on a mat, I found it intimidating to dive headfirst. Instead of curling my body, I would instinctually bow at the waist, converting my body into a giant L. Frozen in this position, I would hit the ground at the wrong angle, an error that registered in a noise, a *clunk*—or more precisely, a *clunk, clunk,* one for the back, one for the butt.

All week long, the coaches and the other students tried to rid me of the habit. Maud suggested I focus on tucking my chin to my chest. My Polish tumbling coach, Ryszard (pronounced "Richard," or "Ree-shard" in French), told me to imagine getting absorbed by the mat. "When you roll," he said, "you think neck into mat. All the way through. Neck and back." (Ryszard's French was a work in progress.)

Boris gave the most logical advice.

"A lot of times the problem is something you wouldn't normally think of," he said. We stood facing the spring-loaded floor. Classes had ended for the day, and the Great Hall was atypically quiet. Only a lone juggler worked near the weight bench, popping three clubs into the air rhythmically.

Boris came and stood next to me. "Here, let's try something." He had a naturally professorial air. He had studied trapeze and judo for years, and, in addition to his circus classes, was working on a degree in philosophy. "When you dive, instead of thinking about your body, focus on your arms." He brushed up the sleeves of his sweater and extended his muscular arms in front of him. "In the air, imagine yourself reaching for the mat. Think of your arms as shock absorbers. Like this." He took a preparatory breath and pounced, elongating himself in the air, curling quietly through his roll. "You see what I mean?" he said, back on his feet. "Really think about *reaching* for the ground."

I nodded vaguely. I could see how it might work. Reaching would automatically lengthen the body, which might keep me from buckling at the waist. It also ensured that the move "traveled," another indication of good form.

I gave it a shot. Envisioning Boris's own roll—the dive, the tuck—I pounced, stretching for the ground.

Clunk, clunk.

At the other end of the runway Boris looked confused. "Did you do what I told you?"

I walked back toward him. "I tried to. I mean, I really reached."

He shuffled his feet. "Okay, try again."

I took my place at the head of the runway. I prepped. I rolled.

Clunk, clunk.

Boris winced. He rubbed a hand against his stubbled jaw. "You know, I might not be qualified to help here."

Naturally, this was all pretty humbling, even dispiriting. Waking, dressing, commuting, all with the certain knowledge that I would spend the next three hours falling on my ass. The experience was physically punishing in a way I had never experienced. I was sore in muscles I didn't know I had. By the end of the week, a permanent scab had formed on my tailbone.

But there was also something redeeming about the effort. It was, after all, why I had come: to get a glimpse of the incalculable amount of effort, embarrassment, and pain behind the seemingly effortless skills. And, in an odd way, I even enjoyed it. The first week felt like an initiation. I felt as though I was learning the circus rudiments, analogous to the knife skills—the paring, the dicing, the chopping—that chefs master in their first week of cooking school. I had the sense I was engaging my body—my joints, my muscles, my core—in a new and complete way. At night I slept like a dead man.

By the end of the week, my sense of the circus's peculiarity—that exotic feeling I had felt in Anny's office—had already started to fade. I came to recognize the school's familiar combination of smells: the sharp brine of sweat, the pungent smoke of hand-rolled cigarettes, the damp musk of the carpet. I came to know its sounds: the rusty squeak of the trampoline springs, the repetitive drone of jugglers hammering silicone balls against the concrete. Everything seemed already like routine, as if I had been part of the world for years.

And then, every so often, the feeling would come roaring back, that old sense of wonder, of the circus as something grand. I remember feeling this strongly once in the middle of the year. Arriving at the Great Hall, I discovered the trapeze rigging had been strung across the space. High above, the students took turns springing off the platform, throwing tricks in the void.

Above all, the whole scene struck me as fascinating and improbable—this collection of government-sponsored acrobats in an unmarked hall in the suburbs of Paris. I don't know how long I watched, until a voice pulled me out of my reverie.

"You know . . ." Gabby, my trampoline coach, said with a wry smile. "It's possible to watch with your mouth closed."

4

Art School

ON MY DESK IN PARIS was a black-and-white picture. In the foreground was a man with a black mustache and a bow tie. In his hand was his infant son, the boy standing on the man's palm. In the background other performers, the man's family, presumably, watch the scene, smiling and clapping. Behind them you can see a line of trailers and a tent.

If you know one thing about circus history, it's likely this: the circus was a family affair. For centuries, families owned the biggest circuses (the Knie Circus, the Ringling Brothers Circus, Circus Krone). They comprised most of the acts. Each had a specialty, a circus skill they passed down through the generations like a gift. For the Ravels, it was wire-walking; for the Franconis, horsemanship. "They don't force their children to join," observed a reporter for *The New York Times* in 1903. "The urge comes almost by instinct. They see their mothers riding or their fathers tumbling and immediately want to do it themselves."

Of course, the circus wasn't the only business to function this way. For millennia, most professions worked according to the family model—carpenters raising carpenters, preachers raising preachers. What made the circus unique is how long the model persisted. During the eighteenth and nineteenth centuries, well after the rise of public education, circus performers continued to educate their children themselves. Being itinerant, circus parents found that it wasn't practical for them to enroll their children in stable schools. The system had technical advantages as well. Over time, each family developed an encyclopedia of practical arcana, what essayist Edward Hoagland once called "a special whirlwind momentum and glory, the craft of a lifetime piled on the craft of previous lifetimes." Circus children, or *enfants de la balle*, as the French call them, received this knowledge from a young age, from birth, basically. "I knew more about timing when I was less than a year old than I did about walking," trapezist Alfredo Codona once noted in *The Saturday Evening Post*. They didn't just learn their skills, they *lived* them, an intuitive experience that translated into astonishing ability. During the eighteenth and nineteenth centuries, the majority of the great international circus stars hailed from circus families. Codona, son of a Mexican circus owner, was celebrated by *Life* magazine as the "Nijinsky of the circus." His wife, Lillian Leitzel, the daughter of a Czech acrobat, starred for Ringling Bros. and Barnum & Bailey, the biggest circus in the world. Circus children so dominated the circus landscape that it was even presumed—to some extent correctly—that only those born into the business could compete.

The family system defined the circus for centuries. But while it provided the source for much of the circus's strength and allure, it also had a fundamental flaw. Ruled by families, the circus was what physicists call a closed system. Although the troupes traveled widely, they remained almost totally isolated from the outside world. On tour, circus families stuck to a consistent rhythm: arrive, set up, perform the matinee, relax for a few hours, perform the evening show, move on. Fraternization with the outside world was permitted, but only to a certain point. "[They live] in a world that is half childlike and half unreal, full of amazing simplicities," Morris Markey wrote for *The New Yorker* in 1927. Some families even practiced a kind of scorn for the outside world. They swindled locals with abandon, fought them in "clems," referred to them by pejorative nicknames—gillys, towners, and rubes. "The families held the world at arm's length for centuries," Steve Gossard, a trapeze historian, told me. "They wanted people's money, but would refer to them as 'lot lice.' "

To be fair, much of this was defensive, a natural reaction to the mistreatment circuses were forced to suffer on the road. But the families also participated in their detachment, and over time it had a deleterious effect. Beholden to tradition, each generation mindlessly duplicated the work of the last. "It would never occur to them to make fun of the gaudy clothes they wear . . . or the prankish things they do for the world's amusement," Markey wrote. In the early twentieth century, a kind of artistic bubble enveloped the form. Technical ability continued to rise, but the art as a whole stagnated. A cheap uniformity ensued. Every show had the same elements: clowns, acrobats, jugglers, animal trainers. Even the details were identical, and to an astonishing degree. In every circus around the world, regardless of size or location, the rings were thirteen meters in diameter. An act lasted five to seven minutes. Ringmasters wore red coats and riding boots. Clowns had red noses. These weren't mere choices; they composed what circus scholars call the "codes" of the form. "You didn't go to *a* circus," French circus writer Jean-Michel Guy once pointed out, "you went to *the* circus."

Of course, some people like these details, and like to claim that the almost aristocratic dedication to tradition is vital to the circus's whimsical charm. The circus, they say, provides the comfort of stability: in our fast-paced, ever-changing world, it's reassuring to know that the circus you shared with your mother will be the circus you share with your son.

But it's also totally bizarre. As a point of contrast, imagine if all music was classical. You could listen to Beethoven or Bach but no Beatles. Or what if the only dance that existed was ballet? This would feel silly and confined. And yet with the circus, almost nobody felt this way. People just took the stasis for granted.

THE STORY OF HOW the circus finally extracted itself from this creative hole is, in large part, the story of the development of circus education. It begins in Russia.

In 1919, Anatoly Vasilyevich Lunacharsky, the newly appointed

People's Minister of Education, summoned to Moscow the key players in Russia's circus industry, including administrators, intellectuals, writers, directors, and performers of various acts. Two years before, the Revolution had swept through Russia. Now the task was to discuss how the new Communist state would handle the art.

It wasn't a straightforward issue. Prior to the Revolution, Russia had known a prosperous circus tradition. As early as 1793, Charles Hughes, a British equestrian and one of the original circus mavens, had quit England to set up shop in the court of Catherine the Great, as her horse trainer. During the nineteenth century, numerous foreign circuses had toured the Russian countryside, and a few had even set up permanent shop in the bigger cities, including Alessandro Guerra, who in 1845 established in Saint Petersburg Russia's first circus building, a heated wooden structure with a Grecian-style pediment and a portico at the entrance. With the arrival of the Communists, however, Russia's circus industry had collapsed. Fearful of being subsumed by the state, most of the families, who were foreign, had fled abroad. If the Soviets wished to continue the tradition, they would have to create a new circus infrastructure from scratch.

Lunacharsky's committee met for two weeks. The debate was surprisingly contentious. Some insisted that the circus was a distraction from public progress and so should be left to die. "It has no place in our society," argued one offended party. "We are building a world free of such depraved exploitation." Others, including Lunacharsky, who was backed by Lenin, strongly disagreed. Rather than abandoning the circus, they argued, the state should embrace and elevate the art. "Our primary task must be to wrest the circus away from the opportunists who play to the baser tastes of the public," Lunacharsky declared during the meetings. The circus, he said, should serve as "an academy of physical beauty and merriment."*

In the end, thanks largely to Lunacharsky's support, the notion of a developed circus prevailed. On August 26, 1919, Lenin signed the decision into law. Over the next decade, the circus in Russia would be transformed. According to the committee's recommendation, all of the circuses were brought under the operation of a single governing body.

* Marx generally approved of the circus. "On seeing a fearless acrobat in bright costume," he once wrote, "we forget about ourselves, feeling that we have somehow risen above ourselves and reached the level of universal strength."

To encourage innovation, the state invited revered artists from other disciplines, including theater director Constantin Stanislavski and poet Vladimir Mayakovsky, to create experimental circus shows. In circus "labs" around the country, artists and scientists developed new circus methods and equipment. Vladimir Durov, a celebrated clown, established "Durov's Corner," a workshop specializing in the scientific study of animal-training techniques. The famous Soviet corps of engineers invented the Russian bar, a flexible balance beam, and the Russian swing, a giant acrobat-propelling swing. As circus historian David Lewis Hammarstrom notes in his excellent *Circus Rings Around Russia*, "Never had tanbark entertainment undergone such thorough analysis, nor received such careful attention."

But the Soviets also faced a peculiar predicament. When the foreign circus owners had fled, they had taken most of their performers with them. The Soviet circus industry was brimming with big ideas, but had nobody with the technique to execute them.

To remedy the problem, the state established the State College of Circus and Variety Arts in Moscow.* Founded in 1927, the school was the first national circus school in the world, and the first large-scale attempt at circus education. Based largely on Russia's famous ballet schools, the program took an interdisciplinary approach to education. The curriculum, which lasted between four and seven years, addressed artistic as well as technical disciplines. Older students took ballet for line and philosophy for inspiration. Younger pupils studied physics, math, and chemistry to develop their intellects.

In the beginning, the school was perceived, by those in the government and even more so by those outside, as a kind of experiment. Circus families claimed it would never work, that acrobatic education had to start early and could not be formalized. The results told a different story. In 1927, the year of the school's creation, 90 percent of all circus performers in Russia came from circus families; by the sixties, that number had plummeted to just 20 percent. By the fifties, upwards of three thousand students were applying annually to fill the school's eighty spots. The Soviet circus—artful, refined, and stocked with circus school graduates—became the envy of the world. When the Moscow Circus

* The official name changes regularly; people in the business call it the Moscow Circus School.

first toured to America in the fifties, *The Wall Street Journal* called it "the most lively, talented, and attractive troupe in the history of the circus."

Today the Moscow School is considered the most successful circus school in history and a fundamental step in the development of an artful circus. It opened the circus to the outside world and provided a model. Other circus schools soon followed. Because of the Iron Curtain, many of the first were Communist. Romania, East Germany, Bulgaria, Hungary, and Cuba all created professional circus programs. In 1974, the model came west. Inspired by the Moscow school, Alexis Gruss, Jr., and Annie Fratellini teamed up with Silvia Monfort and Pierre Étaix, respectively, to create a pair of circus schools in Paris. As happened in Moscow, the Western schools touched a nerve. When Fratellini and Étaix opened their doors, they expected a few dozen students; more than six hundred applied. Circus education spread. In 1977, Paul Binder and Michael Christensen, two former Fratellini students, established the New York School for Circus Arts in a studio on Spring Street. In 1981, Guy Caron, a Canadian graduate of the Budapest Circus School, teamed up with gymnast Pierre Leclerc to establish the École Nationale de Cirque in Montreal, based on the Russian model, which Caron had investigated in Hungary.

The Soviets reinvented the circus. But there was something artistically insidious at the core of their endeavor. The Soviet performers were paragons of craft but in the service of the state. In school, they were forced to study Lenin and Marx. As professionals, the state hired them, placed them in specific jobs, and told them when to retire. The system was a vast machine, with room for creative license, but only insofar as it complied with the specific state directives. A performer who challenged official doctrine or strayed too far outside the box artistically risked repercussions. "My coaches told me that I was too minimalist, too progressive," Viktor Kee, a Ukrainian star with Cirque du Soleil, once told me. "They said I'd never work in a circus."

ONE AFTERNOON EARLY in the year, I sat down with Frédéric Leguay, the director of programming at the National School, to talk about the school's core curriculum.

As a prep student, my classes mirrored the Russian model—a combination of acrobatics, dance, and acting, with an emphasis on technical prowess. As I discovered the first week, however, the school's full-time curriculum was more ambitious. In addition to the core disciplines and the circus specialty of their choice (e.g., juggling), the students studied a bevy of other subjects. Some were academic, like the English language and French literature. Others were artistic. Every student was required to learn how to play a musical instrument, for example. There were also mandatory workshops, hosted by visiting teachers. One afternoon I found the students spread across the Marley floor of the tent in the courtyard, hunched over colorful constructions of paper and ribbon; a sculptor—a thin man in an argyle scarf—offered suggestions. A few months later, I arrived in a classroom to find an easel covered in drawings of stick figures doing flips, with vectors denoting the rotations. Back in the Great Hall, I asked Tiriac, a first-year, what the students had been doing. He looked up from his stretching and replied with a word: "Physics."

The general French term for the educational model was *polyvalence,* which roughly translates as "multidisciplinary." The term was a buzzword in French circus, one of the distinguishing foundational ideas of the school. Created by the French government in 1986, the Centre National des Arts du Cirque in Châlons-en-Champagne was charged with the task of not only educating the students but also resurrecting the circus in France.* In 1991, to further this effort, the school recruited Bernard Turin, head of the French Federation of Circus Schools, to serve as its director. A sculptor by trade, Turin added new artistic classes and workshops taught by contemporary artists. "Bernard gave the school a vision," Anny Goyer told me.

I went to Frédéric to understand how this vision worked. I could understand how a potential circus performer could benefit from learning to play an instrument. But why biology? Why architecture? What did all this superfluous knowledge have to do with making strong *circus*?

Frédéric and I met in his office at the Great Hall, a former maid's quarters at the top of a turret-like stairwell. Like Anny, he had a formal, even phlegmatic, demeanor, and he nodded skeptically when I suggested we play a little game: I had brought a legal pad with a list of the classes; I would say the name of the class, and he would describe its purpose. I started with an easy one.

"Circus History," I said.

* In the beginning there was just one school. The school in Rosny-sous-Bois (often called "Rosny") spun off from Châlons later.

Frédéric repeated the words, as if he were in a spelling bee. "Circus History. Well, I'd say history's always important. We're trying to create artists, and artists need an intellectual grounding for their work. Can you imagine a young painter who never studied Rembrandt? Or a pianist who'd never heard of Chopin? Part of being a serious artist is to have a context, to have references."

I read the next name from my list. "Mathematics."

Frédéric lit his cigarette. Smoke curled up to the skylight above us. "Mathematics. That's more complicated. We believe it helps the students understand the physical principles of their disciplines—how they move, what forces are acting on them." He added that math could also come in handy if a performer wanted to develop a new act. "You might need to design a new structure," he said. "We want the students to have the skills to execute their visions."

And on we went. Sculpting gave the students a sense of space. Music gave them rhythm. English was the language of the world, important for touring and communicating with the press. Anatomy instilled a knowledge of the body, the performer's tool of the trade.

As we checked through the list, it occurred to me that, in one sense, Frédéric's responses were all quite practical. As he pointed out, one of the school's missions was to create performers who could create their own companies, a demanding, multifaceted challenge. "Running your own circus company is basically running your own business," he said. "You have to do everything yourself, from raising funds to putting up a tent."

But there was also a deeper principle behind the school's diversity, which became more evident as he went on. As I noted before, a primary factor in the circus's decline was a lack of innovation. Cut off from society, circus families had a hard time keeping pace with cultural changes, especially as developments in technology accelerated the world. The goal of the National School was to guarantee that this would never happen again. It trained the students to *create* new work, not just *perform* work, in order to keep the circus evolving. This might sound simple, but in reality it's a hugely complicated task, especially in an art in which there was no precedent for creative thinking, and no direct models.

And so the school bombarded the students with information from other sources—from theater, dance, sculpting, math, science. It also introduced them to as much high-quality contemporary art as possible.

During my year at the school, the students took field trips to the Louvre, the Musée d'Orsay, and the École des Beaux-arts. Every month, the school popped for tickets to a theater or dance show. Occasionally the shows were what you'd expect from an academic excursion (e.g., Molière at the Comédie-Française). More often, they were impressively avant-garde, and meant to challenge in some fundamental way the reigning conception of what was possible on a stage. On a drizzly night in October, for example, I accompanied the students on a trip to Théâtre de la Ville, a premier Parisian modern dance venue, for a show by Belgian choreographer Wim Vandekeybus. As I would find out later, Vandekeybus was a staple of the European avant-garde, known for what *The New York Times* referred to as a "tough, brutal, playful" style, and on this night his style was in full effect. The curtain rose on a woman simulating fellatio on an unconscious man. Later, a dancer half-succeeded in sodomizing himself with a peeled banana. In the lobby afterward, surrounded by a buzzing crowd of students, I mentioned to Frédéric that the progressive content of the show surprised me. He seemed bemused. "We want them to see the best," he replied.

Of course, when you look at it from a distance, there's nothing terribly profound about any of this. The school's method is not terribly complex. It teaches the kids a variety of skills, and encourages them to bring those skills to bear on a particular form.

But, then again, who else does this? Where else can you receive such a panoply of experience? Where can you learn to act, flip, speak French, play an accordion, and paint a watercolor, all in one year? It might be the most interdisciplinary education on the planet, and it's a *circus school,* of all places. It's a physical education, where the intellectual reigns. This notion was introduced the first week, and drilled into me the second, when I reported for a course called Analyse du Spectacle.

IN THE NATIONAL SCHOOL CURRICULUM, Analyse du Spectacle, or Circus Theory, was a relatively new addition. In the 1980s, during the school's early years, there had been no call for such a class, because, broadly speaking, there had been no theory of the circus. Writers covered the subject—enough to fill a circus library in Baraboo, Wisconsin—but most of the work was factual or narrative, memoirs and histories and fiction, rather than analytical. Only one man, an anthropologist named Paul Bouissac, could have rightfully printed "circus theorist" on his business card, but he was something of an outsider, since he worked in Canada, a backwater for circus at the time, and since he wrote sentences like "Although jugglers and magicians are frequently praised for the quickness of their movements and, more particularly, for the precision and efficiency of their hand techniques, the meaning of these movements and the fascination they produce can be accounted for only by relating them to uses of hands that occur in everyday life."

In the eighties, the academic sands shifted. As the circus drifted from the carnival to the cultural, critical theory was dragged along. Dissertations were written, critical niches staked. "It was natural but also sort of a shock," Gwénola David, an arts critic for *Libération* during those years, told me. Until then, the circus was seen as a shallow display of prowess, nothing more. "I'd attended circuses my whole life," David said, "but I'd never thought of studying one."

Observing this aesthetic sea-change, the French National School decided to hire a resident theorist of its own, someone to stay abreast of the intellectual developments in the field. They put the feelers out in the circus community, and one name kept coming up: Jean-Michel Guy. In the circus world, Guy was something of a ubiquity, an older, taller Truman Capote. At most show openings, he could be found leaning on the bar in his trademark trench coat and fedora, with a leather valise slung over his shoulder, the modern incarnation of the veteran newspaperman. Like Gwénola David, he had started out as a theater critic, then drifted to the circus as the modern version emerged. When I met him, he was also working for the Ministry of Culture as an *ingénieur de recherche*, a job that required him to compile reports about the modern circus landscape. For one such report, he attended more than two hundred shows in a single year. In practical terms, he was possibly the most modern-circus-aware person on the planet, and when the National School called to offer him the job, he accepted on the spot.

On the first day of class, I arrived early to find him arranging himself at the head of the classroom. He had a narrow, stubbled face and tousled salt-and-pepper hair that flopped messily over his ears. A worn leather valise lay open on the table.

Once the students had settled into their seats, he pulled a videotape from his valise and slipped it into the combination TV/VCR. "I want you to take notes," he said, as the screen flickered to life. "What do you see? What do you think?"

The tape was of a hand-balancing routine, or what the French call a *main-à-main*. In the traditional circus, the act is a classic. One acrobat (the base) muscles a second acrobat (the flyer) through a series of positions. The flyer might do a handstand on the base's hands, say, or the pair might balance shoulder to shoulder, with the flyer upside down. Insofar as the flyer never touches the ground, the act is essentially a display of strength and control, values that acrobats typically emphasize by wearing sleek bodysuits or painting themselves silver. This latter practice ultimately led to the act's other name: the human-statues routine.

That at least was the standard form. Jean-Michel's version was from a modern circus, and so it differed slightly. The acrobats, a man and a woman, wore formal outfits—the woman a sheer satin dress, the man a tuxedo. As they moved from position to position, the man barked commands—"Give me your hand! Place your foot on my knee!"—which the woman obeyed unthinkingly, almost robotically.

The students watched the act with curiosity. Guy meanwhile shuffled around behind the television. He tore off three sheets of paper from an easel and taped them to the wall. At the top of each he wrote a word: "Description." "Interpretation." "Judgment." He was crossing the final *t* as the video came to a stop.

"Et alors . . ." He clicked off the television and faced the class. He asked the students what they saw. A girl raised her hand. She had sturdy shoulders and a ponytail.

"It's a hand-balancing routine," she said.

Guy nodded. "Can you be more precise?"

The girl described the act, the acrobats' positions and movements. While she was speaking, the theorist moved to the board and recorded her words in shorthand on the sheet of paper labeled "Description." "Hand-to-hand stand," he wrote, and "Inverted shoulder stand."

A series of similar exchanges followed. "Talking strange" was a Judgment. "No music," a Description. At one point an acrobat commented on the act's "gender relations."

Guy hesitated. "Say more."

The acrobat twirled a pen in his fingers. "Well, the relationship between the man and the woman is sort of the point, right? The man gives the commands. The woman obeys. They're calling attention to that with their physicality."

Guy nodded. He turned to the board and wrote "gender roles" on the Interpretation paper.

What the students had done, he explained, when the exercise was over and the three pages were buried in ideas, was to engage in the critical process. "First you describe the work, then you analyze the meaning, then you judge it," he said, and he ticked off the three phrases with his marker. As a critic, he noted, he spent his days engaging in this exact process, and he encouraged the students to think similarly, not as critics but as creators.

"In a few short years, you are going to be professionals," he said, slipping into a serious tone. "You are among the best performers in France, and you're arriving at an important moment in circus history. Take it seriously. *Think* about the work you're seeing. *Think* about the work you're making. As somebody who knows the profession quite well, I can guarantee it will be good for your career." He paused and grinned and popped the cap on his marker. "More important, it will be good for the art."

5

Crossroads

IN ADDITION TO Circus Theory, Anny invited me to attend a second freshman course, Circus History, taught by a circus historian, Pascal Jacob. He was one of the world's foremost circus experts, and his obsession with the art made my own look like a passing fancy. Though not yet fifty, he had helped author more than nineteen books on the subject and was writing an additional half-dozen when I met him, including a comprehensive ten-volume history. He taught at three of the best circus schools: the national schools in France, Canada, and Belgium. With a partner, he had amassed one of the world's largest private collections of circus memorabilia ("circusiana"), a museum's worth of circus posters, programs, costumes, paintings, statues, and random circus artifacts.

When his parents passed away, he once told me, he sold their property and sank the money in the circus past. "I might be homeless," he said, "but at least I'll be happy." Needless to say, I was interested in meeting him.

I was not, however, interested in his class. My interest was in the contemporary circus, not the past, which, based on what little I knew about it, I imagined as a sort of grotesque Dalí painting, full of juggling midgets, sword-swallowers, and abused animals. It almost seemed like another form entirely, a tawdry prelude to the more sophisticated modern work. I expected Pascal's class would offer some context, but not much else.

The first class took place in one of the classrooms reserved for academic work. Pascal arrived in dapper fashion. There was something elegant, almost Old World about him. He wore a black velvet scarf and a black silk jacket embroidered with the name of France's biggest circus, Cirque Phénix. His black hair was combed straight back from his brow, like a cinematic duke.

The students entered in a cacophonous parade. When they had settled, Pascal clicked off the lights and cycled through an introductory circus slide show, an illuminated tour of the art's extensive history. He began with an etching of the Roman Colosseum. He talked about the circus arts in ancient Rome, the brutal contexts of their employment. "Look at this," he said, pointing to a church that had been erected in the bleachers of the stadium. "They built it after the fall of Rome, to commemorate all the Christians who died in the ring."

He clicked. The projector whirred. A chubby acrobat appeared. He was dressed in a doublet and diving through a line of hoops held aloft by soldiers. Pascal explained that the image was from the sixteenth century, from the first book ever written about acrobatics, a treatise by Arcangelo Tuccaro, the personal acrobatic trainer to French Kings Charles VII and Henri III.

"But here's the peculiar thing. . . ." He gestured to what looked like a small wooden ramp in the lower corner of the drawing. It was a springboard, he said, an angled plank to create additional height. "But as far as we know, springboards weren't widely used until almost a hundred years after this image. This is the first recorded use."

The show went on. Each image marked an era: traveling performers huddling miserably against the wheel of a covered wagon; a wire-walker perched precariously over a cobbled medieval plaza.

"What is *that?*" a student exclaimed. A Victorian animal trainer had emblazoned the screen. Dressed like Tarzan, the trainer lay sprawled on the ground, a lion huddled over him, its jaws clenched around his throat.

Pascal smiled. Before mass media, he said, before television or the movies, the circus had been the world's most popular spectator event, a combination of professional entertainment and professional athletics. Like we glorify athletes or movies stars today, audiences had glorified circus performers. "This was a celebrity poster for the trainer. It's the sort of thing a child might have hung on his bedroom wall."

I studied the image of the lion-tamer. It wasn't tawdry or cheap. It was oddly ornate. A series of words ran around the outside: "Strength," "Courage," "Power," "Will." It occurred to me for the first time that I might have misunderstood circus history, that the image in my head might have come from the circus of my youth, the circus of clichés. But what if in the past the circus had been something different? What if it hadn't been a punch line, but an actual part of daily life?

Gazing at the illuminated image of the lion-tamer, I worried, quite rightly, that I had tumbled into a new obsession.

BEFORE THERE WAS the circus proper, there were the "circus arts," physical disciplines that date back to the roots of human spectacle. The list of these circus arts is long and imprecise, but it usually includes tumbling, ropewalking, juggling, animal training, and clowning. There is no consensus about which circus art came first. Many of them likely began in religious contexts, before the written record. Acrobatics, for example, was probably first practiced as a hunting ritual. To invoke what anthropologists call "sympathetic magic," a shaman might have imitated an animal's movement, by walking on his hands or dancing nimbly around a fire. Similarly, many sacred myths include characters with clownish features. In pre-Columbian North America, native tribes, including the Nez Perce and the Hopi, celebrated the coyote as a trickster who scandalized, humiliated, and amused the community. In Norse mythology, Loki, a buffoonish figure, jokingly cut off the hair of Thor's wife.

With the classical period, the circus arts shed their religious connotations and became entertainment. Specialists roamed the world, plying the skills wherever they could lure a crowd—at crossroads, in town plazas, in banquet halls. The audiences could be quite regal. In the Middle Kingdom of ancient Egypt (2050–1650 B.C.) jugglers or "ball-dancers," performed for the pharaohs and princes. In Greece, Socrates attended a banquet with a female hoop dancer, who "threw the hoops into the air, making them spin and judging how high she would have to throw them to catch them in time to the music." The performers themselves occupied a low social caste. Their work was demanding, intensely physical and often dangerous. In his *Satyricon*, a description of the Feast of Trimalchio, the Latin poet Petronius (A.D. 27–66) describes a ladder act by a family of acrobats. According to Petronius, the father of the family held the ladder while his son, a small boy, danced from rung to rung. For the grand finale, the father compelled the boy "to jump through blazing hoops while grasping a huge wine jar with his teeth."

Today circus scholars debate whether this ancient work constitutes part of the official circus lineage. It depends, principally, on how you define the form. Some historians take a rather narrow view. They consider the circus a composite art, a collection of acts first brought together in the eighteenth century. This is the perspective of American historian Fred Dahlinger, Jr., who once told me that he sees the circus as "horses around a ring mixed with physical feats."

Others are more inclusive. The circus, they say, isn't a specific collection of activities; it's an experience, even a set of qualities—prowess, risk, physicality, ambition. In David Lewis Hammarstrom's *Circus Rings Around Russia*, the Russian historian Victor Kalesh gives one such model. The circus, Kalesh says, consists of (1) "an artistic model of . . . a festival atmosphere"; (2) "ideal mastership," or prowess; (3) a "wholeness," a feeling of a complete show that combines separate acts. By this definition, the games of Rome were one of the greatest circuses in history. There were staged animal hunts and equestrian demonstrations. Jugglers milled in the corridors, and ropewalkers balanced over the crowds. The Roman Colosseum, the stadium where the games took place, was round. It was known as an amphitheater, but the Romans also had a second type of building—elliptical, like modern football stadiums, with a spine down the middle for chariot races. They called them "circuses."

In A.D. 410, Rome fell, sacked by Visigoths. Performers of the circus arts took to the road in search of audiences. To survive, most performers practiced more than one skill, and so they came to be known by general names: minstrels, *jestours*, *jongleurs*, *histriones*, *bateleurs*, *baladins.** Not much is known about their lives. "It's a historical black hole," Carol Symes, a specialist in medieval performance at the University of Illinois, told me. The performers themselves were mostly illiterate and kept few records. The clergy, the great scribes of the age, considered them base, and so noted little of their doings. Today, perhaps because of the dearth of information, we tend to romanticize their lives. In works of art about the period—films, paintings, and literature—itinerant acrobats and singers are depicted as joyful and free, frolicing in fields of wildflowers. (See Marcel Carné's *Visiteurs du soir.*) In reality, their lives were horrifically difficult. Forced to travel incessantly, they were subject to starvation and disease. Wary of the seductive charms, villagers often treated them with suspicion or scorn.

The tough times continued through the Middle Ages and into the Renaissance. In the fifteenth century, the plague descended on Europe. Fearful of contamination, mayors banned outsiders and public meetings, stripping the *saltimbanques* of their crowds. By the sixteenth century, the contagion had passed, but now feudalism was crumbling. A new migrant class emerged, hordes of merchants, soldiers, and pilgrims who roved from town to town in search of work. Unsure how to deal with this demographic tidal wave, the royal powers panicked. A spate of "vagrancy laws" swept through Europe. Anyone caught without patronage or proof of stable employment could be prosecuted, and the punishments were horrifically gruesome. One vagabond law, passed in 1572, recommended boring an itinerant's ear with a rod of hot iron. Another suggested branding a culprit with the letter *V.*

To protect themselves, *saltimbanques* sought refuge among the elite. For room and board, or even just a letter guaranteeing safe passage, a *saltimbanque* would offer to juggle, sing, or tumble for a nobleman. In 1547, Ivan the Terrible paid 800 bear trainers to perform at his wedding. Some lucky performers even secured permanent positions. During the thirteenth and fourteenth centuries, jesters were regularly recruited from among the minstrel class. Under Charles II, the Duchess of Cleveland paid a salary to Jacob Hall, a famous ropewalker, who "rivaled the king himself" in her affections.

Buoyed by such relations, the fortunes of the lowly *saltimbanque*

* Perhaps the most encompassing term is *saltimbanque*, derived from the medieval Latin *saltare* (jump) and *banco* (bench), because performers overturned wooden boxes or benches for stages.

began to rise. In England, authorities accepted the historical inevitability of migrant labor, and "vagrancy" sanctions waned. On the Continent, French King Louis XIV consolidated power and established domestic peace, allowing for easier travel. The most significant development, however, was the rise of a new venue: the fairgrounds.

In their purest form, the fairs (*foires* in French, *Jahrmärkte* in German) date from the fifth century, when they began as religious festivals, a fixed time and place for pilgrims from across Europe to worship together and swap doctrine. In the fifteenth century, fueled by the new wayfaring class, the gatherings grew. Visitors flocked to hear news from the outside. Merchants from abroad set up booths to hawk their goods: telescopes, spices, miracle potions, exotic birds. Lyon, Cologne, Southwark, Florence, Nuremberg, Naples—they all had their fairs, and by the seventeenth century, the biggest of them—the Saint-Germain Fair in Paris, the Bartholomew Fair in England—were rollicking festivals of commerce, whole barrack villages that lasted upward of a month.

For the *saltimbanques,* who survived on their ability to find a regular crowd, the fairs were a godsend. Because merchants and visitors came from great distances, the fairs were obligated to stick to consistent schedules. An industrious performer could plan his season in advance, hopping from one fair to the next, connecting them like links on a chain. What's more, the atmosphere of the fairs also fit their skills nicely. The foreign merchants imbued the events with an air of adventure. Audiences came with money to spend and the will to spend it.

And so the performers flocked. Records from the Saint-Germain Fair in Paris show them arriving in waves. The puppeteers appeared toward the end of the sixteenth century. Next came the acrobats, including some of the oldest circus families, like the Chiarinis, a group of ropedancers, who arrived in Paris in 1580. The Roma (a.k.a. the Gypsies) arrived around the same time. Originally from northern India, the caste of metalworkers and musicians had fled their homeland in the eleventh century and taken up performing on the road—telling fortunes, dancing, and training bears, monkeys, and goats. In Paris, where they first appeared in 1427, they found a comfortable place among the tumblers, magicians, and jugglers. Over the centuries, the *saltimbanques* and the Gypsies intermarried and swapped customs, leading to the modern associations between the two groups. Nevertheless, it's important to note that the Roma weren't the only itinerant people to make their mark in the performance milieu. As Lord George Sanger, a nineteenth-century showman, noted in his autobiography, in the fairgrounds of his youth, Jewish families "passed the number of goys 2 to 1."

BY NOVEMBER, I had become fascinated by circus history. Weekdays, I pored over pictorial volumes at the city libraries. Weekends, I drifted between dusty antique shops in the Marais, picking over the collections of old circus postcards and prints.

Much of this interest was spontaneous, an instinctual curiosity. But Pascal also played a role. In class, he brought circus history alive. Each week, he would recount stories of the past, of the arrival of Paris's first rhinoceros, of the tragic suicide of the great trapezist, Alfredo Codona. I came to think of him as my circus Virgil, my guide through the circus past. Before long, we started meeting outside of class, for coffee or dinner. Each meeting took a lesson. Once it was the elegant period of the Parisian Belle Époque, when circuses were staged in buildings that looked like opera houses. Another time, it was the great American train circuses of the nineteenth century, the behemoth shows that chugged across the young country at the cusp of the railroads.

The biggest lesson was Pascal himself. He approached the circus with a seriousness of intention that I had never encountered and could never have imagined. Like Jean-Michel Guy, he had intellectualized the form. But whereas Jean-Michel focused on the modern period, Pascal had intellectualized *all* of the circus, from the jugglers of ancient Egypt to the clowns of Soviet Russia. To him, every aspect merited serious consideration, on aesthetic grounds, with regard to expression and form, but also on the "cultural" level: how the circus reflected the values of a given society.

My first inkling of this perspective came during one of our afternoon chats, in a café near the Place de la Bastille. On the way to the café, we had stopped to view a portion of his memorabilia collection at HorsLesMurs, a French circus advocacy organization. As we were perusing the objects, which were piled by the hundreds on metal shelves, an image of a clown caught my eye. It was almost 150 years old, but the clown's hair—a pair of spikes jutting off his head—looked familiar: he reminded me of Bozo.

"Oh, sure," Pascal said, when I pointed out the similarity in the café. "It's the Feast of Fools." Once a year, he explained, certain towns in medieval France had allowed a local fool to replace the mayor or bishop for a day, as a symbolic reversal of power. To mark the occasion, the fool would wear a floppy tentacular hat such as jesters wear, what Pascal called "a crown without the power."

This was a new idea for me. I had never thought of the clown's look as having any particular origin, much less a political or social origin. I asked the historian if other iconic clown qualities also came from specific sources: the red nose, the floppy shoes, the multicolored outfit. "Of course," he replied, "there are reasons for all of it."

A circus show wasn't just a series of acts. Every movement, even something as simple as a back flip, was weighted with history and loaded with meaning.

Another indication of this view came during a conversation about acrobatics in different parts of the world. We were talking about how different countries approached acrobatics. In my naïve view, location mattered little: a handstand was a handstand, a flip a flip. Pascal took an anthropological tack. In the West, he speculated, we tend to consider a back flip an arbitrary pursuit. "It doesn't serve any purpose," he said. "It's just to demonstrate that you're capable of doing it. Its only function is to surprise you, to make you say 'wow.'"

The Chinese take a different view. During the ancient period, Chinese emperors trained cadets to tumble and dispatched acrobatic troupes to perform for foreign heads of state, as emissaries and proof of power. Among the Chinese populace, this courtly attention inspired widespread interest in the skills. Peasants whiled away the frigid winters practicing with household items—tumbling through threshing hoops, spinning plates on sticks. In the spring, they flocked to festivals in the capital, enormous affairs featuring tens of thousands of amateur acrobats eager to demonstrate their skills. Today, acrobatics remains a popular practice in China, but echoes of the discipline's aristocratic history have imbued the practice with a different emphasis.

"The Chinese don't valorize the violence," Pascal told me. "They don't celebrate the danger." They exalt refinement. "It's a little like pulling a bow in Japan: it's about concentration and precision." The acrobat aspires not to glorify himself but to testify to the perfection of the state, even the universe. "It's really related to their culture," Pascal noted. "The body of the Chinese acrobat is integrated into his community, into the cosmos even. People say 'wow' there, but not for the same reason."

The more I got to know Pascal, the more I wondered about him. His unique perspective—the fusion of the past with the present, the high with the low—seemed indicative of the circus today, of an art in transition. I wondered how his obsession had started. Given his elegant bearing, I thought his perspective might reflect his upbringing. (Stories abound of aristocratic children hitching on with acrobats.) In fact, his parents were working-class Parisians. His father was a furniture distributor, his mother a *fonctionnaire*—an administrator in France's byzantine bureaucracy. Neither particularly liked the circus, but, thanks to an old French tradition known as "Arbres de Noël," his mother received tickets from her company every Christmas. When Pascal was four, she took him to see his first show, a one-ring show directed by the Bouglione family, one of France's venerable dynasties. The experience captivated him. "I was fascinated by the smells," he once told me. "The burned gas off the trucks, the hot canvas, the stables with the animals, the sawdust." Another time he said it was the mystery of the circus life, what he once called "the secret." "What's in the tent? What's in the trailers?"

He started attending other shows. Every Wednesday, his grandmother took him to the Cirque d'Hiver, Paris's oldest circus building, where he saw some of the biggest circus stars of the day, including Gunther Gebel-Williams. He quickly grew obsessed. He kept his tickets and the programs, which blossomed into a collection of circus books and memorabilia. In his free time, he constructed intricate wooden circus models, with mechanized equestrians and hand-painted crowds. One model filled his bedroom. When the family went on vacation to London, Pascal insisted on packing it in his bags. "I'm sure my father appreciated that," he said with a chuckle.

Oddly, though, Pascal never wanted to be *in* the circus. "It's strange," he said, "but in retrospect I think I intellectualized the circus from early on." He was fascinated by the circus as an art form and a historical subject. He was able to imagine the extravagant circuses of the past very clearly, and they hijacked his mind. "I used to stay up late in my room and look at pictures of the American circus trains under a magnifying glass. I couldn't get enough of it—the myth of the wagons, of the city on the rails."

What makes this fascination especially noteworthy is the era in which it developed. Pascal grew up in the late sixties, the low point of the art. Across Europe, traditional circuses were collapsing by the dozen. "Modern" companies had just started to form, but nobody really knew about them. "You have to understand that nobody liked the circus back then," he said. "Nobody."

Well, almost nobody. While he was out wandering the antique bookshops of the Latin Quarter one afternoon, a shopkeeper summoned him over to his desk. The man had seen him poking around, ogling the old circus volumes, counting and recounting the change in his pocket, and he asked Pascal if he had ever considered joining the local circus club. Pascal hesitated. Every country has a similar organization: the Circus Friends Association of Great Britain, the Gesellschaft der Circusfreunde. In Paris, it was the Club du Cirque. Pascal of course knew about the club, but the idea of joining intimidated him. The members were serious circus fans and significantly older—of "a certain age," mostly. But it didn't matter. Before he could respond, the shopkeeper had picked up the phone and dialed up the local club's director, a puppeteer named Jean Villiers.

It was the call that changed his life. On the phone, Villiers told Pascal to come to his apartment the following week, and there he sold Pascal the first valuable item in his collection, a Barnum & Bailey program from the company's 1902 French tour. For the next twenty years, Pascal returned to Villiers's apartment every Wednesday. Villiers taught him how to judge circus artifacts and introduced him to the circus club. They talked circus history and argued over shows. "He would call and say, '*Bon*, we're going to Lille, to Versailles. Be at the house at five o'clock. We'll take the car and see some circuses.' " They drove all over Europe—to Switzerland, Belgium, Holland, Germany. They saw all of the great traditional shows—Knie, Krone, Medrano. Villiers was Pascal's mentor and his friend, and when the National School was created in 1985, Villiers became the first historian on staff. "Jean once told me, 'I'm going to do this now, but you'll be the next.' " And he was.

The circus is an art of community. Pascal found his community in the older generation.*

* On Pascal's efforts to connect to his own generation: "I studied theater in college, hoping some people would be interested in the circus. Of course, there weren't any."

But by then the circus had started to change. The *nouveau cirque* was exploding in France. New companies were emerging every year. They garnered headlines in *Le Monde* and filled big venues, like the Cirque d'Hiver in Paris.

Their success led to a schism in the circus community. The traditional community accused the moderns of being upstarts without experience or an appropriate respect for tradition. They said the contemporary work was pompous and extreme, something other than circus—a form of physical theater, maybe. The modernists responded by critizing the traditionalists for being stuck in the past, for letting the art fester. Through the eighties the divisions deepened. Debates turned into animosities. "There were literally fistfights," one participant told me.

At the circus club in Paris, most of the members sided with the traditionalists. But Pascal wasn't so sure. Outside of the circus, his tastes were almost exclusively highbrow. He was a connoisseur of the opera and literature and cuisine. More important, he saw a continuity between the old form and the new. "People said the modern circus was different, but I didn't believe that," he once told me. "I thought it was what it always was: an assembly of incredible forms. Aren't the effects the same? Do we not feel the same fascination, the same surprise?" Even the inciting question—What's a circus?—struck him as an extension of the past. "If you look at the history, we've been having the same debate for centuries. 'This is circus, but that isn't.' The truth is that the circus is like all art—it changes." During another conversation, he compared it to music. "Music changed and we take it for granted. It becomes baroque with Monteverdi in the seventeenth century. During the French Revolution it's Romanticism. One form isn't necessarily higher than another, but there's an evolution. When we talk about Wagner and Mozart, there's a chasm between them."

Over the millennia the circus produced myriad chasms of its own, myriad versions. The ancient games, the *saltimbanques,* the rise of the fairgrounds—these were three of the first. Dozens more followed. The "traditional circus" (or the "conventional circus," as Pascal likes to say) was the version that dominated the first half of the nineteenth century. But it was only a version like all the others, not the art itself.

It took me awhile to accept this sense of continuity. Once I did, the belief had demonstrable effects on my experience. History gave the modern work a different reality. I was able to read the echoes of the past. I took a greater interest in traditional circuses. I sought them out around Paris and was able to watch them with more clarity and respect, less blinded by the clichés.

Pascal understood the benefits of this dual view more than anyone. Because he refused to distinguish between the old circus and the new, he somehow managed to straddle both worlds and was rewarded with an almost fantastical richness of experience, a mix of high art and exoticism. A few years ago, for example, the mayor of Venice invited him to Carnevale to help compose a show for one of the luxurious balls. He was invited because the show was supposed to include a rhinoceros. ("It was a mean rhinoceros, very difficult to work with.")

Another time, he was brought in to broker a deal between a high-ranking emissary from the Chinese government and one of the big American circuses. The circus wanted to acquire a giant panda, the first in Western circus history. "I learned a lot that night," Pascal said with a smile, at one of our dinners. The Chinese government owns all the giant pandas. You can't buy one, but they'll rent you one for the year. "To even begin the negotiations, you have to put $1 million on the table. If you want panda twins, it's $2 million." And of course you have to bring in a zoo veterinarian who can testify that the panda will be well cared for. "You can imagine the trouble if the giant panda died on you."

He was the personification of the circus today: multifaceted, refined, international—as concerned with animals as with art. With this in mind, I once asked him if he ever regretted the changes he had witnessed in the circus during his life. Did he ever miss the old shows that had transfixed him as a boy, the lions and calliopes?

"No," he said. "There are places where I can still see those sorts of shows if I want to." When he's in Russia, for instance, he'll attend a quiet matinee, to be reminded of how the circus smelled when he was a boy, the mix of sawdust and animal fur. Just a few weeks before our conversation he had traveled to India, where touring circuses still take place in gigantic tents, and where animals and freaks still feature prominently. He spent the week touring the country, attending as many shows as possible. One night, after one performance, the director of the troupe, a stern and sober man, invited him into the dressing tent for tea. They spent the night with the troupe talking about circus history. The only light came from a lantern, swaying slowly from the ceiling. Pascal sat on a wooden stool. Contortionists and dancing girls and midgets sat on the ground around them. Outside, on the other side of the canvas, he could hear the elephants shuffling in the dirt.

6

An American Juggler in Paris

JAY GILLIGAN HAD RETRIEVED his duffel from the baggage claim when a middle-aged airport customs official waved him over to inspect his bag. Because he had a connection to make, Gilligan fidgeted as the portly agent snapped on a latex glove and plunged his arm into the duffel. Gilligan watched the hand ripple like a snake over his tube socks, his oversized cotton T-shirts, and his dirty nylon gym shorts. The official, working quickly, almost absentmindedly, flashed Gilligan a warning look, jerking an object free. It was a milky white ring, ten inches in diameter and less than a centimeter wide. After placing the ring on the table, the official plunged his hand into the duffel again and emerged with another ring, and another. When a stack of six wobbled like pancakes on the tabletop, the official snapped the glove from his hand, flicked it into the trash can behind him, and asked Gilligan, "What is going on?"

Gilligan explained that he was a professional juggler and that the rings were part of his act. The official nodded warily. Peeling a ring off the stack, he examined it intensely. "I don't know," he demurred, dropping the ring back onto the pile. "I think I'm gonna need some proof."

Like magicians and comedians, jugglers live with constant requests for impromptu performances. Understandably, they tend to find these demands tiresome. One called such a request the "dancing-monkey routine." The majority, however, accept the attention for what it is: a by-product of the profession, akin to the autographs a movie star has to sign. In a small but redeeming way, the requests even speak to the essence of the performer's appeal: juggling is simple yet magical, accessible yet perplexingly captivating; it's the circus distilled.

Gilligan's own attitude depends on his mood, and in the airport that day he must have been feeling generous, for he plucked the rings from the table and, with a quick instinctive look to the ceiling, began to juggle. The rings ripped through the stale air, cresting near the neon lights, then charging earthward. The official watched, entranced. Soon a woman, her teenage son, and a businessman were watching, too. The whole terminal, in fact, was staring in silence. When Gilligan finished, a small but enthusiastic round of applause rose from the crowd. The officer, beaming like a headlight, slid Gilligan's bag across the counter. "Well, all right," he said enthusiastically. "You really are a juggler!" Gilligan heaved the duffel onto his shoulder and forced a smile. He no longer found such requests to perform flattering. Now he was tired of missing his flights.

THE WORLD IS FULL of professional jugglers. No comprehensive census exists, but an informal estimate based on professional records, booking websites, and a lot of poking around on the Internet would put the number between thirty and fifty thousand. Although Jay Gilligan is a professional juggler, he's different from most because he is a professional "art" juggler, one of the few Americans who can say that.

"Five years ago, I counted for some reason the number of American jugglers doing modern stuff like I do," Gilligan announced over his shoulder while the rush-hour crowd of the Parisian Métro jostled around us. "I think there were six. Today, it's basically me. Oh, and Michael Moschen." (Moschen is the godfather of modern juggling in America and the only juggler to win a MacArthur "genius" award. Incongruently,

Moschen also played the part of David Bowie's glass-ball-manipulating hands in the movie *Labyrinth*.)

Gilligan glided to a stop in front of a scratched map bolted to the Métro's glistening bricks. Raising a long finger, he traced a line around the base of Montmartre, Paris's bohemian butte to the north. Our destination was Accro'Balles, Paris's most popular juggling store. Gilligan, who was in town to teach some workshops at the National School, had heard that the store was carrying a new type of larger ring, and he wanted to see it for himself.

I had tagged along to talk about juggling. As a result of my conversations with Pascal, I had decided to study the circus differently. Rather than analyze the impact of the circus as a whole, I hoped to investigate each of its arts individually. This strategy seemed appropriate given the divergent histories of the arts and also the present state of the circus. Long considered cogs in the wheel of a larger show, many artists of the various disciplines had recently "liberated" themselves from the ring to practice their skills as separate and distinct forms, or what the French called "complete arts" (*des arts entiers*).

The repercussions of this shift in focus are wide. In the conventional circus model, most artists adhered to certain "codes." Unwritten and sometimes unstated, these rules nevertheless dictated everything from how long an act should be (five to seven minutes, as I noted previously) to what a performer should wear (the brighter the better). But now performers were free to reinvent themselves and their disciplines, to pose questions never before possible: What's the difference between an acrobat and a dancer? How can a clown be funny but also tragic? What *is* juggling? For the artists answering these questions, it was a thrilling time. As one modern acrobat told me, "It feels like our art is just being born."

Among jugglers, Gilligan was at the center of this shift, and in many ways he epitomized it. When I met him, he was twenty-six years old. Like most jugglers, he had grown up practicing a conventional and technical form of the art that consisted of throwing balls in the air and catching them when they came down. But with the passage of time, his work became unabashedly avant-garde. In interviews, Gilligan spoke openly about juggling as "art." He experimented with patterns of movement and modes of presentation, incorporating dance and acting. He stopped performing bits and started presenting full-length shows. In one, an hour-long piece featuring a musician with a guitar and a laptop, he wore a gray scientist's smock and simulated a scientist's lab onstage, where he'd discover objects, nudging them experimentally across his body and occasionally tossing them in the air. ("Jay doesn't do tricks," British juggler Luke Burrage explained to me. "He does moves.") Gilligan seemed an ideal spokesman for the changes in the form, and one who could help me answer such questions: What does it mean to be a juggling artist? How can a simple physical skill be "artistic"?

In the dim hall of the Métro, Gilligan stood a head taller than everyone else and appeared to be endowed with a heavy, pliable bulk. He dressed like a BMX racer or a bassist in a rock band, with sagging jeans and tousled hair. He has a relaxed way about him and moves with a rolling, loose-limbed gait, like a man emerging from a hot tub.

"What happened to the other modern jugglers?" I asked him. He shrugged and said, "I guess they decided it wasn't worth it." He recited a list of names followed by phrases like "He's on a cruise ship now" or "He's gone corporate" or "I think he's in Vegas."

For a traditional juggler interested in living by his trade, those are indeed the three prevailing options. Among younger traditional jugglers, work on cruise ships tends to be the most coveted. There are difficulties with such a job, of course, but they are mostly technical. For example, although newer ships come equipped with stabilizers to counteract the roll of the swells, jugglers working on older vessels might find the height of their throws varying by as much as a foot each. But cruise-ship jugglers perform in as few as two shows per week for upward of $1,500 per week, all the while enjoying sunshine, shuffleboard, beaches, and bikini-clad dancers.

Of course, not everyone likes to travel, and for the more domestic set there is the "Vegas gig." This term is technically a misnomer, since the gig applies not just to Las Vegas, but to cabarets around the world. In Paris, the best-known venue of this genre is the Lido, a swanky cabaret on the Champs-Élysées that features jugglers in their topless reviews. (Someone once described it as "naked women and a juggler.") Some of the world's best jugglers perform there, including Anthony Gatto, the self-proclaimed and critically confirmed "Greatest Juggler in the World"; and Vladik, a nineteen-year-old Ukrainian American with a slithering and corporal juggling style in the vein of Cirque du Soleil's Viktor Kee.

The balls roll across his body in trajectories that seem to defy gravity. I met Vladik, who stands five feet seven in thick-soled boots, for an afternoon walk along the Seine. He finds that the "cabaret gig" is a good one, but far from perfect. Though the work is well paid, it's also exhausting—with at least one show a night, sometimes two—and somewhat limiting artistically. "I don't really have to practice anymore," he admitted. "I've been doing the routine for years, so it's basically automatic." He was lifting weights, but "only because I want to do the routine with my shirt off, and so I'm trying to get a six-pack."

The third opportunity, "the corporate gig," is also known by the slang term "corpos."

"So the guys from Microsoft get together to plan the next big team-building hurrah," Gilligan says. "They're trying to think of something entertaining, and somebody raises his hand and says, 'Hey, I saw this weird modern circus thing on TV. Circus Olé, I think it's called. Maybe we could get one of those guys.' So they call me."

Gilligan doesn't do "corpos," though. Nor does he like performing in cabarets or on cruise ships. Just entering Las Vegas makes his "skin crawl"; he calls the city a "graveyard for Cirque du Soleil."

Instead, Gilligan performs his modern juggling shows in theaters. He is based in Sweden and works mostly in Europe and the Far East. In the six years before our meeting, he had juggled in England, Holland, Spain, Ireland, Finland, Norway, Italy, Scotland, Belgium, Korea, and Japan. The preference isn't purely professional, he claims; there's also a cultural element. "In America," he said, "I got calls to do birthday parties or to work at a nightclub. They offered me free parking and a pitcher of shitty beer." He paused as a train wheezed to a stop in front of us. "I'm not saying I'm above it," he said as we boarded. "It's just kind of amazing to come to Europe two weeks later and play in front of six hundred people who know you *before* the show."

I asked him to analyze this discrepancy.

He thought for a few seconds, then replied loudly to be heard above the din. "You know, I think people in America have a preconceived notion of what a juggler is. They think of a kind of clown act, of guys performing a glorified party trick on the streets. The idea of a ninety-minute show of a juggling clown doesn't seem that interesting." He shrugged. "To be honest," he said, "I can't say I blame them."

....

ON JULY 1, 1912, on a clear moonlit night in London, Paul Cinquevalli, England's greatest juggler and a living international legend, enacted what might have been juggling's artistic apex: He appeared as a featured performer during the inaugural Royal Command Performance for King George V and Queen Mary.

At the time, juggling was at a popular peak. A staple of the circus as well as the booming vaudeville and music-hall circuits, jugglers featured prominently on stages across Europe and America. As popular as movie actors or rock musicians today, jugglers were major cultural figures, with newspapers reporting their travels alongside those of generals and princes and describing the prestigious venues where they performed, such as the Wintergarten in Berlin and B. F. Keith's Palace in New York.

And no star was bigger than Cinquevalli. Born to Polish aristocrats, he had joined a wandering troupe of Italian acrobats as a boy and worked his way up through the circus, first as a trapezist, then, after a nasty fall in Saint Petersburg, as a juggler. His routine was centered on his feats of strength. With the neatly waxed mustache of a sportsman, and his muscular frame revealed through an athlete's singlet, Cinquevalli hoisted men above him in chairs, heaved whiskey barrels and bathtubs into the air, and caught a forty-eight-pound bowling ball on the bones at the base of his neck. What made him truly famous, however, was his creativity. "Cinquevalli is a wonder incarnate, a perambulating mass of amazement," said a critic in Adelaide. "You leave the theatre conscious that the English language does not contain adjectives big enough."

For his performance for King George V and Queen Mary, Cinquevalli devised a particularly ingenious routine. He called it his "human billiards" act. With the help of a Regent Street tailor, he crafted a baize topcoat for himself, decorated with five "pockets" containing miniature sacks of cords dangling from brass hoops. According to a captivated critic, "The balls fly into the air like cannon and then descend, only to glide hither and thither, in and out of the pockets, actuated only by a series of sharp jerks on the part of the player."

From high above, the king and queen watched from the royal box. Queen Mary tittered happily throughout the show. According to reports, three million roses decorated the theater for the occasion, tied to the railings and sprinkled across the front of the stage. Never again would a juggler reach such heights.

Today, it's hard to imagine that such a scene ever occurred. As Gilligan pointed out in the Métro, most people perceive juggling as a "glorified party trick," something quirky people do for fun. Before we can understand how the image of this craft fell so precipitously, it would first be instructive to examine how it originally reached such a pinnacle.

Like most circus arts, juggling has experienced a long arc. Its origins can be traced to the third millennium B.C. Most ancient societies practiced some version of the skill, usually at an amateur level, in accordance with local customs. On the steppes of China, for example, peasants spun plates on sticks and manipulated spears and swords in an effort to while away the hours of their interminable winters. ("It was a bit like going out and tossing a Frisbee with your friends," Mark Golden, a historian of classical games, told me of similar practices in Greece.) A few professionals survived by the craft, but they lived hard lives as they performed for change in plazas and at crossroads and the occasional banquet. In his *Symposium*, set in 421 B.C., Xenophon describes the appearance of a juggling girl at a dinner presided over by Socrates. To the tune of a flute, the girl danced with twelve hoops and "flung the hoops into the air—overhead she sent them twirling—judging the height they must be thrown to catch them, as they fell, in perfect time." According to Xenophon, the guests were impressed. Socrates himself considered the routine proof that "woman's nature is nowise inferior to man's."

And yet juggling persevered, which elicits the question of why its appeal is so enduring. In some sense, the skill's early popularity speaks to its simple drama and basic beauty: the rhythms are captivating, and the circular patterns are appealing to the eye. (As Luke Burrage likes to note, each juggling toss creates a moment of tension. "There's a question posed: Is he going to catch it?") But there might be a deeper reason as well. In societies around the world, juggling has long been hailed as a meditative, even magical practice. The first recorded images of jugglers were carved into the fifteenth tomb of the Beni Hasan necropolis, overlooking the Nile in central Egypt. These images, dating from roughly 3000 B.C., were dedicated to a priest, and the tomb contains decorations depicting women—slaves, likely—juggling leather balls stuffed with reeds. These women jugglers are first standing and then mounted on piggyback, the action building as in a cartoon strip.

Janice Kamrin, a Cairo-based Egyptologist with the Smithsonian Institution, told me that when an important figure died, the Egyptians liked to bury the person with objects and images that had brought the person pleasure in life. They believed that the joys might be transported to the afterlife. The images might also illuminate the burial process. In their mortuary cult, Kamrin noted, Egyptians used round objects to represent celestial spheres—planets, moons, and stars. It's possible that the pictured jugglers performed at the priest's funeral. With their nimble tricks—tossing and catching the balls, which looped steadily—jugglers might have represented a universe in balance. In a symbolic sense, jugglers held the world in their hands.

With the advent of the Dark Ages, jugglers in Europe were scuttled just like everyone else. For almost eight hundred years, professional juggling became a lost practice, save for a few minstrels who included juggling in their repertoire. This remained the situation until the beginning of the circus proper in 1768. The majority of early circus producers, including Philip Astley, the father of the form, considered juggling too "small" to fill a ring, and instead encouraged the skill as a kind of spectacular condiment to flavor other acts. One early poster, for instance, testifies to "juggling on the rope." John Bill Ricketts, the father of the American circus, juggled four oranges while standing on the back of a galloping horse.

Only in the 1860s did the juggler begin to assume the spotlight, thanks largely to the advent of music halls in Europe. Founded as British beer and song halls, the venues evolved into full performance halls, featuring nightly variety shows, mostly built around singing, but with room for other acts. For jugglers, the music halls proved ideal. Theatrical lighting and the contained space of the stage made their work seem bigger and more spectacular, while also fostering an intimacy that played to the juggler's solitary endeavor. Immune from the effects of wind, rain, and other inclement weather, jugglers could develop more subtle and complicated tricks, such as "bounce juggling," made possible by the levelness of the stage and the discovery of rubber.

The demand for jugglers skyrocketed. Because local European performance traditions were still recovering from the Dark Ages, many of the early stars came from abroad, especially from Asia. As early as 1832, Lau Laura, a Chinese specialist in balancing, contortion, and the manipulation of balls of twine, made a much-discussed appearance at London's

Drury Lane Theatre. Fifty years later, Awata Katsnoshin, the official juggler for the Mikado court in Japan, performed a stick-and-ball routine at Niblo's Garden on Broadway.*

With the boost of exoticism that captivated European audiences in an age of imperialism, juggling continued to prosper, and by the 1880s it had reached what many consider the golden age of the craft. Across America and Europe, any self-respecting circus or music hall included at least one juggler on its bill.

In 1885, Benjamin Franklin Keith, a retired circus performer, provided another boost when he created the first vaudeville theater to run continuous performances, in Boston. The new venues that followed provided a glut of professional opportunities. At one point thousands of jugglers were occupied in America alone. To distinguish themselves, jugglers began to diversify. "Weight jugglers" heaved and balanced heavy objects—anchors, cannonballs, and chariots. "Foot jugglers" popped balls, barrels, and people into the air while lying on their backs. There even emerged a sort of "juggling theater," in which jugglers wove their tricks into theatrical narratives, with characters and plot lines. The Rambler Comedy Juggling Company performed one such act in 1900. According to an article in *Sandow's Magazine of Physical Culture,* the men, who were costumed as waiters and guests in a restaurant, juggled "lamps, loaves, knives, forks, dish-covers and serviettes." Writing about the Rambler routine, a critic noted "the musical quartette with the wine bottles is distinctly original."

During the golden age of juggling, which lasted roughly from 1880 to 1920, what audiences treasured most was creativity. Audiences wanted a juggler who could surprise them by developing a new character or skill to earn their affection. And in this regard nobody was greater than Cinquevalli. He was quite simply the most original juggler the world had ever seen. Dressed in his trademark billiard jacket, Cinquevalli had a repertoire that included an array of tricks involving an impossible number of objects—coins, cigars, umbrellas, barrels, billiard balls, cups of hot tea, turnips, lighted candles, daggers, bottles of soda water. In 1893, he finished training himself to catch an egg on a plate—a feat that had taken nine years to master.

* One article from the period claims Katsnoshin sired the first Japanese children born outside of the imperial mainland.

In part, his natural determination fueled his work. "If I can't figure something out I lie in bed all night thinking about it," he once told an interviewer. "The papers sometimes say that I do not bring out enough new tricks," he said on another occasion, "but they do not understand how difficult I make my feats." Cinquevalli became one of the highest-paid performers in the music hall and a star in Europe. He purchased diamonds for journalists and bought a château. "Exhibitions of this kind are not new," noted *The New York Times* in 1889, "but no one has ever equaled Cinquevalli within our memory. His feats . . . are simply bewildering."

Which brings us back to the original questions: What destroyed the prestige of juggling? After such a meteoric rise, how did juggling fall so steeply?

With the advent of cinema and radio, vaudeville houses plunged into decline. Many jugglers fled to the circus, but by then most shows had mushroomed into three-ring spectacles, behemoth extravaganzas where jugglers found themselves overwhelmed. Their subtle tricks were no match for a parade of elephants and fireworks. On television, a few jugglers found a reprieve, especially on variety shows like those hosted by Ed Sullivan and Red Skelton. But the gigs were few and far between. They were nothing compared with the vast opportunities available before.

Jugglers also deserve some of the blame. As their popularity began to wane, they shifted their approach. Sacrificing novelty and theatricality, they emphasized athleticism rather than showmanship. Instead of "What new object can you juggle?" the operative question became "How *many* objects can you juggle?" The trend took root before World War I, but it wasn't until the twenties that the movement from juggling creativity to juggling quantity burgeoned, largely through the work of a single juggler, Enrico Rastelli.

Today, Rastelli is widely considered the greatest juggler in history, the Nijinsky of the discipline (an ironic epithet, since Rastelli actually trained with Nijinsky's father as a boy). Born in Siberia in 1896, he was the son of a family of touring Italian acrobats. His parents coached him as a boy to carry on the family tradition, but juggling mania seized him when he was six, and he began training in secret. By the time his parents discovered his preference, he was so good that they were forced to acquiesce to his desires and began booking him gigs. His first solo job came in 1915 with Circus Truzzi in Russia. The revolution in 1917 caused the family to flee abroad to Italy, where Rastelli's professional stock exploded. By 1923, his name was headlining the marquees of the biggest venues in the biggest cities, from the Hippodrome of London to B. F. Keith's Palace Theatre at Broadway and 47th Street, where he was billed as "Europe's Greatest Music Hall Artist."

As a man, Rastelli was famously ebullient—according to legend, he had to will himself *not* to smile for photos—and that manifested itself in his juggling as volcanic dynamism. Dressed like an athlete, in nylon shorts and a rugby jersey, he was an avatar of virtuosity, racing between tricks, hurling his balls into the air with maniacal abandon, beaming, posing, pouncing. His single focus was keeping objects in the air. To this end, instead of incorporating a diverse range of props, he concentrated on a few—inflatable balls, plates, and wooden sticks, all selected exclusively for their properties of flight. This narrow approach, combined with a herculean work ethic—his practice sessions could last ten hours—led him to achieve feats previously deemed impossible. In 1893, less than two decades before Rastelli's rise, George Fielding had made international headlines at the world's fair by juggling six balls at once. Like his predecessor, Rastelli could juggle six balls—while skipping a rope, bouncing a ball on his head, and spinning a hoop on his leg. Without such distractions, he could juggle ten balls. He could also juggle eight plates, or eight sticks, or three cantaloupe-sized balls on his head. Even by modern standards such feats are extreme. In 1930, they were borderline supernatural.

Rastelli died young: In 1931, one of his sticks sliced the inside of his mouth during a show at the Apollo Theater in Nuremberg, Germany, resulting in a fatal hemorrhage and infection. His legacy lived on in the form of a statue in his adopted hometown of Bergamo, Italy, and in the wave of jugglers who rushed to copy his kinetic, technical style. The Rastellian mode, with its emphasis on what is known as "toss juggling" and a limited range of objects, became a benchmark, so widely practiced that it literally defined juggling as a pursuit.

Before Rastelli, a juggler was a creative manipulator of objects; afterward, he was a person who could throw a lot of objects in the air and catch them. He threw bigger objects both higher and faster than had been previously done. Before Rastelli, a "trick" was an ingenious stunt (e.g., throwing a knife such that it sliced open an envelope mid-flight);

after Rastelli's performances, a trick was defined by an object's pattern of movement.

This definition of a trick still holds today. There are literally thousands of these juggling tricks, or "patterns," as they are sometimes called, categorized online and in books including *The Encyclopædia of Ball Juggling.* The basic juggling trick, wherein the objects loop from hand to hand, is called "the cascade." Throwing one ball over the top of the other two is termed "tennis." Tossing two balls vertically while shuffling the third between your hands is a "box." For traditional or "technical" jugglers, these skills constitute the essence of the craft. A "strong" juggler knows lots of tricks and completes them with a large number of objects—balls, rings, or clubs—like Rastelli.

But this traditional definition of a performance is precisely where juggling runs into trouble. By hinging their craft on virtuosic execution, jugglers painted themselves into a corner. Although it is thrilling, this kind of technical juggling is also tough for audiences to appreciate. The tricks themselves can seem indistinguishable. Many tricks are harder than they look, and vice versa. It's even accepted that, when there are more than a certain number (some say five, some say seven) of objects, audience members have trouble identifying how many are in the air simultaneously. The result is this awful Catch-22: the more a juggler improves, the less accessible he becomes to an audience.

This issue—call it the problem of disassociation—is nothing new. Cinquevalli spent nine years learning how to catch an egg, as I said previously, only to drop the trick from his act when he realized audiences had no appreciation for the superhuman skill the trick requires. Nor is the issue unique to juggling. "There's such a moat between what a performer is able to do and what the ordinary person is able to do," Aloysia Gavre, an American acrobat, once told me. "Even if the spectator has some experience using his body—even if he does yoga—a strong performer can still leave them cold." (This problem is at the root of the annoying habit of ringmasters who call attention to ambitious tricks. "Now, in ring one, the famous quadruple somersault, the most difficult maneuver known to man.")

But jugglers wrestle with the problem with particular acuity. Though other disciplines can seem remote, they also offer secondary pleasures: the danger of a woman walking on a wire, say, or the majesty of a man flying on a trapeze. Jugglers have no such joys to fall back on. The only danger a juggler faces is the danger of looking foolish. His dynamism is real, but the performance is also limited and self-contained.

Jugglers know this, of course, and have all sorts of strategies to bridge the divide. Dick Franco, an American master, told me that he varies the rhythm of his throws and staggers the level of difficulty so that audiences can feel the difference. "The object is to create a situation where the viewer knows you are doing something different even if he cannot actually perceive what you are doing." But this happens rarely enough, and the sad truth is that skill can be a handicap.

This irony was once made clear to me in a conversation with American juggler Steven Ragatz. A longtime performer with Cirque du Soleil, Ragatz was discussing the work of another Soleil star, Anthony Gatto. By any technical measure, Gatto is the greatest juggler in the world and maybe the greatest juggler in history. Son of a vaudeville juggler, he started juggling at the age of four. By eight, Gatto had won the Junior National Championships among kids twice his age. When he was thirteen, he could, amazingly, juggle seven clubs. Seven years later, he set the world record for rings with twelve. Since then, he has held world records in twelve different juggling categories. Other jugglers uniformly discuss his achievement with a mix of awe and bafflement. The English juggler Luke Burrage once captured Gatto's reputation very well: "If there's something Anthony hasn't done," he said, "it's only because he hasn't tried."

And yet, at least according to Ragatz, this mountain of skill, this once-in-a-generation talent, is almost completely lost on an audience. "Imagine stopping somebody in the lobby after Anthony's act and asking them what he did," Ragatz said. "Probably they'd say something along the lines of 'Okay, well, he did the balls, and he did the pins, and he did a whole lotta rings. Oh, and there was this girl, and she was really hot and she was dancing around a bit.'" Ragatz chuckled at the indignity of it. "I mean, it's a shame but it's also the truth. People just have no fucking clue."

EMERGING FROM THE MÉTRO, Gilligan thrust a hand into his pocket and pulled out a scrap of crinkled paper.

"Rue Duuunkerque," he read in an exaggerated American accent as he glanced around. Montmartre, Paris's famous bohemian mound, rose above us to the north, capped by the Sacré-Coeur Basilica like an ivory glacier. It was a gray day, the sky hanging low above us.

We headed south, and within minutes found ourselves standing in the doorway of the juggling shop. It looked like Santa's workshop circa 1953: Every inch of the space was slathered in toys, and we relished the simple joy of the store's inventory. Pogo sticks and unicycles leaned against wooden columns. Sacks of marbles hang like grapes from the ceiling. I was basking in the ancient smell of the place—lacquer mixed with dust—when a shopkeeper came scuttling around a low counter.

"Bonjour," he greeted us. He was in his forties and well accoutered for his role as resident Geppetto, with scraggly hair and a beige cardigan pulled over a blue oxford button-down. In a docile voice, he asked if there was anything we desired. When Gilligan mentioned the rings—the bigger-than-average size he was looking for—our host smiled grandly and whisked him toward the back of the shop.

Like golfers, chefs, and mechanics, jugglers are notoriously finicky about the tools of their trade. According to legend, Rastelli used to carve his own clubs from trees growing near his home in Bergamo. Francis Brunn, a German star, commissioned his sticks from a cousin who also manufactured ball bearings for Mercedes-Benz. These days such strategies are unnecessary. Juggling objects are rendered by computers, manufactured by robots, and sold in bulk online by dealerships like Dubé, based in New York City.

Still, Gilligan has his requirements, and in the shop he peeled a ring from the wall and set to appraising it with the squinting, lip-pursed air of a jeweler. He bobbed the ring up and down, then shifted it from hand to hand. A second ring came down from the wall. Each got tossed—right, then left. Being thin and hollow, these rings were both easier to grab and less likely to collide in midair, and so among professionals are often employed for what is known as "high numbers"—roughly, juggling more than seven objects. But even here in the shop, Gilligan's competence was clear. There's a precise yet casual disregard in the way Gilligan handles rings, and like those of a tennis player with his racquet, his smallest tosses resonate with practice.

He let the rings come to a rest, and made a satisfied smack with his lips. In slow English he asked the shopkeeper if the store carried an identical model in white.

"Oh no," the shopkeeper replied, wincing. "I am sorry. I have no white." Then he eagerly added, "But if you are coming back today, maybe I have some white for you later."

Gilligan nodded vaguely, gave the ring another instinctive toss, and returned it to its metal hook. He told the shopkeeper he would think it over. The truth, he told me later, is that he prefers to work with white, a color that triggers no "preconceived notions" (as opposed to neon orange, say, or flashy silver). In his early years, Gilligan wouldn't have been so picky, and his change in attitude says much about the changes in the craft.

Born in 1977 in Arcadia, Ohio, a rural farming town with a population of five hundred, Gilligan began as a technical juggler of renown. He started juggling when he was nine, after discovering the skill at a unicycle convention, and plunged headlong into obsession. He juggled seven, sometimes eight hours a day, in a "juggling lab" in his converted barn. After some introductory lessons with a vaudeville juggler-turned-boxer from Michigan ("this really old dude"), he began performing.

Not surprisingly, while experiencing his bliss, he also grew quite skilled, and as word of his skills leaked to his neighbors, they began inviting him to perform. He did the local Cub Scout banquet. He did Christmas at the firehouse. The shows were nothing special, usually a medley of tricks set to the music and theme of whatever movie happened to be big that summer (*Indiana Jones and the Temple of Doom* was one), but the local audiences loved them. Before long, his phone rang with offers from farther afield. At age seventeen, he had his own business card and headshot and had embarked on his "word-of-mouth American tour."

At the height of this activity, Gilligan received a call from a producer in Las Vegas with an offer to perform there. For most young jugglers the offer would represent the culmination of a dream, but Gilligan's feelings were mixed. By then he had become aware of certain limitations inherent in juggling. He found himself growing bored during practice. "With numbers juggling, you can kind of turn your brain off," he said. "What comes after nine? Oh, ten—it's not hard to figure out." More troublingly, he wondered about the place of juggling as a form of performance. Jugglers developed a specific kind of rapport with the audience: "There's a power thing that happens. It becomes: Watch me. I'm going to impress you." Juggling, he felt, was reduced to technical show, a concern thrown into relief when he saw his first ballet.

Like jugglers, he noted, dancers cultivate a skillful form of bodily movement. Yet audiences approach the work from a vastly different perspective. "You don't go to a ballet and say, Wow, he jumped super-high," he pointed out. Instead, the audience is expected to consider the totality of the performance: the themes and composition of the dance, the expressiveness of the dancers, the lights, the stagecraft. "Although I hadn't realized it, that's how juggling always was for me," Gilligan said. "I was always more interested in the performance than the skill."

Gilligan's qualms came to a head one night in Vegas. After a show, a Scottish producer knocked on his door. He was interested in hiring Gilligan to perform in Scotland. To help cover the costs of the flight, Gilligan booked other gigs around Europe. All told, he spent six months performing and meeting other jugglers in England, France, Germany, and Scandinavia. What he discovered there changed his life.

In Europe, Gilligan found jugglers who practiced a completely different form of juggling. They moved in odd ways and according to odd rhythms, and on the whole seemed to be thinking less about tricks than about creating shapes—shapes among the objects in the air, between the objects and the body, and between the objects and the environment. There was an intellectual quality to the work that he appreciated. "For the first time I had to sit down and think: Why am I going to use this technique? Or how could this technique join *this* technique?" The work seemed to come from a different place. Gone was the emphasis on pure displays of skill. In its place was the notion of juggling as a vehicle for creative expression. The European jugglers "weren't just trying to impress people."

The "modern" (or "art") juggling he found in Europe felt like a revelation, a scene he missed out on growing up in rural Ohio. ("I was eighteen years old and just beginning to figure things out.") Unbeknownst to him, however, the modern form dated back almost sixty years, and, as he later discovered, its roots were actually American.

During the thirties and forties, as most jugglers propelled themselves headlong toward virtuosity, a select few had taken an opposite tack. One of the first of these so-called minimalists was Bobby May. Born Ludwig Mayer, May, who debuted as a professional in 1922, was in many ways a throwback to an even earlier time. Dressed like the gentlemen jugglers of yore, in black tie and tuxedo, he created routines using elegant props: top hats, canes, pool balls. What made his act unique was his approach. Instead of creating routines with *more* objects, May deliberately worked with fewer, often as few as three—three hats, three balls, three canes. In his posters, he rarely specified what he did, working instead to cultivate an air of mystery. In one ad he listed his name, "Bobby May," followed by the line, "or he may not."

As juggling historian Alan Howard told me, May thought of himself first and foremost as an entertainer. Francis Brunn, another minimalist, took himself more seriously. Son of a champion diver, Brunn learned to juggle from his father, who had taught himself using stones while a prisoner during World War I. Performing first in Germany, later in the States, Brunn worked his way up the cabaret and circus circuits, often appearing with his sister, Lottie. Like May, Brunn usually juggled a small number of objects. (He's quoted as saying, "I am fascinated by controlling one ball.") But whereas May saw himself as an entertainer, Brunn considered his work closer to dance. Though many jugglers had trained in dance before him, they viewed the skill as preparation, a means to an end—namely, bodily control. For Brunn, dance was part of the performance. In one of his most famous pieces, he played a flamenco dancer, prancing through his moves like a matador with an inflatable ball, his chin aloft, spine erect. More broadly, Brunn approached his work as a dancer might choreograph a number. "Everything had a flow," Howard said. "Every move was a picture." Between tricks, Brunn struck balletic poses. He was obsessed with the shapes his body made during routines, with line and rhythm.

In videos such moves can make him look cheesy and overwrought (Pascal once called him "kitsch"), but their inclusion marked a fundamentally important shift. By incorporating his body as a central element of the performance, by refusing to "hide behind" his objects, Brunn changed the emphasis of his juggling. No longer was the work a mere demonstration of skill. Now it was about the *juggler himself*, about the visual and potentially poetic presentation of his body in dialogue with objects as well as the connection between its movement and his personality. "Francis used to stress this to me all the time," Viktor Kee once told me. Kee, the Cirque du Soleil star, was a Brunn protégé. "He told me never to compete, literally or metaphorically. Your real act is who you are."

This was one of the central tenets of the modern circus movement, and the first essential point in understanding how the circus evolved: the circus isn't just a series of skillful displays; it's a vehicle for personal expression, for the conveyance of an artist's ideas and emotions. Perhaps this truth seems obvious, but for a long time it was rarely voiced. Traditional circus performers took their acts seriously, investing a tremendous amount of themselves in those acts' execution. But their interest was in a kind of classical purity. Perfection was produced by conforming to the codes, attaining the correct form. It was an admirable approach, but for the circus to become a modern art, something more was needed; the performers would need to apply their skills as a means of personal communication with an audience.

Personal expression can take myriad forms. Like a dancer, a circus performer might attempt to express a negative feeling in the routine—pain, loss, sadness—or an idea or a concept. As with most modern art, the concept doesn't have to be obvious, and in most cases it isn't, but the audience still feels the effects. For "Light," one of his more popular routines, Michael Moschen manipulated a crystal ball across his body, rolling it over his arms, his chest, and his back. The act was supposedly a tribute to Moschen's sister, who had died in a car accident several years before. To Moschen, the crystal ball symbolized her soul; he endeavored to communicate the idea that, for the two or three minutes the ball was in motion, she was alive.

Among jugglers, Brunn was the first to aspire to create such work, and it's this intention that makes him important. By declaring himself an artist, by aspiring to make work that meant something to him personally, that spoke to his own ideas, his own experiences, his own past, his loves, anxieties, attitudes, he willed modern juggling into being.

After Brunn, the movement continued to develop through the seventies and eighties. Many of the practitioners were American. In the East, Moschen was big. Out west, in Colorado, a group of jugglers called Airjazz created theatrical juggling shows, combining the skill with dance, character work, and physical theater, and they eventually landed on Broadway.

During the eighties and nineties, the art of juggling sputtered in America, largely for reasons of cultural funding. (On the vagaries of American funding, more later.) Europe, however, carried the torch. In England, one of the earliest and most influential groups was Gandini Juggling. Founded in London by Sean Gandini and Kati Yla-hokkala, the group, according to their company mission, was born of the desire to create full-length juggling shows, "fueled by the belief that juggling is an exciting living art form." In France, where much of the early action centered on the National School, modern juggling became so popular that, by the time Gilligan visited, it was the art's dominant form. The majority of French schools taught at least some "art" juggling, and professionals could expect to live off their work through shows and grants and teaching.

After his exposure to modern juggling, Gilligan deliberately set out to learn the form, primarily by talking to as many European jugglers as he could. He cultivated a style of his own, which he billed in America as Postmodern Juggling. People didn't know what to make of it.

"Because they have never been to Europe, most performers in the States have no idea of the possibilities," Gilligan told me that day in the store. "The bar is still set really low. The typical reaction was two-part. First they'd say, I've never seen anything like that. Then they'd admit, I liked it. Which I guess is a good thing." Nevertheless, Gilligan eventually tired of the "hustle," of educating people about the work, and returned to Europe, where he had made a name for himself.

I asked if he could ever see himself living in the States again.

"Sure, I'd love to," he replied, "but the work's just not there yet. It's the kids now, the first wave who know about Europe, mostly through the Internet, who are making the changes. In fifteen years, it is going to be the kids with that experimental spirit who are really badass performers," he said. "We're just going to have to wait fifteen years, that's all."

JUGGLERS ESPECIALLY ENGAGED the issue of what "modern" circus means. On the Internet, where they collected in droves, there were long debates over the recent changes in the field, and how the new "modern" forms differed from more technical forms. The issue had become so prevalent that a backlash had emerged. "Can't we just shut up about this whole thing?" one forum poster wrote.

Initially, I didn't know what to make of this discussion. Listening to a juggler talk about Marcel Duchamp, I would feel my ironic knee start to jerk, the product of my own stereotypes about the craft. But I was overlooking an essential point. The circus had "absorbed" juggling during the twentieth century, which was a period of immense artistic changes. There was a chasm between the classical art of 1900, when Cinquevalli made his mark in London, and the art of 1980, when the art broke away. In the intervening period, modernism and then postmodernism had swept through the world. As a reaction to the destruction of two world wars, and the sense of increasing instability brought on by accelerated industrialized life, the old codes fell away, yielding to a more fractured, individualized approach to art.

This shift affected most forms of creative human endeavor. Take painting. From the Middle Ages until the end of the nineteenth century, painters had adhered to strict rules of composition and restricted themselves to the representation of subjects largely culled from the natural and religious world. But with Impressionism, painters stopped trying to convey a realistic image of the world and instead tried to capture their subjective experience—their impressions of a moment, how a subject made the artist think or feel. Other forms went through equivalent transitions: Composers developed atonal chords. Poets abandoned rhyme and meter.

This unshackling of artistic rules occurred in all the arts at roughly the same time, and yet the circus and its component art remained unaffected. Enslaved by their own traditions, the forms of circus art failed to evolve. Only in the 1970s did the circus finally wake up, like a man emerging from a mythic slumber. Only then did artists engage with the essential modernist questions that other disciplines had long since resolved: What is juggling? What defines it? What are its limits? What can it be used for?

No wonder jugglers were excited. In a small but justifiable way, they felt they had arrived at a historical moment in their discipline. And it was all happening so quickly. Changes that had occurred in other forms over decades were happening in the circus arts in a few years.

Of course, nobody knows where this is headed. Technical juggling is still the dominant form of the discipline, especially in America, and perhaps it always will be. As I was reminded in the shop with Gilligan, for all the changes in the form, the new overlay of intelligence, the fundamental appeal remains the same.

We were standing near the back of the shop, perusing a shelf laden with juggling paraphernalia of every conceivable shape and size—clubs, balls, scarves. Feeling inspired, I had decided to buy some juggling materials of my own, and Gilligan agreed to help pick them out. I plucked a beanbag off the shelf. It was round and plum-sized, with blue and white panels. "Yeah, that's good." Gilligan squeezed the beanbag. "You're gonna suck in the beginning, so it's better you don't spend half your time chasing shit."

Just then the door to the shop clanged open. A postman backed into the shop, his arms wrapped around a cardboard box, which he delivered to the shopkeeper at the counter. I couldn't make out what they were saying, but when the shopkeeper pried open the flaps of the box, his face lit up. *"Merci! Merci!"* he said fervently to the postman, then shuffled quickly over to where we were standing.

"Eh, *excusez-moi.*" He approached Gilligan tentatively. "If you want, I have some white rings for you now." He held one up.

The juggler's face erupted into a smile. "You are my new best friend," he said to the shopkeeper.

We moved to the register in a pack, where the shopkeeper pulled four more rings from a box and handed them to Gilligan, who gave them his jeweler's appraisal. The shopkeeper watched him. "You are Mr. Gilligan, *non?*"

Gilligan nodded.

"We have some films of you," the shopkeeper said as his wife appeared from a back room behind the counter, watching Gilligan wordlessly.

"Merci," Gilligan said.

"We have also this," the shopkeeper's wife chimed in, picking up a colored flyer from the counter and handing it to Gilligan. Since Gilligan's initial trip to Europe, he'd been back to France several times. This time he had been invited specially to create a new juggling show with a French troupe led by Jérôme Thomas, an artistic-juggling legend. The flyer was for the upcoming show, and Gilligan stared at it with seemingly genuine astonishment, like a rookie admiring his own baseball card for the first time. "Wow," he said. *"C'est moi."* He thanked the woman and put the flyer in his bag. He'd started to do the same with the rings when the shopkeeper stopped him with a hand and a playful grin.

"First, a figure, maybe." The shopkeeper and his wife stood shoulder to shoulder, beaming.

"A figure?" asked Gilligan.

"Yes, just one figure, one trick, please."

Gilligan shrugged. Nowhere, not in airports, not in hotel lobbies, not even in Accro'Balles, was he immune. He picked up the white rings from the counter, and we all took a step back to watch as he casually performed a basic five-ring trick. The shopkeeper, his wife, and I all applauded. Then the juggler laughed and, rings in hand, executed an overly dramatic Shakespearean bow.

7

Juggling Clubs

A MONTH AFTER MY EXCURSION with Gilligan, I still couldn't juggle. When I tried, I quickly grew frustrated. Practice seemed willfully Sisyphean: I threw balls in the air and then scrambled after them as they fell. Depressed, I stopped trying to learn, and the balls began to gather dust on my mantel. In retrospect, I think I might never have learned to juggle had an unexpected meeting not spurred me to action.

Nestled in a cobblestone side street on the Left Bank is the Librairie Bonaparte, a boutique shop specializing in *littérature de spectacle*—anything related to the performing arts. To drum up business, the owner, an imperious woman in her forties, had taken to hosting readings by local performing artists in which they read passages that had "marked" their work. One week it was a choreographer reading Nerval. Another reader, a director, shared Dostoevsky. The week I attended, the guest was Jérôme Thomas.

I had been hearing about Thomas since the beginning of the year. In circus circles, as I said, he was a living legend. Jean-Michel Guy openly referred to him as "a master" (*un maître*). Back in the eighties, Thomas had been the form's primary progenitor in France as well as the creator of the country's first full-length juggling show, *Extraballe*.

What really made Thomas famous, though, was his personality. In interviews he was animated and eccentric. He talked about juggling the way Picasso discussed painting. "The ball is the master," Jérôme once told a reporter. "One must understand it like a shell discovered on the beach and listen to it in order to hear the sea." When I asked other people about Thomas, they described him with a mixture of amusement and admiration that made me curious.

On the night of his reading, I took the Métro to the bookshop after my final class. I had arranged to meet a couple of other students there and found them sitting on a staircase in the back, among a crowd of forty or so. Patrons were crowded into folding chairs and spilling onto the floor.

Thomas arrived and took a seat in a high-backed wooden chair. He was tall and sinewy, with an angular face and black hair flecked with gray. Professionally cool, he fielded a series of typical questions ("Are you going to juggle for us?") with professional *sagesse* ("It's true that one could make a show with objects in this room"), and then turned to his selected passage from *If This Is a Man*, by Primo Levi, an account of Levi's time in Auschwitz. The passage described an informal market prisoners had established in the camp to exchange bits of food and clothing. Thomas read the words in the slow and somber voice of a poet.

When he finished, he placed the book on his knee and related his own trip to Auschwitz. He described the cold rain that fell as he boarded the van in Kraków, and his expectations for the visit, and how paltry those expectations proved to be when he was confronted with the horror of the camp as expressed in the smallest details: where the fence burrowed into the dirt, a line scratched into the plaster wall. "As an artist, you ask yourself what can be done in the face of such insurmountable evil—what can I do? The answer is, very little. I can only try to tip the balance away from all that evil, toward something better, something more hopeful, toward the beautiful."

From my perch in the back of the room, I listened intently to his monologue and tried to grasp the sentiment he was expressing. On the one hand, Thomas made a clear and serious point about the function of art and an artist's ability to add light in the war against the world's dark forces. But to me Thomas was just a juggler pontificating on the evils of Auschwitz. Despite all my research and conversations with Gilligan, I was still stereotyping jugglers: there was still a limit to how seriously I could take them.

And so I approached Thomas after the reading. We chatted briefly at the front of the store, the crowd buzzing around us. I told him about my classes at the National School, my interest in the circus, and my meeting with Jay Gilligan. He listened attentively, nodding sharply and interjecting "Hmm-hmm" and "Umm-hmm" with distracting regularity. The man had what pulp novelists call a "penetrating gaze," exaggerated by his height. But he also seemed congenial and genuinely curious about my activities. At the end of our conversation, we agreed to meet again in three weeks, when he would return to Paris for another performance.

I thanked him, and was heading for the door when I heard his voice behind me.

"Hey! American!" He was staring at me over the crowd, his lips crimped into a wry smile. "Are you a juggler?"

I winced. What Thomas was asking was whether I was part of his tribe of jugglers—an "insider." I had been confronting this question since the beginning of the year: Do you merely like the circus, or do you actually perform in it? Invariably, when I mentioned my attendance at the National School, I would be treated with the informality of camaraderie. There was still a low wall around the circus.

Influenced by such concerns, I found myself exaggerating to Thomas: Yes, I told him, I juggle a bit.

His face unfolded perceptibly. *"Excellent!* An American juggler!" He cast his eyes about the shop. "I don't often get to juggle with Americans!"

I hedged. "Really," I said, "I only juggle a little bit."

But the damage had been done, and when the juggler gazed at me, there was a glint in his eye.

"Oh, don't worry." Thomas smiled sardonically. "Just be sure to bring your balls when we meet."

....

I HAD THREE WEEKS to learn to juggle. To the layperson this time frame might not seem like an issue, given my enrollment in the best circus school in Europe, but there were complications. For starters, the school offered no regular juggling classes. Occasionally there were workshops, usually for the advanced students, but for the most part jugglers were left to their own devices. Frédéric explained that jugglers learned mostly by doing. Though I knew this was a reasonable way to learn, it was not exactly helpful in my case.

I thought about approaching the students themselves for help, but after several months of making a spectacle of my failings as a tumbler, I was reluctant to add juggling to my list of public embarrassments. The jugglers were also a peculiar lot. Historically, they had a reputation for being self-motivated and solitary; they generally ate and trained alone. I saw hints of this reclusive behavior at the National School. At night, after the other students had retired to the campfire in the courtyard to swig wine from bottles and swap stories, the jugglers would slip into the empty hall to practice. To observe this ritual, the habits of this rare and lanky species of circus performers, was to conduct a piece of circus ethnography.

"The jugglers are the crazy ones," Ryszard whispered in my ear during one such session. We had been lounging on a mat, discussing his trip to New Orleans ("I was hoping to use my French"), when a pair of sophomore jugglers, Alex and Julien, entered the hall. I knew both in passing. Alex, who was lean and muscular with a delicate air, specialized in "bounce juggling"; he hurled white silicone balls at the ground rhythmically, as if squishing bugs. Julien was more unconventional and was quiet to the point of being stern. I had previously encountered Julien juggling two balls and a rusty sickle. Later in the year, he would shave his head with a razor and spend weeks trying to catch a ball on his barely visible hairline.

On this night, Julien marched to a box in the center of the floor, peeled off his shirt to expose a muscular torso, and began stretching his arms across his body like an Olympic swimmer preparing to dive. Alex, meanwhile, had constructed a fortress of crash pads and began whipping his silicone balls against the cement floor. His drumming simulated a metronome: *bum-bum-bum-bum-bum-bum-bum.*

I asked Ryszard why he thought the jugglers were crazy.

"They are always here," he said, not diverting his eyes from the two. "I think sometimes they break into the building at night. Maybe they cut the lock, then fix it in the morning." I didn't know what to say to this bizarre comment, although I was amused by the image of Ryszard waving a flashlight in the courtyard after dark, on the watch for nefarious jugglers. Anyway, the two strange students were out as instructors. Fortunately, I had another source. Shortly after arriving in Paris, I had learned that an old friend from college, Mose, was also in town, teaching English. When he came to my apartment, he spotted the pyramid of dusty balls on my mantel and popped all five of them into the air with astonishing ease. He was a juggler!

The day after my encounter with Jérôme, I called Mose and asked if he could teach me to juggle in three weeks.

"Sure, that's no problem," he said. "I mean, it depends on how good you want to be."

I asked him if I could learn to juggle five balls in the time I had available. After a pause, he answered that it had taken him a year to learn to juggle five balls. "You should probably stick with three."

We agreed to meet the following Friday. For our first lesson he proposed an unexpected venue: the École Normale Supérieure (ENS), one of France's most prestigious universities—Harvard, Princeton, and Yale rolled into one aristocratic ball. Every week, Mose had heard, the school hosted a juggling club, technically for the students but open to anyone. It was purportedly the biggest gathering of jugglers in the city.

As part of the aforementioned "liberation" of the circus arts, circus skills, once purely professional, had been made available to the French masses. All of the circus arts had experienced this broadening, but juggling had *really* exploded. Almost every college hosted a juggling club, and most decent-sized towns had juggling meetings, a preposterous notion just twenty years before. I thought visiting the club would be a good opportunity to explore the movement. Learning to juggle among unskilled newbies seemed sensible.

Alas, that's not quite how it worked out.

IN 1977, shortly after moving from a Stanford education to a job as a river rafting guide, John Cassidy had a brainstorm that would alter both his life and the history of juggling. Several years before, Cassidy had learned to juggle from a hitchhiker. This wasn't unusual. Juggling was in the midst of its boom. Membership in the International Jugglers' Association, founded by a group of magicians in 1947, had exploded. In 1975, *The Wall Street Journal* dedicated a front-page story to the association's annual convention in Youngstown, Ohio, and membership promptly doubled again.

In many ways, juggling was the most accessible circus art. Compared with other circus skills, it was relatively cheap and required minimal equipment. ("Find three balls behind a tennis court and there you go," was how juggling historian Alan Howard once described it.) Juggling also held a social appeal, especially among supporters of the counterculture. "It was something you could do sports-wise that didn't necessarily involve competition," Tim Roberts, an American juggler and circus administrator who grew up during this period, told me. "It was progressive. Everyone could participate at their own level. It was this perfect activity."

In California, Cassidy knew about this trend—his own lesson from the hitchhiker had been a part of it. He also knew, however, that juggling remained outside the mainstream. For the masses, the skill was still esoteric, like yoga or meditation. But then, during one of his rafting trips, he decided to teach a few of his charges how to juggle, using stones by the river. Dentists, lawyers, salesmen, teachers—they all loved it! At every opportunity they would pile out of the boat and practice.

Inspired, Cassidy made juggling lessons part of his guiding routine. With a group of ambitious friends, Cassidy compiled in a book a collection of illustrated lessons for the juggling amateur. Entitled *Juggling for the Complete Klutz*, the book promised to teach juggling to anyone who could "scramble an egg, find reverse in a Volkswagen or stumble onto the light switch in the bathroom at night."

Technically, *Klutz* wasn't the first "how-to" book for the craft, nor was it the first effort to bring juggling to a wider audience. Cassidy's book was, however, the first effort to address directly the aura of impenetrability surrounding the craft. That was reinforced by its casual title, and by three small beanbags attached to the spiral binding.

The book was released in 1977. Initial interest was small. But as word of mouth spread, sales skyrocketed. Within a year, *Klutz* had landed on the *New York Times* best-seller list. The manual would go on to sell more than two million copies, and it still sells well today. With the proceeds, Cassidy founded a publishing company specializing in the sort of "experiential reading" he brought to juggling (e.g., *The Klutz Book of Balloon Twisting*). Meanwhile, *Klutz* altered forever the American public's perception of juggling, catapulting the skill into the mainstream. As Penn Jillette, the speaking half of the famous magic duo Penn & Teller, famously quipped, "When you pulled out three balls in 1973, what was going through people's minds was, 'I saw a deformed midget do that once.' But when you pulled out three balls in the '80s, it was, 'a guy in my dorm room used to do that.' "

Today there are no official statistics about the number of practicing jugglers, but informal estimates put the world total as high as ten million. Juggling conventions, once quaint affairs held in church basements, are now major events. The European Juggling Convention (EJC), the Woodstock of the discipline, annually attracts upward of sixty-five hundred jugglers and fans. The festival takes place over a long weekend. Days are consumed with workshops and leisurely matches with strangers. Nights fade into shows and booze-fueled banter. The highlight of every festival is the juggling competitions. Some of these are what you might expect, with prizes for "best routine" and "most objects juggled." Others are more peculiar. In "Endurance Juggling," contestants vie to see who can juggle the longest. In "Combat," a juggler tries to knock his opponent's balls while somehow maintaining his own pattern. Matches can last hours.

In their diversity, sociability, and outright absurdity, these activities testify to the spread of juggling as an amateur practice, and especially to its rise as something you *do* instead of *watch*, as was once demonstrated for me with comedic clarity on a Sunday morning in New York. I was watching the New York City Marathon near the eighteen-mile mark and admiring the flow of panting humanity when—lo and behold!—a pair of jugglers came jogging around a bend. They wore mesh tank tops and kept up a steady flow of three orange balls each, rotating in front of them.

At conventions, where the practice is common and completed at varying speeds, such men are known as "jogglers." How far juggling had come. In surprise and delight, I found myself whooping the New York duo on. "Yeah, joggling!" I called. "Wooo-hoo! Go, jogglers!" I thought the men would appreciate the recognition, but they must have thought I was mocking them, because as they hustled past—chests heaving, balls awhirl—one of the two cut me a nasty look. The other just joggled on by.

OF COURSE, not everyone has the time or the resources to rent a Cessna and go convention-hopping every weekend, and for the less fortunate souls there are juggling clubs, such as the one whose meeting Mose and I attended in Paris. Like the juggling conventions, juggling clubs are ubiquitous. Tokyo has four, London ten. In America, where many of the nation's 191 juggling clubs are associated with and sometimes funded by universities, these clubs double as social organizations. In Europe, most clubs are more straightforward: they provide a high-ceilinged room and, if you are lucky, a box of juggling equipment. Fortunately, the club at the ENS provides both, and after fishing five balls and three clubs from a trunk labeled "Help Yourself!," Mose and I wandered onto the gymnasium floor.

"So . . . I guess we should start with the basics," Mose suggested, dropping his armload of objects to the green parquet floor. I had never stood in a juggling crowd before, and it was an odd feeling. There was an unfamiliar verticality to the room's energy. The objects in the air pulsed like a swarm of hummingbirds, and the space echoed with a cacophony of clicks. Few of the jugglers at the "amateur" club seemed like beginners. Searching for a position on the floor, I spotted three jugglers working with more balls than I could count. Across from us a young girl, no more than ten years old, worked with four clubs. Such professionalism was disheartening.

Mose stooped to pick up a single ball. "Most people think juggling is about catching," he said. "In fact, it's the opposite. Get the tosses perfect, and the catches take care of themselves." To illustrate his point, he demonstrated the ideal toss, lobbing the ball from one hand to the other, his arms bent at the elbow. "There should be a lightness to it," he said, watching the ball drift in front of his eyes. He told me to pay special attention to his hands, which rotated in alternating outward circles: the right hand should move clockwise while the left hand rotates counterclockwise. "It's like *The Karate Kid*," he explained. "Wax on. Wax off."

I gave it a whirl. Retrieving a ball from the parquet, I lobbed it back and forth while focusing on the height of the tosses.

"That's good," Mose said. "Now let your shoulders relax. Work on keeping your hands low."

I did as I was told, tossing and tossing again. The act's rudimentary rigor reminded me of the first days of dance class at school, and of the hours spent drilling the basic ballet steps, the *tendus* and the *dégagés*. I had raised a foot a few inches off the floor, replaced it, raised the foot, replaced it. Our instructor had told us that it was necessary to establish the essential "vocabulary of movement" before progressing to more difficult fare, and I found juggling similar.

But juggling was also similar in the persistence it required. Mose made me throw the ball for what seemed like an hour. It came to feel less like a lesson and more like occupational therapy. The ten-year-old girl eventually stopped juggling and, with open curiosity, watched me move the single ball back and forth, over and over.

Finally, Mose granted me a reprieve. "Lesson two," he announced merrily, reaching for another ball.

Lesson two was all about rhythm. To keep the objects from colliding in the air, jugglers stagger their throws, tossing alternately with each hand.

"Wait for the first ball to reach the top of its arc, and then throw the second," Mose said. "Toss, toss, catch, catch." With each toss, he scooped a ball into the air. Because of the delay, they created an "X" in front of his eyes. "Toss, toss, catch, catch."

I gave it a try. The motion was easy at first. I threw the first ball, waited for it to reach the top of its arc, and then tossed the second. Whereupon I was hit with juggling's basic dilemma: With two balls in the air, which one should you focus on? The ball going up or the ball coming down?

I chose the ball coming down. Lurching toward it, however, I failed to make a proper second toss. Instead of loping upward leisurely, the ball zipped forward almost laterally, striking Mose in the thigh.

Mose scolded me with his eyes. "What did I tell you?"

He retrieved the ball graciously. "Tosses, not catches." The golden rule.

I tried again. It went better. The first toss arrived noticeably higher than my second, but the balls knit their ideal "X," each hovering for an instant before cascading into my open palm with a satisfying smack. Mose encouraged me to count the rhythm aloud. "Toss, toss; catch, catch," I repeated, tossing and tossing, catching and catching.

In discussions, jugglers regularly mention the satisfying "circularity" of the activity—the movement of the arms, the casual drift of the balls. There is a meditative quality that jugglers like to cite, as in the book *Zen and the Art of Juggling.* On paper this seemed like New Age drivel, but, even working with a lowly two balls, I understood the claim better. There was a continuous rhythm to the motion, a drumlike feeling, that made it easy to achieve what psychologists refer to as the "flow state," when you feel yourself being absorbed by an activity. There was even something relaxing about it, and I was basking in this calm when Mose plucked a water bottle from his backpack and took a swig.

"Right on," he said, drawing his sleeve across his lips. "Now do that for another half-hour and you'll be ready for lesson three."

JUGGLING WITH MOSE brought to the foreground a question I had been pondering since the beginning of the year: On a purely physical level, what was happening inside me when I learned to perform in the circus? What was going on in my body and head that allowed me to acquire these new skills? In essence, how does the repetition of an action translate into physical efficiency, and eventually into art?

Later, I went to a professional—Marie-Claude Després—for some answers.

"Technically, I'm a body person," Després said. "But of course it's all relative. Two-thirds of what I do takes place upstairs."

What Després "does" is physiotherapy, the nebulous profession of manipulating bodily behavior. She was based in Montreal, and her client roster had included professional hockey players, ballerinas, and rock stars, all working in the upper echelons of their fields. Before going into practice for herself, Després spent six years as the head physiotherapist for Cirque du Soleil's *Quidam,* where she counseled jugglers ("lots of neck problems"), clowns ("like actors"), and enough Russian acrobats to guard the Kremlin ("so adorable, the Russians"). I asked her how circus performers become practitioners of such unconscious exactitude. Her response was one of the more elegant metaphors I ever heard on the subject.

Human beings, Després told me, are essentially complex machines operated by computers. Our bodies are the machines; our brains are the computers. And, just like a computer, a human brain has two types of memory: the hard drive and the working consciousness.

"Your hard drive is here." Després tapped herself on the back of the head. "This is your cortex. It's where information is stored—memories, movements, anything unconscious. The other type of memory is your prefrontal cortex. That's up here." She skimmed her fingers to the top of her head and buried them in her cowlick. "The prefrontal cortex handles all the processing, anything happening in the minute. Like this conversation."

What matters for the circus performer is how these parts relate. As we navigate through the workaday world, the two types of memory are in constant conversation: old information gets retrieved, new information is stored. As he or she practices, Després said, a circus performer refines this conversation. The movement is basically "downloaded" from the prefrontal cortex to the cortex, from the performer's short-term memory to her long-term memory. First a connection is made; then each repetition deepens the impression a bit more; in time, the connection forms a habit. "Eventually, all you have to do is initiate the movement," Després explained. "You start the throw, and the long-term part of the brain immediately takes over the rest of the action."

In popular lingo we refer to this as the development of "muscle memory," but it's an inaccurate term. Circus performers aren't just training their muscles; they are training their minds, too. With each toss or tuck, they're creating the interior conditions for exterior achievements.

Of course, circus performers aren't the only masters of muscle memory. Chefs learn to chop with lightning flourishes. Piano players measure their finger movements by the millimeter. All of us employ it every day when we parallel-park a car or walk and talk on a cell phone simultaneously. But circus performers show us how precisely a person can train himself. Argentine juggler Marco Paoletti once told me that in his training sessions he aimed not to perform a move successfully but, rather, to discover a "consistent feeling" connected with each, a sensation that he could access onstage and use to reproduce the movement. Over tens of thousands of hours of practice, he had amassed an encyclopedia of these feelings. This was *his* juggling, this index of interiority.

"Whether I'm holding a ball or not," Paoletti said, "the movement should be exactly the same."

....

IN THE ENS GYMNASIUM, I watched the jugglers pack up their equipment and drift to the exit. Mose had already disappeared. I kept tossing two balls until I eventually grew bored and decided to track down Marc Espie, the lanky, Einstein-haired director of the club. We were talking about juggling as a social discipline—"The school thought we might be troublemakers, but of course we're mostly nerds"—when Mose appeared again, jogging.

"Sorry," he said, out of breath. "There was this dude with glass balls doing some crazy contact in the hallway."

I had no idea what he was talking about. We resumed practice: three balls.

The idea, Mose said, was to create the same "X" in the air. He suggested that I start with a "flash," a single throw and catch of each ball. He demonstrated the move: "toss, toss, toss; catch, catch, catch." "As each ball reaches the top of its arc," he dictated, "throw the next one." With my own three balls, I tried the pattern jugglers call the cascade, and found it surprisingly easy: right, left, right. True to Mose's plan, the interminable two-ball scooping had carved a track in my brain.

"Of course, that's just the beginning," Mose said.

To really have the sense of juggling, I had to create a continuous flow, not just a sequence of catches. This flow is what jugglers refer to as a "run."

Mose held two balls in his right hand and one in his left, and lobbed the balls into the air, alternating hands—right, left, right. Only this time, instead of catching each ball and holding it, his hand immediately cycled the ball into another toss. The balls crossed in the air in a seamless rhythm: toss, toss, toss, toss, toss.

Watching him, I had the sense of *seeing* juggling for the first time. As Michael Moschen once put it during a talk on juggling at the Technology, Entertainment, and Design conference (TED) in California, to the untrained eye even the simplest juggling patterns looked like "a mess that this guy's got his hands around." Now my experience gave me a new perspective. I could *see* the rhythm—how high each ball flew and in what direction it moved. I had heard about this moment from other jugglers. They often spoke of the first time they "understood" juggling. The American legend Dick Franco once told an interviewer for Juggle-Now, a juggling website, that "the feeling I had was profound," and "a lot of things came together and made sense." Tim Roberts saw a juggler on television while lying in a hospital bed as a teenager. "It was like he was in 3-D," Roberts told me. "It's the only thing in my life that I've understood right away."

For Roberts, the moment led to a professional juggling career. My own insight was more intellectual. The circus, I came to understand, was a kind of connoisseur's art. To fully appreciate it, you have to know the forms, through either experience or exposure. Pascal later confirmed this. "Going to the circus is like going to the opera," he said. "You already know the story beforehand. You go to hear the performance, to hear how a singer interprets the specific role."

But there is also something tremendously basic about the circus arts. They are really just physics; each act is about bodies exerting themselves against unseen forces, about wills and forces colliding. The tension is beautiful: an act seems at odds with everyday reality and is yet natural and satisfying. The lesson applies most concretely to juggling. Balls travel in arcs, and every toss is a little science experiment. This simple power goes a long way in explaining why, even in airports, the work of a juggler can leave security guards dazzled. The circus has a simple, inherent loveliness that is easily recognized.

My grand epiphanies did not make learning any easier. In the hall, my first run was a mess, the balls popcorning all over the place. After a few pointers from Mose, I made progress, and on my tenth attempt or so, I managed a run of seven scrambling throws. That simple act felt like an accomplishment. By the end of the night, I had managed ten throws—and I felt downright heroic.

The feeling of competence escalated over the following weeks. From online tutorials and a booklet that came with the balls, I learned the basics: how to throw a ball over the top of the pattern ("tennis"); how to snatch a ball with an aggressive downward swipe ("the claw"). Each new success brought a jolt of positive reinforcement. It was a pleasure unlike the experience of tumbling. Tumbling felt like a sport, like skiing or rock-climbing—I felt the rush of adrenaline. My athletic triumphs were tinged with a sense of having evaded some physical catastrophe. In contrast, juggling was difficult but not dangerous. It was less muscular and more "outside the body." There was an intellectual and technical component to the exercise. Each new trick was a puzzle to be solved. Success, when it occurred, was easily defined and satisfying, like fixing a bicycle, the appeal of a simple process competently enacted, of imposing yourself on the world in a small but measurable way. In short, juggling feels like play more than practice.

By the end of the first week, I was juggling all the time. I juggled in the morning, before breakfast, and at night, after dinner. I began taking juggling breaks throughout the day—five minutes here, ten minutes there. This obsession wasn't uncommon. Almost every serious juggler experiences a similar period. Eric Haines, a Washington-based juggler, once told me he used to sneak out of his room as a teenager and tiptoe down to his basement to practice at night, juggling over a sofa so his parents couldn't hear the balls land.

Still, the strength of the feeling surprised me. It was an oddly tactile fixation, unlike anything I had previously experienced. Objects developed magnetism. I wanted to juggle everything. Walking through the kitchen, I would spy an empty plate in the dish rack and desired to see it in flight. Nothing was off limits—pans, pens, books. In the grocery store, I was a mess. Daniel Schultz, an American juggler I would later meet in Berlin, described this particular curiosity well. Schultz noted that juggling gave him a "new measure of the world," which he called "the jugglability of things." He'd once found himself in his front yard juggling stove grates.

With a week left before my meeting with Jérôme, I had nailed down a dozen tricks or so with three balls—including the "robot" and "Mill's mess" (I picked tricks for their evocative names). But anybody could juggle three; that was child's play. I wanted to learn four. With time running short, I attempted to teach myself, but this proved impossible: the balls kept colliding in the air. Mose was out of town. I decided to look for a teacher at the National School. Finding one didn't take long. Hauling open the hall's rusty door, I found myself facing Yohann, one of the first-year students. He stood in the center of the carpet, in a black tank top, purple socks, and a pair of hot-pink boxer shorts. Eight balls whirled melodiously above him.

Of all the students, Yohann was the most intriguing, and possibly the school's finest circus prospect. As a juggler, he was among the best in his year. He could chuck seven balls over his head with the ease of a man tying his shoelaces. As an acrobat, he managed a grace and polish that most other students lacked. On the trampoline, with his shock of black hair spilling over his ears and wafting when he bounced, Yohann catapulted himself with fluidity and economy of motion. "If he keeps this up, he could be one of the greats," Ryszard commented once, watching Yohann improvise a routine. "There's a difference between being strong [*fort*] and being beautiful [*beau*]. Yohann could be both."

At the same time, Yohann had an intensity that could be troubling. Like other jugglers, he sometimes stayed late to train, but his practice sessions lacked those performers' breezy camaraderie. Instead, Yohann adopted the wild mannerisms of an athlete playing an important match. Between attempts, he paced and picked at the balls' stitches. If he messed up, he berated himself under his breath. The other students didn't know what to make of this erratic behavior. "You never know what he's thinking," confessed Odilon, a freshman acrobat. "He has this way of just staring at you with these intense eyes."

It all made me curious. I had tried to strike up a few conversations with Yohann, but he always seemed disengaged, answering in clipped phrases. I hoped that asking him to help me master four balls would be an opportunity to get to know him better. And, sure enough, when I approached him, he tossed his own equipment aside and readily agreed to teach me.

"The key is in the pattern," he said. I stood barefoot next to him on the carpet in the center of the hall. He still didn't have any pants on. "Unfortunately, the pattern is also the one thing you won't figure out yourself."

He started juggling two balls in his right hand, circling them skyward in an oblong pattern called the fountain.

"Can you do this?"

Yes. I showed him.

"What about the left?"

I showed him the left. The balls meandered, causing me to scramble a bit, but Yohann nodded. "That's good. Now let's put them together."

What followed was a small bit of circus alchemy. Starting with his right hand, Yohann began juggling two balls, whirling a fountain as before. Then he juggled two balls in his left hand to produce a second fountain. At first the patterns were distinct, his hands at least two feet apart. But as he brought his hands slowly toward the center of his body, the patterns began to merge. I thought the balls would collide, but the staggered rhythms fit the patterns inside each other like a pair of gears.

Yohann taught me a critical bit of juggling wisdom: with odd numbers, the balls changed hands, stitching the "X" Mose had shown me in the gym; with an even number of balls, they only *appeared* to change hands.

"Of course, that's just the beginning," Yohann observed. "Later, there are more complicated patterns." He cycled through a few quickly. "But you'll get to that."

We juggled for a half-hour or so, long enough for me to realize that four balls would require some practice, and then we took a break. The hall was relatively quiet. The other first-year students had already taken off for the day. From my class, only Maud remained, sprawled in the corner as if she was making a snow angel. Across the hall, Maurice, the school's docile janitor, was helping a workman bolt a heating duct to the wall.

In the lazy calm, Yohann and I chatted. I told him about my recent plunge into juggling obsession and the conversations I had had with other jugglers, including François Chat, one of France's young superstars, discovered by theater director Robert Wilson when Chat was just a teenager. Though still only in his twenties, Chat had confessed that he might give up juggling, because he found the practice too "intense" and potentially unhealthy. When I relayed this to Yohann, he started to nod.

"Yeah," he said tiredly, "I wish I could quit myself." His narrow face had assumed a serious look, and his eyes were pinned on the janitors working across the hall. "I juggle a lot, but I'm not sure it's good for me."

To assuage him, I commented that he seemed okay when juggling at the school—deeply focused, sure, but not unhealthy. He shook his head and looked down. "Here it's different. There are people around. It's more of a social experience. At home, it's easy for me to get locked in."

"Locked in?"

He paused before responding. He drank from his water bottle and pursed his lips, as if debating his answer. Several years ago, he finally began, he had heard there was a juggler from one of France's most famous companies who had lost control of his obsession. He juggled all day, every day. "His life disintegrated," Yohann said. "He stopped seeing his friends, stopped going out. He barely ate. Then, one day, he disappeared."

"Disappeared?" I said.

Yohann nodded. "He just went missing. For seven years."

"*Seven years?* Where did he go?"

Yohann shrugged. "Nobody knows. If you ask him, he says he can't remember. He can't even remember how he supported himself or what he ate. Just that he was juggling."

I asked Yohann if he believed the tale.

He paused to pick a piece of lint off his boxers, and then said, "You know, I don't know. At first I thought it was ridiculous. But then I saw him perform. And there's something going on there. You can see the seven years in his movements. They say he's never dropped a ball onstage."

The history of the circus is littered with apocrypha, with stories concocted to sell tickets or build mystique. Probably this is one of those stories. I can't say for sure. But it confirmed what I was beginning to understand: some people took the circus very seriously indeed. This applied doubly to jugglers. They were the philosopher kings of the ring, and some of the most passionate, eccentric, intelligent, energetic, and downright peculiar people I had ever met.

And I had yet to juggle with Jérôme Thomas.

8

King of the Juggle

A FEW YEARS AGO, in a declaration noticeably lacking in pomp, the French government added juggling to its institutional registry of *beaux arts* (fine arts). To be among the *beaux arts* in France is to be taken seriously, and so it was with no small amount of pride that Jérôme Thomas served as the art's official representative at the induction ceremony.

The choice of Thomas was natural. Today many critics consider him the most important French juggler alive—the godfather of modern juggling in France. In the eighties, when Gilligan was just beginning to learn his skills, Thomas was part of the vanguard, developing a style that was as much ballet as juggling, as much mime as manipulation. In 1990, with the help of choreographer Hervé Diasnas, he created *Extraballe,* an hour-long show inspired by the improvisational nature of jazz. It was the first full-length juggling program performed in France. Every year or two since, he has premiered a new piece of "juggling theater," each an experimental approach to his three-thousand-year-old craft. In *Rain/Bow,* his juggling ballet, performers moved through showers of white light and paper snow. In *Cirque Lili,* his solo ode to the circus, he played every character in a traditional show, from the ringmaster to the strongman. For the ethereal beauty of his work, critics are wont to refer to him as a "juggling poet" or a "poet of space." "He offers us an hour of poetry in the midst of so much tumult," wrote a critic after an appearance in Shanghai, "an hour of suspension among the skyscrapers."

Jérôme takes himself very seriously. He is openly arrogant, even egotistical, and he occasionally refers to himself in the third person, in a way that might be ironic but probably isn't. People tend to have strong opinions about him. Collaborators tell horror stories of his tirades over missed steps or early exits. This doesn't bother Jérôme, since he tends to have strong opinions himself. Perhaps more than any other juggler, he subscribes to the notion that juggling is a high art, even a spiritual practice. I first observed this attitude when he'd read about Auschwitz in the bookshop. The full extent of it became clear as I researched him prior to our meeting. In interviews he talked about juggling the way Picasso or Warhol discussed painting. For instance:

"Juggling is a language—dramatic, poetic, humorous, theatrical. It participates in the mysteries of gravity and the cosmos."

"I've studied this relationship between object and body for twenty-five years, and it's ungrateful work, comparable to the study of the violin."

"The object is the master. When you fight against it, you don't get much from it."

"One must understand an object like a shell discovered on the beach, listen to it to hear the sea."

"The ball is a note—yes, a note of music, a 'La.' "

On paper this kind of pontification can seem incongruous, like a plumber eulogizing his wrench, but the effect is quite different in person, where Thomas's words are carried by charisma. I discovered this firsthand when, on the day of our appointed visit, I joined him in the Centre Culturel Aragon, a theater on the outskirts of Paris.

"You can call it a passion, but that doesn't do it justice!" Jérôme said, hunched in front of a mirror in the theater's dressing room, rubbing lotion into his cheeks. He was in his boxer briefs, in the middle of changing for rehearsal. Normally he practices where he performs, in his tent, a small one-ring structure that he had set up behind the theater. But it was a chilly afternoon, and so the cultural center's director had offered the use of the stage.

"You understand what I'm saying?" He lit a cigarette, his leg propped on the counter. "You don't find your passions. They find you."

I had come to juggle with Jérôme, but also to understand how his artistry expressed itself in his past and his approach to the work. Like Gilligan, he wasn't born into the circus, but discovered juggling when he was a boy. One summer afternoon in Angers, where he'd been born in 1963, he happened upon a juggler practicing behind the tent of a circus that had installed itself near the river that cut through town. For years Jérôme had struggled in school. He'd been bored by piano, soccer, horseback riding, and judo. But the sight of the levitating balls captivated him, and he marched up for an impromptu lesson. The juggler complied. He taught Jérôme how to juggle three balls and afterward dismissed him by saying, *"Maintenant, démerde-toi"* (Now go play by yourself). The line struck Jérôme as an epiphany. "For the first time, someone insisted I rely on my own creativity."

Then came the usual obsession. Mornings, Jérôme awoke at four and juggled in the predawn darkness, tossing the balls over his bed to muffle the sound. At night, when he was supposed to be doing his homework, he juggled to the music of John Coltrane and Miles Davis. In the dressing room, I asked Jérôme if he ever got lonely. He shrugged. "I felt alone, yes, but never lonely. *C'était plus grand que moi.*"

The phrase *plus grand que moi* was one of his mantras. The literal translation is "bigger than me," but in the Tao of Jérôme, the notion referred to anything intuitable but not comprehensible—an idea, an emotion, the force of a natural or historical event. I first heard him use the term in the bookshop, then in interviews while describing the artistic experience. In this case, he was referring to his progression from an inexorable compulsion to juggle, to Annie Fratellini's circus school in Paris, and then out into the professional world three years later.

The year was 1981, and the options for a professional juggler were limited to circuses and cabarets. As a student, Jérôme had worked on a minimalist routine—seven minutes of Weimar-style juggling inspired by Bobby May—which he performed in tour with the circus associated with Fratellini's school. Afterward, he opted to go the cabaret route, striking a deal with a producer who established him as a regular in the circuit of Parisian parties, discothèques, and lounges.

The life of a cabaret performer is unconventional, not unlike that of a chef or a rock musician. Shows start late, invariably followed by early-morning dinners and predawn drinks. Drugs are omnipresent. The sleaze factor is high. "It was my darkest period," Jérôme said. "I saw real human exploitation."

But the cabaret life also offers a tremendous upside: time. The hours are minimal and well paid, if inconvenient. During the day, Jérôme studied ballet and modern dance, and enrolled in Jacques Lecoq's theater school, a Mecca for European mimes. He started hanging out with musicians, especially jazz musicians. Invariably, the influences bled into his work. He had always been interested in the relationship between juggling and movement: As a kid he had instinctually blended the two, in his room and sometimes in front of his bathroom mirror. "My body had a need to express itself," he said. Now he began to codify his ideas, to develop a style. His juggling became more physical and abstract. He started improvising, playing with rhythm and pacing, and struggled with the existential questions that would later plague Gilligan: What is juggling? What constitutes a trick? How did the codified differ from the creative?

"Here, let me give you an example," he said in the dressing room. He stood above me, holding a white silicone ball. He had found a pair of pants, but still no shirt. His body resembled that of a triathlete, thin and muscular, with the thick mottled skin typical of a physically active man in middle age.

"Take the five-ball pirouette. That's a standard move. Beginning from a cascade"—the basic juggling pattern—"you throw all five balls in the air, spin, and catch the balls when they come down." He mimed the action—the tossing, the spinning, the catching. "That's a codified move. Everyone knows how to do it, even if few people can."

But that was only one approach. An alternative, he said, was to create an original move. It could be an original pattern; Mill's mess, for example, was a mind-boggling three-ball move created for Steve Mills in the seventies. Or it could be an entirely new technique.

"In my latest show, I balance a ball here," he said, pointing to the topside of his wrist, where a watch face would usually rest. "I balance a ball there and spin." At which point, to my surprise, he demonstrated the move. Raising his arm, palm-down, he cocked his hand upward a few degrees, creating a small trough at his wrist. He nestled the ball in the trough and extended his arm to the side. In this position he started to spin, slowly at first, then with gathering momentum, his carriage erect, his feet pivoting precisely on the carpet. As his arm zipped above me, whipping circles in the cramped dressing room, I thought for sure the ball would fly off. But it didn't budge. Centripetal force combined with the upward tilt of his arm to pin it in place.

"That's an original point," Thomas declared as he eased to a stop. The pace of his breath had increased. His eyes glinted. "The move is just as difficult as a five-ball pirouette. The only difference is that one move is codified and the other isn't, so one is seen as technical and the other is artistic. But they're both juggling."

This might seem like an obvious distinction today. But at the time of Jérôme's first experiments, it was revolutionary. Traditional jugglers followed certain codes. The new model meant breaking away from those codes. Jérôme had to carve his own path. Nobody else was thinking that way.

Well, almost nobody. In 1984, Jérôme received a visit from Karl-Heinz Ziethen, a juggling historian, who showed him a video of an emerging American juggler: Michael Moschen. Like Thomas's, Moschen's path was atypical for his era. Born in Greenfield, Massachusetts, he learned to juggle as a teenager with his neighbor Penn Jillette of Penn & Teller. After high school, he didn't opt for college or the traditional circus, but instead migrated to New York. There he made a name for himself juggling in less traditional venues, such as the steps of the Metropolitan Museum of Art, and later for a group of circus upstarts recently arrived from Canada, Cirque du Soleil.

Like Thomas, Moschen worked to expand the definition of juggling. He tried to find novel uses for traditional objects—balls, rings, clubs. In 1984, for a performance called *Light*, he invented what he referred to as "dynamic manipulation," a method of rolling crystal balls along his body such that his skin appears magnetic. Then Moschen branched out into atypical objects. In his 1991 performance, *In Motion with Michael Moschen,* he worked with metal rods. Later, he danced with and manipulated S-shaped pieces of metal.

On the surface, the work sounds derivative: vaudeville jugglers had long before invented original routines (e.g., Cinquevalli's baize billiard jacket). But whereas the vaudevillian jugglers sought novel stunts to impress their audience, Moschen thought of his objects as "visual instruments." What interested him were an object's aesthetic possibilities: What did it look like? How did it move? What patterns could be created with it? As a critic for *The New York Times* commented, "He is a movement artist . . . a sculptor in motion."

Jérôme considered Moschen an artistic brother, an *alter-ego outre atlantique.*

"I once told Michael that," Jérôme said in the dressing room, now zipping up a sweatshirt. "We were driving in a cab and I said, 'Michael, you are the little brother to Francis Brunn, and I am the little brother to you.' "

For fifteen years, the jugglers spread their ideas across their respective continents. In America, Moschen lectured in "innovation and creativity" at MIT and demonstrated his method at the prestigious TED conference in California. In France, Thomas went on to become, well, Jérôme Thomas. Together, the men helped change the definition of juggling. Today "toss juggling" is just one form of the wider discipline, which has become known as "object manipulation" or "dexterity play." During my time in France, I saw "jugglers" perform with plastic bags, leather boots, glasses, feathers, swords, sofas, sawhorses, tea bags, cups of yogurt, slide rules, plastic bags, origami cranes, and a pair of unruly khakis.

Today, this spirit of innovation can be found in all the circus arts. Being a modern practitioner means searching for new and different approaches: new moves, new techniques, new equipment. "It's not *l'exploit pour l'exploit,*" a member of Les Acrostiches told me. "From our very first show, we wanted to present things in a different manner."

But, in my experience, jugglers take ideas more seriously than other performers. Discussing their work, they can sound like explorers heading into the great unknown. The term "discovery" is common. So is scientific jargon. In 1992, Jérôme founded a group called the Workshop for Research in Object Manipulation (*Atelier de recherche en manipulation d'objets*). Jörg Müller, a German juggler, conducted "Performance Research Experiments," including one investigating the possibilities of juggling in a zero-gravity plane. At Gilligan's invitation, I once attended an "Object Manipulation Lab" in Stockholm, a series of workshops he'd organized with funding from the Swedish government, with the aim of conducting "research" into the art of creative manipulation.

For three days, Gilligan and three other jugglers experimented to elucidate fundamental presumptions of their craft. The process was rigorous and concrete. The jugglers worked individually to see what movements an object could yield, gathering in the center of the room afterward to discuss their observations. Gilligan scribbled notes on a legal pad and filmed the exercises with a digital camera. "If a manipulation isn't in line with the one that came before it, it's weak," concluded Gilligan to the group. Added Luke Wilson, a British juggler, "I try to find the best solution for any given situation. Not just a solution. The best solution." The other jugglers nodded in agreement.

The pronouncements sound heady, but they have practical effects. As Henry Moore once wrote, "A sculptor is a person who is interested in the shape of things, a poet in words, a musician by sounds." Jugglers are interested in the motion of objects. To train as a juggler is to receive a unique education in the material that surrounds you, to be an expert in what Moschen once called, in an interview with *The New York Times*, "the emotional resonance objects have with people."

Carried to the extreme, you might even say that juggling isn't a type of performance so much as a way of interacting with the world. My own understanding of this came from watching Jörg Müller perform his piece *Mobile*, in which he manipulated a series of steel pipes hanging from the ceiling by steel cords, thus resembling an enormous wind-chime. Each pipe was as big as Müller himself. Watching him dash between the pipes, knock them with his knuckle, toss them in complex trajectories so that they missed each other by inches, I thought: Who else could do this? Who else could control these objects so precisely? What other kind of training could lead to this art?

....

IN THE THEATER, two enormous pieces of white canvas cloaked the stage, one hanging down the rear wall, the other rolling across the floor, both glowing brightly under rows of halogen lights. Jérôme and I paused in the wings to slip out of our shoes and admire the environment, our rehearsal space. It had a quiet, cathedral-like elegance. Light from the stage spilled over the rows of empty seats. Across from us, a woman in paint-splattered overalls eased a roller across the floor, marking strips of glistening white on the black surface. Cupping his hand to his mouth, Jérôme called to her across the canvas expanse.

"Is it safe to walk on?"

The woman looked up and smiled warmly. "But of course," she said, and made a low "be my guest" sweep of her arm. With his black nylon bag of juggling balls knotted around his knuckles, Jérôme tiptoed barefoot onto the canvas, advancing carefully, as if laying the first tracks in freshly fallen snow. "Somebody's going to be lucky to work in such a beautiful space," he announced to nobody in particular. "To dance on, it's paradise. To juggle on, paradise!"

The woman grinned. "I like my work."

A juggler's work demands that he be both an athlete and an actor, and so training can prove tricky. There is no standard practice routine. Much depends on age. At nineteen, Vladik, a Ukrainian American star, can afford to spend his days mixing hip-hop music on his computer. Older jugglers can't be so cavalier. Although a juggler can continue to work well into his fifties and sometimes even his sixties—decades longer than acrobats—practice becomes progressively more important as he eases toward what Dick Franco once called "the age bomb."

At forty, Jérôme referred to his practice as "hygiene." In a good month, he averaged twenty-six days of juggling, a respectable total, he felt, given the distractions of being a living legend. Most days, he would pad through his newest routine, reviewing the rhythms, reminding himself of transitions, or polishing a move that had been giving him trouble. Sometimes he studied new techniques. A few years ago, Jérôme decided to learn five clubs. Back in the 1980s, when he was breaking into the scene, five clubs was a rarity and a high benchmark, the four-minute mile of the craft. With the Internet, however, things changed. Kids started posting videos of themselves performing seemingly impossible tricks, which they never could have pulled off in person. Nonetheless, the videos had an effect: worldwide, the skill level went up.

Jérôme practiced five clubs every day, paying attention to his footwork and body position, drilling his double flips until he was sure enough of the trick (95 percent accuracy) to include it in his show. That was three years ago, but he was obviously still pleased with the achievement. He was, he said, "pretty damn proud" of hanging with the kids.

"How about we start with a little warm-up?" Jérôme had dumped his balls from his bag, and he started popping four of them above him with a childlike joy, working up an energetic lather as he counted the rhythm of the tosses. *"Tac, tac, tac, tac."*

Nervous, I lingered at the edge of the stage. I dug out three of the balls that I had purchased with Gilligan and lobbed them around, trying to find the flow. The process reminded me of jogging: the first few minutes are rusty, then you feel the grease ooze into the gears. When I felt comfortable, I ran through a series of tricks I had choreographed for the meeting: claw, claw, reverse cascade, tennis, columns, yo-yo. By professional standards, my routine was a remedial display, one Gilligan might have performed long ago at one of his preteen Cub Scout banquets. But I was proud of it, and wanted to get it right, and so, in my corner of the stage, I tried to summon Mose's sage advice: "Scoop in a relaxed fashion. Keep your hands low." I also thought about my expression. I had come to believe that all good jugglers developed a "latent face," a look of practiced nonchalance reserved for particularly difficult moves. Jérôme's latent face included a narrowing of the eyes and a pursing of the lips. Gilligan's was staid, his jaw unhinging to breathe. I aimed for something like baffled amusement. I imagined myself saying, "Oh, would ya look at that!" Which is what I was thinking when Jérôme summoned me to action.

"So why don't you show me what you're working on?" he said. We stood in the center of the stage. Jewels of sweat had already appeared on Jérôme's forehead. He was swigging from a plastic water bottle. I assumed the starting position: two balls in my left hand, one in my right. I could feel my heart knocking against my rib cage. I started to juggle, beginning with my left hand. Things quickly went south: before I could even find a rhythm, one of the tosses came off wrong, and in my distraction I felt another ball glance off the side of my hand, then heard it hit the stage with a shameful thud. "Sorry about that," I said. I retrieved the ball and started again, careful to avoid Jérôme's penetrating gaze.

The balls now settled into their familiar rhythm: toss, toss, toss, toss,

toss. With a bracing breath, I launched into my routine: cascade, tennis, cascade, claw, reverse cascade, columns, yo-yo. I don't remember performing the routine at all. It was a blur of zipping balls and flagging arms—my arms but somehow not my arms—whipping around like tentacles. The panic-stricken voice in my head struggled to keep pace with the action: *grab it, yes, claw, go, yes, next*. Miraculously, I emerged from the routine with the pattern intact, the balls looping jauntily in front of me. A great bell of pride clanged inside my chest. But not for long: for the first time all day, Jérôme had fallen silent.

"Bon" was what he finally said, in a notably flat tone. "You have some nice tricks there. Now let's work on the *quality* of the gesture."

He told me to start juggling again. When I had found the rhythm, he began pacing a circle around me, like a sculptor examining a statue. In the beginning, he explained, what mattered most was the relationship the juggler cultivated with his body. "You have to be aware of yourself all the time," he said. "You have to be checking yourself constantly." He stopped and stared at my feet. "For example, without looking down, can you tell me how your feet are positioned?"

I had no idea. I was too focused on my hands.

Jérôme made a clicking sound. "Your right foot is pointed out, your left foot straight." He nudged my left foot into position with his toe. "Try to keep them both slightly pointed out. When you practice, find this position first."

We repeated the exercise with other parts of my body. Was my spine straight? My shoulders? My chin? Jérôme adjusted me physically, as if I were a pliable doll.

"Now try changing something yourself," he said, after nudging my chin a few centimeters upward with his knuckle. "Try rolling your shoulders forward." He demonstrated by hunching his shoulders over his clavicle.

I followed his lead. Still juggling, I drew my shoulders into my chest.

"*Bon*. Now pull them back."

I complied, squeezing my shoulder blades together. But the new position separated my hands, which altered the rhythm of my tosses. Instead of the usual scoop, the balls whipped in a low, wide pattern. I yanked my shoulders forward, but it was too late, and the balls rained to the ground.

Jérôme cocked a pedagogical eyebrow. A smile pushed at the corner of his lips. "See that? You learned to juggle in one position, so anything else gives you trouble." He scooped my balls from the canvas and started juggling them himself. "Remember," he said, "juggling's not a static operation. It's dynamic. You're not moving the balls. You're moving *with* the balls."

With the balls still bubbling in front of him, he started contorting his body, twisting at the waist, bending at the knees. "Think of the balls as an extension of your body. Whatever motion you begin the balls continue."

I gave it a shot, starting with the vexing shoulder move. Trying my best to imagine the balls as an extension of my body, I retracted my shoulders slowly. Instead of forcing a rhythm, I let the pattern grow wider, using my wrists to toss rather than my arms.

"Et voilà!" Jérôme chimed. "Now do it again, all of it, forward and back."

I did, curling my shoulders forward, drawing them back. At first the motion felt unnatural, like an awkward hip-hop dance. But after a few repetitions, the move became easier, my body more supple.

"You see that? You're freeing up your body. Now try moving around freely."

I started moving around, twisting with the balls, left, then right, bending at the knees. I even dared an improvisational kick. Jérôme almost exploded.

"Et voilà!" he said again. "He's beginning to understand!"

I grasped the lesson. It was related to Jérôme's speech in the dressing room. Juggling isn't just hands and arms; the entire body is involved. By thinking outside the usual position, you could also move beyond the traditional definition of the craft. But there was a subtler lesson, too. For Jérôme, juggling was defined by space, not objects. He regularly coached me to "explore the space." "If you're thinking about the objects, you've lost half the game. This is about the space."

With this in mind, he had developed a training system for himself and other jugglers. He called it *jonglage cubique,* cubic juggling. In cubic juggling, the space around the juggler is divided into three-dimensional planes, like a Rubik's cube. The juggler's body is similarly dissected. To train, a juggler works the parts individually, targeting each with unique exercises. Some of the exercises involve objects, some don't. The latter, considered part of "zero-ball juggling," can look like dances, but the system as a whole is closer to tai chi or biomechanics. At first the trainee practices the exercises separately. After three years, he begins to combine them. The idea is to build the juggler's awareness of the space and his energy, to help him develop a "poetic sense of movement." "It will be my legacy," Jérôme told me.

For the rest of the afternoon I worked with my three balls, exploring different trajectories, patterns, and movement. Jérôme, meanwhile, drifted nimbly across the stage, juggling and dancing on the canvas, cycling through objects—big white balls, little white balls, clubs.

At one point, feeling inspired, I decided to follow his lead. My balls aloft, I shuffled across the stage awkwardly, not moving anywhere specific, just relaxing into my juggling groove. Jérôme loved it. *"Mais oui!"* he shouted *"Formidable! Impeccable!"* He swooped up next to me, juggling and moving, moving and juggling. *"Ah, oui! C'est beau! Vas-y! Lache-toi!"* Let yourself go!

It felt ridiculous at first, but once I got over my self-consciousness the motion was pleasant. Juggling in a single position, usually over my bed with my knees plugged against the side of the mattress, I could feel constricted. Juggling with Jérôme felt more like dancing. I felt loose and expressive. I came to appreciate juggling in a new way, as a form of bodily motion.

One sticking point remained, however. In the circus, jugglers might have the worst experience of failure. There is something noble about the failure of an acrobat—he earns your sympathy with his bravery. And clowns are supposed to be ridiculous. But when a juggler drops a ball, when he stoops or scurries after it, the audience just feels embarrassed for him. If he insists on trying again, you hope he succeeds, mostly to have the whole thing done with.

Of course, every juggler has a way of handling such a moment. Most comic jugglers have what they refer to as "drop lines," quick jokes that cover the flub. ("Now let me show you my floor show!") Other jugglers I spoke with try to find their failures motivating. Greg Kennedy, a juggler with Cirque du Soleil, told me he aims for one or two drops per show, as a measure of how hard he's pushing himself: any more means he's being sloppy, any fewer and he's playing it safe.

"Don't you ever worry about it?" I asked Jérôme after one of my own mistakes.

A wry smile spread across his face. "Worry about what?"

"About the balls falling."

He recoiled in mock surprise. "But of course they're going to fall. You couldn't juggle if they didn't."

WHEN I FIRST CONSIDERED the changes in the circus, I thought of them as a question of modernity: how had the circus become "modern"? Talking with jugglers, I had come to understand that art lay at the center of the changes. What is art? What makes something artistic? At the National School, these questions were paramount, implicit in every aspect of the curriculum. Professionals argued the issue regularly, and used the dialogue to fuel their creations. Jugglers generally refer to it as the "art versus sport" debate.

From a critical perspective, there were obvious answers as to how the circus had become a modern art: the shift from technical virtuosity to personal expression and meaning; the rise of longer forms; a willingness to be creative; the intellectualization of the acts. But these were concerns of process, not product. I was more interested in practicalities: What did an "artistic" circus *do*? What unique experience did the "artistic" circus afford?

Over espressos after our rehearsal, I put the question to Jérôme. He chuckled as if he knew it was coming.

"I would say that in art there's the notion of work." We were in an empty café near the theater. An icy chill ran through the place. Near the front a window had been propped open with a small block of wood. "In my shows," he went on, "I make the spectator work. In a spectacle of pure entertainment, that's not necessarily the goal."

I asked him what he meant by "work."

His eyes narrowed. Art, he said, forced the audience to ask itself certain questions. "First off, where are we?" The juggler ticked off the point on his thumb. "That's number one. Place. Next is time. What year is it? What day is it? *Who* is the artist that you are watching? *Why* are you watching him? What's he doing? What's your perception of him?" Falling back in his chair, the juggler blew out his lips. "*Oooh, la la*. And of course that's just the beginning. After that there are historical questions. What is the history of this thing you're seeing? What is it referring to?

What movement? Why does it refer to that and not to another movement? You see what I mean?"

He paused to light a cigarette and took a drag. "So now think of your spectator. He's confronted by all this at my show, by these questions, and he *works* on them. He thinks about them, sometimes without even realizing it."

I found this confusing. "How do you make a person think about something without realizing it?"

The juggler smiled. For his reply, he leaned forward a few inches, as if sharing a secret. He spoke in a near whisper. "You make him work his imagination," he said, and then he repeated the words, slower this time. "You make . . . him work . . . his imagination. You make him *dream*!"

Over that year, I would hear innumerable explanations of the line between art and what is often called entertainment. Some refused to answer the question. "Ultimately, I don't think it is for us to define our work," Philippe Copin of Les Acrostiches said. "If there are those who wish to call what we do art, that's fine. I do handstands and balances. It's as if you pointed to a painting and asked the painter, Is that art? The painter could tell you, That's a painting."

Certainly no one cast the divide in such sharp relief as Jérôme. Of course, the circus has always made people dream. That was one of its charms. As Ernest Hemingway wrote in a 1953 program for Ringling Bros. and Barnum & Bailey, "The Circus is good for you. It is the only spectacle I know that, while you watch it, gives the quality of a truly happy dream." But happy dreams are often facile dreams, and audiences returned to the circus every year not to experience something new, but to see something old. The circus offered stasis as a virtue. If it gave you pleasure, it was by distraction. If it made you think, it was by confirming what you already knew: that everything would be all right; that man would triumph and succeed. Jérôme was talking about a different type of dreaming. Art, he was saying, pushes you beyond yourself, into ideas or history. It encourages you to question your sense of the world, or how the world could be.

"But, you know . . ." Jérôme paused to puff on his cigarette. Outside, a light rain had started to fall. A man was scuttling down the street, holding a folded newspaper over his head. "This whole argument—'What's art? What's not art?'—there are more important things."

This from a man who had spent his life dragging his craft up an artistic mountain.

"No," he continued, "what matters is the dedication, an artist's work. How I got to where I am. How any great juggler gets to where he is. By the work."

This was one more concept vital to my understanding of the circus as an art. With very few exceptions, Jérôme was reminding me, all the great performers abandon themselves to their craft. They view their art not as a practice, but as a prism through which to experience the world. As Marco Paoletti told me, "Juggling is my lifestyle. It's my way of being." This defining quality, the mad desire to work, cut across all time periods and all forms of the discipline. Technical jugglers burned no less for their work than creative jugglers. Modern jugglers practiced no more than the historical greats, than Cinquevalli or Rastelli. And in this sense, I realized, the circus has always been an art.

9

Father of the Circus

OVER AFTERNOON ESPRESSO in a cramped café near the Place de la Bastille (I drank a lot of coffee in Parisian cafés), I asked Pascal which figure in circus history most fascinated him.

"Astley," he said, without hesitation.

The answer came as a surprise. Philip Astley is often dubbed the "father of the circus" for the shows he performed in London during the 1760s, medleys of stunts on horseback and "feats of activity." But in my readings about Astley, nothing struck me as particularly intriguing. Asking the question, I had been hoping to discover some new quirky star, another Cinquevalli or Mazurier, the nineteenth-century monkey man. Astley was a soldier and a businessman. In an art of armless trumpet players and wire-walking lions, what was so exciting about that?

"It was his resiliency," Pascal said. "He was obsessed. There's no other word for it. He lived his entire life inside the circus."

PHILIP ASTLEY WAS BORN on January 8, 1742, in Newcastle-under-Lyme, a market town in the West Midlands of England. About his mother, nothing is known. His father, Edward, worked as a cabinetmaker, though poverty seems to have converted him into a kind of working-class Renaissance man. He introduced his son to the family trade at the tender age of nine, but the tutelage didn't last long. Edward was big and domineering, and as Philip blossomed into his own imposing physical presence, the two men frequently quarreled. Often Philip ran away. Then as now, Newcastle-under-Lyme served as a crossroads for farms on the western periphery and villages to the east, and according to legend, the lanky teenager could often be found sitting on the city's wooden gates, ogling wagons as they passed through town. The spirit of the circus was born on these delinquent afternoons. On the fence, Astley made his first contact with the eccentric wayfaring class, the tinkerers and fairground performers who would later populate his shows. There he developed his thirst for travel and adventure, what P. T. Barnum once called life beyond "the ordinary trade."

Most critically, the fence-sitting provided Astley his first exposure to horses. Mingling with the travelers, he learned to groom and feed. When a merchant popped into the local tavern for a drink, Philip would sit outside with the man's mount, running a currycomb through its mane. If the horse needed food or drink, Astley would scamper to fetch it. This interest soon became a fixation. He dreamed of working with horses full-time, and of owning a horse. In 1759, he got his chance.

Five years before, the country had tumbled into war with France. Now word reached Newcastle-under-Lyme that George II, England's aging monarch, had ordered a cavalry unit to be formed in Coventry, less than sixty miles away. Astley didn't hesitate. With only a satchel of clothing and food, he kissed his sisters goodbye and absconded under the cover of darkness, hitching a ride with a passing traveler. Once in

Coventry, he quickly located the regiment, the 15th Light Dragoons, and enlisted under the command of Lieutenant George Elliott.

The lieutenant was happy to have him. In an age when the average private stood five feet seven, Astley towered over six feet tall, with what historians describe as "an oaken chest" and "the proportions of a Hercules." Recognizing the new recruit's passion for horses, Elliott put him to work breaking the mounts and readying them for battle.

Such techniques date from the ancient period. As early as 4000 B.C., armies in Central Asia were training horses to pull their chariots and wagons. Around the first millennium B.C., nomads on the Iranian steppe developed the first cavalry techniques, employing their horses not just for transport but as implements of battle. Over the centuries, these methods, collectively known as horsemanship, became progressively more complex. The Romans, for example, invented vaulting as a means of mounting and dismounting quickly. In the Middle Ages, knights taught their horses "war moves"—how to kick and rear up, how to wheel and caracole.

As a soldier under Elliott, Astley became a master of such techniques. He also studied more acrobatic routines made possible by the advent of gunpowder, which rendered heavy chain mail obsolete. Astley learned to pluck a pistol from the dirt at full gallop and to slide himself perilously under the belly of a horse. He practiced slipping out of his saddle to avoid an enemy bullet, lowering himself against the horse's haunch. In the military, soldiers referred to such stunts as "trick riding."

Later, when these exercises composed the beating heart of the circus, they were collectively called vaulting or *voltige*. Instead of snatching pistols from bloody dirt, riders plucked lace handkerchiefs from sawdust. Instead of dodging enemies, they hurdled colorful silk ribbons held aloft by quaking clowns. The practicality was gone. What mattered was daring and flamboyance. One of Astley's early circus posters advertises him "play[ing] an air on the violin, and display[ing] a flag in many comic attitudes." A later performance promised "a young Lady nine years old . . . which Mr Astley will carry on his head." But these feats were still down the road.

All told, Astley spent seven years trooping with the army. By the few extant accounts, he was an admirable soldier. The official regimental history notes his "peculiar power over animals." On June 21, 1766, Astley submitted his resignation, captivated by a force even more dazzling than war. Stopping in London on furlough, Astley had observed former cavaliers trick riding for money in makeshift arenas sprinkled through the fields of Islington, Lambeth, and Mile End, and it struck a chord in him.

The notion of equestrian theater wasn't entirely novel. At the Roman games, acrobatic riders known as *desultores* would race four or more horses abreast and hop from one to another. During the Renaissance, court equestrians trained their horses for lavish exhibitions, including a "grand ballette-dance," choreographed by Louis XIII's riding master, Monsieur Pluvinel. But never before had such entertainment been so ubiquitous. With the end of the Glorious Revolution of 1688 and the resultant flood of horses into the marketplace, prices for the animals plummeted. For the first time in history, anyone could own his or her own horse. English nobles closed their private manèges. To support themselves, several of the royal trainers took to performing, first outside taverns and in village greens and later in more permanent venues.

And though today the names Thomas Price, Jacob Bates, and Thomas Johnson have been forgotten, if Astley is the father of the circus, they are the art's great-uncles. In their arenas, simple pastures cordoned off by circles of rope, they traced the contours of the circus's form: a series of equestrian displays based on spectacular prowess. These men are also responsible for the circus's shape. At palaces and on battlefields, equestrians trained in rectangular pens; in London, they chose rings, allowing for more difficult tricks; as the horse galloped around, the centripetal force naturally pushed the rider's feet into his mount, granting him stability.

In honor of his valiant service, Astley's regiment presented him with a horse, a milky charger, which he named Gibraltar. On his back, Astley clopped off for London, his chest garlanded with medals, in pursuit of the one thing more seductive than the smell of gunpowder: the glare of the spotlight.

LONDON WAS BOOMING. Long a center of Europe, the city was fast emerging as the center of the world, the capital of commerce and industry, thanks to the Industrial Revolution and the strength of the British naval fleet. Factories and warehouses were rising up in place of corner shops and dusty streets. Migrant workers flooded in from the countryside, to live in vast and deplorable ghettos. It was an age of growth and discovery, of action. In short, it was an age and a city tailor-made for a man like Astley.

On arriving in London, Astley found himself a reasonably priced room and struck out on Gibraltar in search of work at one of the theaters that had inspired him. These enterprises survived by offering riding lessons in the morning and public shows in the afternoon. Astley quickly landed a job at the Jubilee Gardens, under the direction of "Old Sampson," one of the city's original equestrian stars.

Paul Bemrose, Astley's only biographer, refers to these years as Astley's period of "industrial espionage." In fact, he was participating in a rite dating back to ancient Rome: mentorship. From Sampson, he learned the rudiments of running a business and luring a crowd. With his wages, he purchased a second horse from the Smithfield Beast Market, a little "learned" miniature pony named Billy, and managed to win the hand of a "fine horsewoman," Patty.

At the age of twenty-six, ambitious, experienced, and indomitably energetic, Astley decided to strike out on his own. After investing in Glover's Halfpenny Hatch, a boggy grove between Blackfriars and Westminster Bridges, he paid a gang of local toughs to build a deck of risers and rope off a ring. On a plank of wood he painted a sign: "Philip Astley's Riding School." His shows were a copy of Sampson's model: lessons in the morning, shows in the afternoon. For motifs, he borrowed heavily from his military days. The year was 1768.

By the following autumn, gazing back on his first season, Astley felt his life was marching along according to plan. The summer at Glover's Halfpenny had turned a small but meaningful profit. A small buzz of respect had started to circulate around the city, with praise for his ambitions as an equestrian and a producer. And so, in preparation for his second summer, Astley did what any burgeoning capitalist would do: he expanded. Transporting his show six hundred feet up the road, he commandeered an old sawmill near Westminster Bridge, where he built a new outdoor amphitheater, this time with a roof over the bleachers to protect his patrons from the capricious London rain, as well as three stories of luxury boxes. From a business perspective, the move was ideal. The expansion of the bridge in 1763 had opened a new swath of the city for business, and Astley's circus was smack in the center of the action.

The capital improvements, however, had shackled Astley financially. To break even, he needed a tremendously successful second season.

This was easier said than done. With each passing year, more equestrians were setting up shop in the city. To stay on top, he needed something unique, something novel. He needed to distinguish himself. He found his answer in the theaters across town.

Concurrent to his own rise, the city was experiencing a theatrical revolution of sorts, the biggest boom since Shakespeare's career nearly two hundred years before. For centuries, the city's theatrical action had been confined to the so-called legitimate venues subsidized and indirectly managed by the king, the Theatre Royal and the King's Playhouse.* With the Industrial Revolution came wage increases and the standardization of working hours, and a new theatergoing population: the working class. To cater to them, a new sort of venue emerged: the commercial, or "illegitimate," theater. Unlike the royal houses, these theaters survived on ticket and beer sales, and so tailored their entertainments to fit the clientele. In place of high drama, they offered far less heady, more spectacular fare, often imported from the fairgrounds. Sadler's Wells, for instance, founded in 1683 as a music-and-dance hall, became known for its popular operas and pantomimes.

For the *saltimbanques*—that class of itinerant entertainers—the rise of the commercial venues marked a turning point in history, a shift at least as important as the rise of the fairgrounds two centuries before. By inviting the *saltimbanques* onto their stages during the interludes between longer comedies and melodramas, theater directors essentially sanctioned their profession for the first time. Granted, the theaters were ramshackle and crude compared with the royal venues, but they were theaters just the same, complete with advertisements, infrastructure, and a stable clientele. Instead of cadging donations in a muddy field, a performer could play to a paying crowd with a roof over his head. It was the first step on the road to cultural integration.

Astley regularly frequented commercial venues and couldn't help noticing their success. Soon he found himself ruminating on their model of dramas punctuated by entertaining interludes. He realized his own equestrian shows could profit from a similar system: his "feats of horse-

* Both venues still exist. They are familiarly called Covent Garden and Drury Lane, respectively.

manship" interspersed with "feats of activity," old fairground acts he'd loved as a boy.

Beginning in 1769, Astley branched out. Short on cash, he performed the first acts himself, comic routines and some horse-mounted sleight-of-hand, and later experimented with audience participation: he erected an obstacle course in the ring and invited spectators to race through it in burlap sacks. When these endeavors failed to take, Astley contracted out. According to one report, his first outside hire was a fourteen-year-old tumbler by the name of "Master Griffiths." Later, he hired a "clown to the wire," followed by the Ferzis, a family of Italian acrobats poached directly from the stage at Sadler's Wells.

Astley's timing was impeccable. Less than a decade before, King George II had started closing the city's fairgrounds, citing a lack of sanitation. Disinclined to return to the itinerant life, the fairground performers flocked to Astley for work. Under their influence his shows diversified even more. In 1773, a poster testifies to his addition of a "sagacious dog" capable of responding to a question such as "Does Beauty or Virtue in the Fair Sex more attract our Affections?" In 1776, he found a slack-rope walker who could spin on his line like a "roasted pig."

In time, the show became an amalgam of exoticism, spectacle, wonder, skill, and fascination. There were "Philosophical Fireworks" and "Men piled upon Men." There was Signor Rossignol, the bird imitator, and a wire-walking monkey named General Jackoo. Throughout, however, horses remained the show's focus. In the equestrian age, when horses were integral to human life, the public appreciated Astley's routines and understood the difficulty of his moves. Watching the show, they experienced what Pascal refers to as a "mirror effect": "A man would go to the circus and see Astley performing these amazing stunts. Then he would go home and see his own horse in the stable and think, Why not me?"

Philip Astley created the circus as we know it. But he wasn't an artist. He was a businessman, a master of promotion and pastiche, and as British chronicler George Speaight noted in *A History of the Circus,* the sergeant's reputation rests "not so much on what he originated, as on how he developed the elements of entertainment that he had inherited."* During his

* According to Pascal, records indicate that another London equestrian, James Woolton, staged a spectacle that combined horsemanship with "feats of activity" a few weeks before Astley's premiere. "But it doesn't matter," Pascal said. "He performed a few weeks and disappeared. Astley persevered."

fifty-year career, he became a central figure in London society. He built four different circuses, including his Royal Amphitheatre, with purportedly the biggest stage in London. He also toured extensively. In 1774, he introduced the circus to Paris, where he first performed in a manège on the Rue des Vieilles Tuileries. In 1788, he pitched a "Royal Tent" in Liverpool, the first big top.

All told, Astley constructed nineteen circus buildings across Europe, as far east as Belgrade, and in the process he defined the circus as we know it. He determined the circus's colors (red and gold, from the British cavalry), its music (brass military marches), the size of the ring (forty-two meters), and even the smell (sawdust, which he used to cover the ground when he took the old mill on Westminster Bridge).

Astley also inspired a wave of followers who carried the circus around the world. The first was Charles Hughes, one of Astley's equestrians, who defected in 1772 to establish his own amphitheater near Blackfriars Bridge. After nearly two decades of acrimonious rivalry (at one point Hughes hired Astley's own father as a ticket taker), Hughes absconded to Russia, where he became a favorite of Catherine the Great. Other equestrians followed, filling in the gaps of Europe. In 1780, Spaniard Juan Porte brought the circus to Vienna, where he installed his show in a grain-market plaza. By 1787, English equestrian James Price had sailed to Stockholm, where he constructed Sweden's first circus, an open-air amphitheater. Because the circus was primarily a visual spectacle, unencumbered by linguistic barriers, there were few places where it was not welcome. John Bill Ricketts, America's first circus mogul, managed to construct twelve circus buildings in America before he fell into the hands of French privateers during a trip to the West Indies in 1799.

Philip Astley was the "father of the circus." Without his insistence on growth and prosperity, historians claim, the art wouldn't be what it is today. But there are also indications that Astley himself was just a sign of a trend sweeping the world, and that the circus was in fact a product of its time.

Before the emergence of the circus, European society had been divided according to class lines for hundreds of years. A person's class influenced every part of his life, from what he ate, to how he talked, to how he earned his living. In the eighteenth century, however, these walls were crumbling. As part of the great economic and social upheaval leading to the modern age, classes began to mix. Inevitably, this homogenizing spirit flowed into art. In 1760, not long before Astley's premiere, French choreographer Jean-Georges Noverre staged the first *ballet d'action*, combining the movements of dancers with character and action. In 1770, Jean-Jacques Rousseau and Horace Coignet staged the world's first "melodrama," *Pygmalion*, a mix of music and drama that would serve as a progenitor of the opera and later the Broadway musical.

The circus emerged as part of this same trend, and no art epitomized it better. Early circus audiences included every class and creed. In America, John Bill Ricketts was a riding partner to George Washington. In France, Astley performed his stunts for Marie Antoinette. More symbolically, the show itself was a melting pot, a fusion of the highbrow equestrians and the lowbrow fairground performers. Less than a hundred years before, aristocrats had hunted performers like animals, boring their ears and branding their chests with *V*s. Now the world was changing. As Pascal noted, "If the circus didn't exist before, it was because the world wouldn't allow it."

WHAT A LIFE Philip Astley led. When he wasn't busy with his entertainment endeavors, he was publishing hand-illustrated maps of Central Europe and writing books on horsemanship, such as the bestselling *The Modern Riding-Master*. On holidays, he served as the unofficial chief of fireworks for King George III and the purveyor of some of London's first hot-air balloon rides. In 1793, when England hurtled yet again into war with France, Astley gleefully took up the charge. Re-enlisting with his old regiment at the age of fifty-one, the now famous theatrical maven shipped off as the company's "horse-master, celebrity morale-booster and war correspondent."

For all his swashbuckling success, however, there's something tragic, perhaps even pitiful, about Astley's story. He is almost totally forgotten outside the circus. Even at the National School his name usually elicited only vague nods.

In a way, this is not surprising. The history of the circus has long suffered from neglect. Writing in the seventies, Edward Hoagland noted that the circus "remains a private passion for children and loyal fans; among sophisticates it occupies a niche similar to that of primitive art." That is still true today. Circus museums are rare and starved for funding. The Circus World Museum in Baraboo, Wisconsin, for example, has closed multiple times; the International Circus Hall of Fame in Peru, Indiana, is open only from May to August. In academia, where professors dedicate whole books to the examination of an obscure painter, the circus is considered unworthy of serious attention. Until the twentieth century, circus history was almost entirely ignored. (In the introduction to their 1890 study, *Acrobats and Mountebanks*, Hugues Le Roux and Jules Garnier claim to be the first to examine the disciplines closely.) In America, where nearly every major university has a theater department, only a handful of schools offer an accredited circus history course. (One is the University of Virginia, where LaVahn Hoh, a stagecraft professor and amateur circophile, advocated relentlessly for its creation.) Internationally, there is almost no such thing as a professional circus historian. At one point Pascal was teaching at four different schools *and* designing costumes on the side. Steve Gossard, the author of the only complete history of the trapeze, worked another job while he was writing, as a ticket salesman at the Amtrak train station in Bloomington, Illinois, where he also cleaned the bathrooms.

The neglect might explain some of the circus's power to fascinate and consume. "There's a certain siege mentality that can set in," one historian admitted to me. I experienced this firsthand while I was studying Astley. I had come to see Astley's oblivion as a proxy for centuries of intellectual neglect.

And so I decided to seek out Astley—as he exists today. Somewhere in Paris, I thought, there had to be some surviving Astley artifact or shred of tribute. This wasn't as crazy as it sounds. A. H. Saxon, Barnum's premier biographer, once confessed to slipping into the showman's old suits. Pascal had visited Barnum's grave twice. "You hope he'll jump out and tell you something he's never told anyone before," he said. He called it "ghost-hunting."

And so I spent two weeks hunting every Astley ghost I could think of. I visited his house on Rue du Faubourg du Temple. I visited the site of his first Parisian performance, on the old Rue des Vieilles Tuileries (today roughly Rue du Cherche-Midi). I visited Versailles, where he once performed for Marie Antoinette. I called the Louvre, the Musée d'Orsay, and the Musée Rodin. But I came up totally empty.

The closest thing to a victory came at the site of his original Parisian circus building, 16–18 Rue du Faubourg du Temple. Founded in 1783, officially known as the Amphithéâtre Anglais des Sieurs Astley Père et Fils, the building once had been a marvel of circus architecture, with a roof, a stage, and thirty candelabras blazing with two thousand candles. Today it's a mess. Entering through a pair of iron gates, off a street of kebab stands and discount-jewelry dealers, I found myself standing in what looked like a truncated alleyway. Industrial and commercial businesses lined both sides of the dirt lane. Loose garbage and dried leaves accumulated in piles. I walked around for a few minutes, trying to conjure up a sense of communion, before retreating to the sidewalk, where my eyes happened to fall on a sign. It was shaped like a shield on a post and embedded in the pavement like a parking meter. It began, "Philip Astley, former officer with the British cavalry, founded here in 1782 the first permanent circus in Paris." I stared at the sign in despair, not elation. The thing was in rough shape. Dirt blotched the lettering. Across the top someone had scrawled an illegible but presumably unflattering word in silver paint pen.

I decided to give up looking. Which is of course when I found him.

At home one evening, reading the latest addition to my circus library, Earl Chapin May's *The Circus: From Rome to Ringling,* I came across the following quote:

"The first circus owner of modern times celebrated his seventy-third year of adventuring by recovering and remodeling his Paris property, only to die in his house in the Faubourg du Temple. Within a few months his son and successor also died, in the same house, the same room, and the same bed as his father, and was buried with him in Père La Chaise."

Père Lachaise! It was the biggest and most prestigious cemetery in Paris—and less than a mile from my apartment!

I verified the facts online, then grabbed my coat and headed into the street. It was a gorgeous day. The sun blazed in a cloudless sky. The parks brimmed with children.

Feeling chipper, I stopped into a flower shop. After Astley's performance for Marie Antoinette in 1783, the queen, impressed and perhaps a little smitten with Astley's son, John, had awarded the young cavalier a "rose of Paris," a golden medallion inlaid with pearls. According to several sources online, when John Astley died in 1821, his wife buried him in

Père Lachaise next to his father. For his epitaph, she chose: "Here lies the once Rose of Paris."

In the shop, I picked out the healthiest rose I could find. I thought it would make a fitting tribute.

ENTERING PÈRE LACHAISE from the south, through a narrow stone stairwell, I found myself gazing over a rolling sea of graves. Trickles of camera-toting tourists, including a pack of Italian teenagers, drifted through the narrow lanes. I found a placard with the names of the cemetery's famous graves and ran my eyes down the list: Apollinaire, Balzac, Bernhardt, Chopin, Colette, Delacroix, Duncan, Ernst, Montand, Ophüls, Piaf, Pissarro, Proust, Seurat, Wilde. But no Astley.

The omission seemed odd, though not exactly shocking, given my experiences at the other sites. I flagged down a guard and asked him if there was a more complete record somewhere. He pointed me toward a little house in a wooded grove, which turned out to be the cemetery's house of records, and where I found myself facing an ancient-looking woman in a conspicuously red dress.

I explained my mission: Astley, the circus, the grave. The woman regarded me skeptically. Behind her another pair of elderly women shuffled between a half-dozen rows of enormous bookshelves. I was, I realized, still clutching my rose.

"The inventor of the circus, eh?" the woman said, scratching the counter. "I've never heard that one before. When did he die?"

"Eighteen fourteen," I said.

She recoiled. "*Oooo la la*. Do you have the date?"

I didn't, actually. I wasn't expecting a scavenger hunt.

I decided to take a guess. I told her it was sometime in July.

The woman gave me another skeptical look, pivoted on her heel, and marched into the forest of bookcases. Scanning the top shelf, she rose onto her toes and hauled down what appeared to be a Gutenberg Bible, as big as a phone book and bound in leather. Cradling the tome in her arms, she spidered her fingers to the appropriate page, ran her eyes down the list, flipped to another page, nodded, then slammed the book shut.

"*Non*," she said, back at the counter.

"*Non?*"

She shook her head. "I even checked August as well. You're sure he is buried here?"

I didn't know how to respond. It wasn't like circus historians to make such an egregious error.

Trying to be diplomatic, I asked the woman if perhaps one of her colleagues might have some insight. Begrudgingly, the woman turned and called over her shoulder, "Martine." The woman at the computer looked up. "Astley," said the older woman. *"Ça te dit quelque chose?"*

"No, pas vraiment."

The older woman looked at me. "How do you invent the circus anyway?"

Outside, I noticed all the crows for the first time. They were dispersed across the tombs, dozens of them, obtrusive splashes of black. In the distance, a line of tourists had started herding toward the exit by guards. It was almost forty-thirty. The cemetery would be closing soon.

I considered my options. Quitting seemed reasonable—I had grandparents whose graves I had never visited. But I wondered about the grave. The search had started to feel like a mission. Once I found it, I would write to the cemetery, alerting them of the oversight. I would demand that Astley's name be added to their map.

I raced home and looked up his death date online. January 27, 1814. I double-checked. Yes, January 27, 1814. I wrote the date on a piece of paper and hustled back to the cemetery, where I again found myself standing across from the woman in red. "Ah yes," she said, wearily. "The circus man."

I slapped the date on the counter. The woman looked at it for a long moment, before peeling it up and shuffling again into the shelves. One of the other librarians, a younger woman, looked up from her computer and held my gaze. I had the distinct sense that I had been talked about.

I heard a book slam shut. The woman came waddling back.

"Non."

I felt myself recoil. "What do you mean, *non*?"

The woman shrugged. "He's not here."

"Listen—"

"Monsieur—"

"No, please." I was insistent. "There must be some kind of mistake."

A cloud rolled over her face. "It's not a mistake, *monsieur.*"

I didn't know what to do. It seemed impossible that the historians would be wrong about the grave. Was there no electronic record? No comprehensive list? I looked pleadingly to the other librarians, but they were conveniently absorbed in their work. I pointed foolishly to the date on the paper. "I don't understand. This is it. I mean, is there even a grave?"

And at this, the woman sighed. She must have registered something sad or desperate in my tone. Her face softened, and she looked at me with sympathetic eyes.

"You know, it's a long shot, but there's one other thing we can do."

"What's that?"

"We can look in the book."

I had no idea what she was talking about, but the way she said it made it sound serious. "Okay, of course."

She nodded and walked solemnly to the end of the counter. Stooping, she retracted what looked like a dictionary from beneath the cash register. It was, she explained, a list of all the famous people buried in France. "If he's buried in France, he'll be in the book."

She opened the book and scaned the pages. "Archley."

"Astley," I corrected.

"Astley, right."

I watched her finger scan the page, then come to a slow stop. "No, I don't see it."

I felt something die inside me.

"But you know," she mused, returning the book to the shelf, "it's possible that he is buried here but that the grave was lost."

"Lost?!" I said a little louder than I should have.

The woman nodded. "It happens, you know. We do our best, but there are so many graves—over ten thousand." She shook her head—at the historical weight of her position perhaps, at I don't know what. "And, you know, it's the circus . . ."

In the end, the librarian's suspicion proved to be correct. In 1814, Astley was in fact buried in Père Lachaise, followed by his son seven years later. For a century, their graves remained a site of circus pilgrimage. (According to Pascal, the French circus-historian Henri Thétard had once paid a visit.) But things changed. The circus fell on hard times. For years nobody cared about the dead showman, and his grave fell into neglect.

Sometime in the 1940s or 1950s, the grave "disappeared." Nobody had bothered to record its location.

I learned this later. That day, as I slumped toward the exit, rose in hand, my eye fell on a pack of Italian teenagers that I had seen earlier. The girls wore big Jackie-O sunglasses, and the boys had glossy hair, and everybody wore pants two sizes too small for them.

I went over to investigate. They had formed a half-moon around a grave, a flat stone almost completely invisible under a mound of flowers and other diverse tributes—unlit cigarettes, a Yankees baseball cap, a rolled joint, postcards written in a half-dozen languages. A couple of the teens were engaged in a heated conversation in Italian. I heard the words, "Cam un baby laht my fiyar."

Standing a few feet back from the scene, surveying the horde with a bored look, was the guard who had directed me to the house of records.

"Pretty crazy, huh," he said. He was portly and demure. "Jim Morrison. People love him."

I asked him who had the second-most-popular grave in the cemetery.

"Hard to say," he said. "Édith Piaf. Chopin. Maybe Proust."

They were all artists—not politicians, not scientists, not generals. But they were also artists who had left legacies. For Chopin, there were scores. For Piaf, recordings. For Proust, his books.

But circus performers of the past left no such legacy. Their art was physical and largely ephemeral. Critics rarely reviewed shows. Acts were rarely filmed. Instead, we are left to piece together the stories of their lives from secondary sources: photographs, advertisements, programs with lists of acts and mysterious names written next to each.

Some consider this ethereality part of the circus's charm, a quintessential part of the "here today, gone tomorrow" magic. Personally, I find it tragic. The circus is among the oldest art forms in the world, and yet so much of its past remains an empty canvas. No wonder circus historians are so obsessed with "ghost-hunting." With so little tangible history, you have to cling to what remains—the clothes performers wore, the graves that hold their bones. And no wonder circus families cling so steadfastly to tradition. If your children fail to carry on your name, your reputation might be lost forever.

Loving the circus, I thought, is like loving a fictional character.

10

Tradition

ONE OF THE INTERESTING ASPECTS of learning to juggle was how systematic the process is. This is doubly true for acrobatics, the discipline that circus historian Tristan Rémy called the "substance" of the show. Every aspiring acrobat submits himself to a sometimes harrowing hierarchy of exercises, each building on the last. The path is challenging but also reassuring: if you trust the system, it will take you where you need to go.

My own engagement with the system occurred three days a week. Mondays and Fridays were with Ryszard and Luc, respectively, both of whom taught tumbling. Ryszard handled the "power moves," like hand-standing and hand-balancing. Luc taught more dynamic moves, like round-offs, back handsprings, and back flips. On Wednesdays, under the tutelage of Gabby, a Spaniard, we studied rudimentary moves on the trampoline.

The classes stuck to a fairly consistent schedule. We started with calisthenics, followed by stretching. The first day, Ryszard advised stretching at least twenty minutes before every class. This struck me as a lot, but by week's end I understood. Acrobatics is a full-body exercise. Every muscle and every joint has to be coaxed into action, from your neck to the cartilage in your toes. (This is no joke: I dislocated my toe halfway through the year.) We also stretched to build flexibility. For this, partner stretching was helpful, because it allowed for what was called an "active" stretch, in which your complementary muscles worked against the muscles being used. It was one of the pleasant fringe benefits of the school: watching physically perfect women tug each other through vaguely tantric positions. Pleasant, that is, when I wasn't involved myself.

"Ow! Goddamn, Ryszard! Seriously?"

I had been stretching peacefully, legs splayed, nose nudging gingerly toward the industrial carpet, when, without warning, I felt a weight pushing against my back, pressing down against my shoulder blades. I didn't know what was going on. Then I realized: Ryszard was sitting on me, a buttock on either side of my spine, such that my torso was now pressed painfully to the floor. I heard a crunching noise above my head. Was Ryszard eating an apple?

Shards of pain shot up the inside of my groin. The dank musk of the carpet invaded my nostrils.

"Um, Ryszard . . ." My voice was pinched.

"Shut up." He chomped at his apple. "Try to breathe."

Ryszard was of the old school. He specialized in ground-based moves, what's known as "carpet work" for the threadbare rugs *saltimbanques* used as makeshift stages (and sleeping mats) in the Middle Ages. In his native Poland, Ryszard had trained as a gymnast until the wall fell and Europe opened up. Like a lot of Poles, he headed west in search of work—and then wandered into the circus. ("I never think I end up in circus. Not in million years.") In style, he adhered to the Eastern European sportsman's look: the knock-off Adidas tracksuit, with hues that varied according to the season. As a person he was harder to read. Over the year I came to find out that he had followed avant-garde Polish theater quite closely when he was younger and now read Chekhov in his spare time. He would come to be a friend.

I felt my muscles ease into the stretch. It felt good but not good. "Um, Ryszard . . ." I repeated.

"Shut up." He polished off his apple. "You'll thank me later."

The stretching was initially mostly left up to us. (After my first embarrassing day, I had researched maneuvers on the Internet, and nobody ever corrected me.) Standardization came when we tackled the moves themselves. The Greek term for "acrobatics" literally means "to walk on the extremities"; indeed, learning acrobatics often felt like relearning to walk. Before attempting difficult moves, as I said, you had to master the basics. On the trampoline, for example, we spent the first week learning the correct bounce, a sort of a vertical breaststroke—arms shooting upward on the ascent, fanning outward on the way down.

In tumbling class, the basics included the old classics: somersaults, cartwheels, round-offs. Mastery was a matter of refinement and reminding my body of what it already knew but had buried in adulthood. Perched by the padded runway, Ryszard would usually bark one piece of advice with each turn, a single physical idea to focus on.

"Dive. Go to the floor. It's like woman—you must *go* to her."

"Why you are falling into cartwheel? You are not tree. You are human."

"Point toes in somersault."

"Chin tucked all through! Tuck, tuck."

At first, much of the advice felt nitpicky, little points of body position. (Ryszard was forever reminding me to point my toes.) Later, I came to understand that even the simplest training occurred with the higher moves in mind. Once, as I was jogging back to the end of the line, Ryszard pulled me aside yet again to coach me on the position of my hands after my round-off.

"Why I always have to tell you—finish round-off, you put hands up." I nodded, out of breath and only half paying attention, the adrenaline still churning.

"Hey! I am serious. Repeat. Hands up."

"Hands up."

"Show me." He thrust his hands in the air. "Hands up."

I followed his example. "Hands up."

He nodded and dropped his hands. "Yes. You know why?"

I didn't, actually.

"Because—if no hands, no next move." In the not-so-distant future, he explained, we would connect a back handspring to the end of the round-off. If I didn't train myself to put my hands up now, that connection would be harder to make and maybe even dangerous. "You no learn round-off with hands, you break neck on handspring. You want to break neck?"

I did not.

"I didn't think so," Ryszard said.

On the whole, I liked the system and made quick progress. Within a month, my acrobatic repertoire included a somersault, a cartwheel, and a pretty solid round-off, none of which I would have expected to achieve even six months before. I liked having a coach. This was especially the case as the moves got more difficult. Instead of teaching the maneuvers in their entirety, which would have been dangerous, Ryszard broke the motion into component parts, the way you might deconstruct a golf swing or a dance step. These exercises were known as *éducatifs*. In the best cases, *éducatifs* could lead to surprising successes. Training for back handsprings, for example, I began with so many backward somersaults and back walkovers—to get used to the position and going backward—that when I attempted my first actual back handspring, the ease of the move caught me off guard. Pitching backward, with Ryszard supporting me on one side and Boris on the other, I was shocked to find myself suddenly back on my feet. Almost before I left the ground, I felt my palms make contact with the floor, felt my feet follow. I must have looked dazed, because Boris smiled wryly. "Congratulations," he said. "You shouldn't look so shocked."

That said, the process could also be frustratingly gradual. There was a sense of going two steps forward, one back. This was especially true with handstands.

As I discovered early in the year, handstands as practiced in the circus require a certain technique: the body is bullet-straight, clenched in a sturdy line from your hands through your pointed toes. To get the hang of this, we began by forming countless handstands against a wall. Once we were inverted, Ryszard would maneuver our bodies into position, shaping us like lumps of clay. It was a strange and somewhat uncomfortable feeling. Upside down, my palms pressing into the ground, I would see Ryszard's Keds park themselves a few inches away and then feel his muscular hands grip my ankles. "Hold still," he would say, and started to pull, raising my feet toward the ceiling. I felt the weight ease off my palms, and my body lengthen. I felt the blood rushing out of my feet, falling through my chest, pooling in my face, pressing against my eyeballs.

By lengthening my body, Ryszard was modeling the proper position. He was demonstrating how a handstand should feel, how my shoulders should "extend" from their sockets, how the spine should "stack" into a single column, vertebra on vertebra. And against the wall the instruction worked. Once Ryszard had pulled me into position, I would often feel my body "lock." When he released me, I would stay upright, perfectly straight, a few inches from the wall. In such moments the position felt easy—natural, even. I thought I was getting it.

Unfortunately, the operation went to hell on the open floor. My particular difficulty was what Georges Strehly, a turn-of-the-century circus sage, referred to as "the block," the moment when, after kicking your legs up, you lock into the position. Gymnasts make the block look easy, but, on a purely physical level, it's actually completely bizarre. When you kick up, the entire energy of your body is headed forward. To arrest this motion, you have to "block" the movement—using the *same muscles* that you're trying to stop. In essence, you have to prevent yourself from falling forward *by* falling forward—and while balanced upside down.

The whole thing evaded me. Kicking up, I would either come up short and buck like a mule, or else kick up with too much energy and go sailing over the top, which was frightening and ultimately painful, since it meant crashing to the ground upside down and directly on my tailbone. I tried focusing on specific pieces of practical advice. If I felt myself going too far, I would clench my stomach and my backside, as I understood was necessary. But this just made the landing harder. I practiced for hours at the school and in my apartment. (The practice resulted in one of the stranger, more linguistically tortured conversations I had in France. When my downstairs neighbor asked me, "What is all the crashing?" I was forced to reply, "I am all the crashing.") But with the exception of those magical moments a few inches from the wall, not once was I able to hold the position on my own.

After two months of failure, I took my frustrations to Ryszard. We were eating lunch in the tent outside the Great Hall, a spot that was normally reserved for dance classes but which Ryszard and I had taken to commandeering with our Tupperware on account of the microwave in the corner.

Like myself, Ryszard lingered on the periphery of the school's social circle. He liked the circus spirit, the laid-back atmosphere. But his move to France from Poland had come with sacrifices, most notably the two sons he left behind. (One of the sons came to visit and shamed us with his brawn.) His life was now tinged with a certain disquietude familiar to expatriates who head abroad later in life. Because of an unfortunate real-estate transaction—something involving a French woman he cared for—he had been forced to give up his apartment in Paris temporarily. In the meantime, he had taken to sleeping on a cot in a closet at the school. "It's not bad," he said. "I have little television. I read before I go to sleep. I'm usually tired."

I wasn't quite as isolated, but I did feel like an outsider, and over this shared foreign status we forged a bond. During the midday break, we often joined each other for lunch, and after classes I would sometimes stick around and lounge on the mats with him, shooting the breeze in broken French. ("This is why we friends," he once said. "Nobody else understands.") He told me illustrative stories about his training in the old country and supplied me with additional tips. I liked to think of him as my private tumbling sensei.

"So what is problem?" he asked on this day, popping the top off his lunch, the same goulash he brought every day. Steam poured from the Tupperware. In the corner of the tent a heater churned, muffling the sound of a trumpet playing in the distance.

I described to Ryszard my progress when I was next to the wall, my near-total regression on the open floor. He waved his spoon dismissively. "It's work," he said. "You want to do handstand but you don't want to work." I told him that work wasn't the issue, that I was putting in the time. He tipped his chin down and eyed me over his glasses. "The work is always issue."

Still, he conceded, there were a few things I could do to hurry the process. Practicing every day could help—ten minutes in the morning, ten minutes at night. He also showed me a stretch. Rising from our table, he bent down in front of its bench, placed his palms against the seat, and pressed down with his arms straight. To perform a proper handstand, he said, you had to be flexible in the armpit and shoulder regions, since the move required pulling the shoulders back.

"But this is small thing," he said, returning to the seat. "It not change a lot. The important thing is work. And patience. It's not like playing the piano."

"The piano?"

He nodded, chewing his food. "Yah, you know, piano player, maybe he wants to work for ten hours every day. So he work for ten hours. It's not problem. Every song is different. His fingers hurt, yes, but he is working mostly brain." Acrobatics, he went on, is more physical. You have to develop certain muscles in your shoulders and your back. You have to learn to compensate for subtle shifts in balance with shifts in muscular tension. In a very literal, physical way, your body is recalibrating itself, and that takes time. Or it should take time. "I hear recently about Chinese girl," he said. "She learns to walk the wire in a week." He winced and shook his head, as if the idea pained him. "This is bad. This is very, very bad. It is bad for girl, but it is also bad training." Learning the basics incorrectly, he said, led to bad habits, which could ruin an acrobat later. "This is probably number one problem. I get acrobats from other coaches and have to start over. Too many bad habits from before."

I pointed out that, according to this line of thinking, I was his dream student.

A bushy eyebrow cocked over his glasses. "Yah, you know, maybe it's exception this time."

BECAUSE ACROBATICS IS so physical, I got in great shape, a different kind of shape. I wasn't buff; I was flexible and agile. Because the muscles developed naturally, from supporting my body in movement, there was no unevenness. Recently, the circus has started to take off as a recreational fitness activity, like yoga or aerobics, and it's not hard to see why: the classes never seemed all that rigorous, and yet I saw amazing results; it was a perfect workout.

What caught me off guard was how challenging the mental preparation for acrobatics could be. Enormous focus was required to execute the moves. And there was a fear factor. I tangoed with it throughout the year on back handsprings, the flying trapeze, and other disciplines, but the fiercest struggle came on the trampoline, when I set about learning to back-flip.

The word "trampoline" probably evokes images of common backyard equipment—round, black, surrounded by a protective mesh netting. The school's trampolines were of another order of magnitude. Big and rectangular, their surfaces consisted of thick strips of white webbing capable of vaulting a trained acrobat twenty feet in the air. Though rare in shows, the devices were popular in training rooms, as a means of developing the kind of "aerial awareness" essential in more high-flying disciplines: the Russian bar, the Russian swing, the flying trapeze.

My guide in such maneuvers, as I said, was Gabby. Like Ryszard, he came from the world of gymnastics, but his style was totally different. He was methodical, almost clinical. His jogging suits were always impeccably crisp; his head was shaved clean. When explaining a move, he liked to employ the chalkboard bolted into the brick wall by the trampolines, diagramming stick figures in stages of movement. In his explanations, he often used scientific terminology, words like "leverage" and "rotation." For the back flip, his word was "torque."

"For a back flip, you want to rise gradually," he noted, tapping the stick man's hips with his nub of chalk. "Wait until you're parallel to the ground. Then pop your knees to your chest. That pop—that's where the torque comes from."

The back flip was relatively simple, a matter, as Gabby said, of rise, tuck, and open. From a purely physical perspective, the back flip was no more complex than any of the other basic moves—cartwheels or round-offs, for example—except for one essential difference: it went backward. We hardly ever hurl ourselves over backward, so our brains rebel against it. I first experienced this reaction when I was drilling back handsprings. A few minutes before any attempt at the move, my heart started to pound. I felt my body resist, right until I bent at the knees and started rocking backward.

"Oh yeah, that happens to everybody," Ryszard said. He also said that my age probably made the issue worse. "A kid watches and repeats. He doesn't know enough to be afraid."

To conquer my problem, he gave me *éducatifs*, aimed at acclimating my subconscious to the idea of flinging myself over backward. I rolled through countless backward somersaults on the padded floor; I stretched into innumerable back bends. To train for the takeoff, I repeatedly flung myself backward into a crash pad the size of a small automobile.

The moves felt vaguely ridiculous (especially when performed in the shadow of an acrobat doing a double somersault on the trampoline), but they had a positive effect. After a week, I noticed that my heart wasn't beating quite so hard when I stepped onto the runway. That was on the ground, however. On the trampoline, following Gabby's instructions, I could feel my heart drumming in my chest. Sometimes the fear would come in the middle of a move. Professional acrobats call this "casting" or "getting lost in the trick." Trapezist Alfredo Codona once compared it to "a sharp knife drawn against the strings."

My worst experience with this occurred while I was attending my second class on the back flip. Gabby worked with me for a few flips and then hopped down. Without him, the trampoline felt empty and grand.

"Same as before," he said, standing at the edge of the trampoline, his fingers gripped around a foam pad, safety protection in case of errant flips. "Whenever you're ready."

I was actually feeling quite calm. We were fine-tuning the rotation, since I had a tendency to jump back instead of up. By this point, I had established a reputation for intense precision. Perhaps because I was still working on a few simple moves, I was very conscious of the little things I could control, such as pointed toes and correct posture, and in this spirit I had developed a little prep routine of arm circles and toe-pointing, which I now performed. The other students got a kick out of the routine—I imagine it made me look as if I had some kind of compulsive disorder—but I ignored the titters and focused on the move. I gave myself a little pep talk—hips out, knees tucked. Then I flipped.

The start was fine. I kept my arms above me. My hips rose until I was parallel to the ground. But just as I was about to tuck, I seized up. My chest tightened and the air rushed out of my lungs. I began to flail. My legs kicked, my fingers clawed for purchase. Completely panic-stricken, I came crashing earthward. I heard Fanny gasp, and from the corner of my eye saw Gabby launch the pad underneath me. Landing headfirst, like a duck shot out of the sky, I folded into the trampoline, my knee barreling into my mouth.

The next few moments are vague. I remember the rafters in the hall spinning, then dissolving into a nebulous wash. For a moment the world was black. Then I heard a voice:

"Is he okay?"

The world came swirling back. Light from the overhead lamps sparked in my eyes. After a moment, a dark object hovered into view—Fanny's round face.

"Oh, mon Dieu," she said. I could see her brow flexing. "He's bleeding." As she said the words, I felt a brackish worm inch across my tongue.

The accident rattled me. For a week afterward, I couldn't go near the trampoline without feeling fear. But in the longer term it was almost calming. I had made a mistake, but all the proper precautions had been in place: Gabby was watching; the mattress was ready. As a result, the damage was minor: my neck was sore for a few days, but my lip healed quickly.

The old circus families had an expression: "eating sawdust." It referred to a performer's first accident and marked the aspirant's official introduction to circus life. ("Now that you've eaten the sawdust, you might, with a lot of work, become an artist," the famous clown Footit's grandmother told him when he fell off his first horse.) My frustration, my impatience, my bumps and bruises—I realized that they were all part of the system. Possibly hundreds of thousands of people had undergone identical training, had suffered the same mistakes.

The depth and specificity of this lineage was confirmed during a research trip to Milner Library at Illinois State University, home to one of the world's largest collections of circus literature. I went to the library to see a specific document, what circophiles affectionately call "the Tuccaro": *Three Dialogues on the Practice of Jumping and Flying in the Air,* by Arcangelo Tuccaro, *saltarin du roi,* "Tumbler to the King." Published in 1599, the book is important to acrobatic history on a number of levels. Like the circus generally, acrobatics was long considered a marginal discipline and so was only ever mentioned peripherally. The Latin poet Terence, for instance, once complained about people deserting his theater to watch ropewalkers. Acrobats rarely wrote about their skills or experience themselves.

The Tuccaro was the first book to remedy this, and the first treatise in acrobatic history. Tuccaro himself was an acrobat and a royal trainer.

After serving Holy Roman Emperor Maximilian II, he was recruited to work with France's Charles IX. When he was fifty-nine, just two years before his death, he published his manifesto. Structured as a dialogue, the book is essentially letters to a young acrobat, with each chapter detailing instructions for various maneuvers—how to somersault, how to flip, how to flic-flac (what Tuccaro calls "monkey jumps")—interspersed with Tuccaro's musings on the craft.

Today, fewer than thirty copies of Tuccaro's book exist, and at the library at Illinois State I had to don white gloves before handling one of them. Delicately, I opened the book. The cover was vellum; the pages were yellow and brittle. Inside, the text was interspersed with woodcut illustrations, depictions of a conspicuously chubby tumbler performing various maneuvers. Other illustrations showed a teacher leading a student through the requisite preparatory exercises—helping the student bend over backward and grab his own ankles, contorting the boy over his knee as if breaking in a baseball glove.

As I turned the fragile pages, admiring the wash of images, what struck me was how familiar they all seemed. Ryszard might have kept a copy under his pillow and referred to it before each lesson, so similar were the exercises. In writing this book, Tuccaro was arguing for acrobatics to be taken seriously as a discipline, on the level of ballet, which had just begun to emerge as a noteworthy art. His argument was based on the beauty of the craft but also on its history, which he was finally recording on paper. This resonated with me. What I was receiving as tradition, Tuccaro himself had received as tradition four hundred years before. For all the innovation (the flying trapeze, 1859), all the evolution (the triple somersault, 1859), the acrobatic rudiments remain the same. The back flip that captivates us today is nearly identical to the flip that a slave used to wow Aristotle at a banquet in Athens.

I asked Pascal why, in a world bursting with distraction, such simple moves continue to hold sway over us.

"It's the human body," he replied. "We changed the world around us, but we haven't changed ourselves."

11

Physical Theater

PHILIP ASTLEY DIED in 1814. His art, however, lived on, and in the fifty years following his death entrepreneurs spread the circus around the world.

Europe succumbed first. In 1805, Christoph de Bach settled in Vienna, where he set up a permanent riding and ropewalking show. Joseph Beranek, a trick rider, brought the circus to Prague. In 1827, Jacques Tourniaire, one of Astley's best riders, installed the circus in

Moscow. Around the same time, another French equestrian, Louis Soullier, extended the circus to the Balkans, then to Turkey, where the sultan appointed him the master of his stables.

These were extraordinary lives, and, for circophiles, this period of expansion ranks as one of the great heroic periods in history. Men suffered mightily to bring the circus to the world. John Bill Ricketts, the father of the American circus, watched two of his theaters burn, then perished at sea on his return to England. During Giuseppe Chiarini's first Asian tour, he lost a crew member every week, including a tiger trainer to smallpox in Calcutta and a canvasman to cholera in Malaysia.

But the rewards outweighed the risks. In an age of limited possibilities, an age of class restrictions and geographical isolation, before the radio or even the telegraph, the circus offered a life of potential almost unfathomable adventure and wealth. Born to a family of poor fairground acrobats, Chiarini played to Emperor Maximilian I of Mexico, Tsar Nicholas I of Russia, and King Rama V of Siam. The son of poor wire-walkers, Ernst Jakob Renz built opulent circus buildings across Europe, in Berlin and Milan. When he died in 1891, his fortune was estimated at more than $16 million ($384 million today).

The beginning of the nineteenth century also marked a time of unparalleled openness and creativity, because the circus was still defining itself as a theatrical form. On the road, circus owners adopted local traditions to woo audiences. In Turkey, Soullier rebranded his show the Cirque Impérial and adopted a Turkish colonel's uniform. In 1854, he packed off to Asia, where he discovered Chinese acrobatics—plate-spinners, hoop-divers, and perch-pole balancers. In Europe, circus moguls experimented with form. They constructed buildings featuring both rings and stages. They hired writers to pen circus scripts with characters and plots. There was almost no distinction between genres. Equestrians graced royal stages. Ropewalkers recited soliloquies on their cords. Almost a century later, the great Russian theater director Vsevolod Meyerhold would proclaim that there was "no true dividing line between the circus and the theatre," and for a brief time this was true.

This period of experimentation encompassed most of the capitals of Europe, from London to Berlin. There was, however, one spot where the innovation was most developed: the Boulevard du Temple in Paris.

Located on the eastern edge of the city, less than a mile from Astley's circus, the boulevard, also known as the Boulevard du Crime, which began as a quiet walkway for Sunday strollers, had emerged by the turn of the nineteeth century as the most eclectic corner in Europe. One writer called it a "perpetual fairground" inside the Paris city limits. "How could I even try to enumerate all the action?!" wrote Victor Fournel in *Le Vieux Paris*. "The hand-balancers, the learned fleas and dogs, the ferocious animals, the midgets, the giants, the colossal women and savage women, the Hercules, the card-sharks, the acrobats, the torch swallowers, the puppets, the monsters, the freaks."

Initially the *saltimbanques*, most of whom came from the fairgrounds, installed themselves on the city sidewalk, on wooden barrack stages, where they harassed the passers-by, trying to summon them to their shows. As the sidewalks filled, a few ambitious entrepreneurs ensconced themselves more permanently. In vacant lots, they constructed full theaters, venues specializing in hybrid productions of their skills. At the Théâtre de la Gaîté, founded by puppeteer Jean-Baptiste Nicolet in 1759, ropewalkers sang operas. At the Théâtre des Funambules, the house specialty was acrobatic pantomime (*pantomime sautant*), scenic fairy tales starring tumblers and mimes. Some of the theaters were hugely extravagant. The Cirque Olympique had enough room for a full orchestra and a team of elephants. All were hugely popular. Wrote Nicolas Brazier, a singer and playwright from the period: "It was stunning, it was deafening . . . But it was crazy . . . original . . . varied . . . it was exciting, it was alive!"

Reading about the boulevard, I became fascinated by it and the era of circus history it exemplified. One of the defining qualities of the *modern circus* was how it combined circus skills with theatrical techniques—plot, character, and stagecraft, such as lights and sound. Suddenly it struck me as a throwback as much as an innovation.

I decided to visit the site. Baron Haussmann had razed the theaters in 1862, as part of his great Parisian renovation. But I didn't care. After my failed pilgrimage to Astley's grave, I had become increasingly interested in what Pascal once referred to as "ghost-hunting"—of connecting to history through tangible experience, even if that experience was sparse. Astley's grave had disappeared, but I found myself returning regularly to the former site of his theater, the courtyard on the Rue du Faubourg du Temple. I liked the buzz of historical connection that I felt when I entered.

After a few trips, I became custodial about the place. I picked up the cigarette butts and empty beer bottles in the entryway, and eventually brought a soapy rag in a Ziploc bag and cleaned off the plaque. It was a small contribution, more symbolic than real, but it felt good.

And so, on a sunny Sunday in December, I ventured out to see what remained of the Boulevard du Temple. Joining me on my pilgrimage was a college friend, Tina, an American expat and actress. I knew a lot about the circus by now, but less about the theater, and I thought she could offer some insight into this genre-bending period.

I also had a more selfish reason for inviting her. After cleaning up the site of Astley's theater, I had brought friends to see it. I would walk them through the grounds and tell them the story of Astley, of his creation of the circus and his more colorful adventures. I enjoyed telling the stories. I came to feel they were important in a small way. I had come to understand that the circus's reputation suffered because of a lack of historical perspective; people were ignorant of circus past, so they misjudged its present. The guided visits were my attempt to help remedy the situation, to demonstrate to others what Pascal and the books had demonstrated to me: that the circus past was richer, more varied, and more culturally important than they thought; that it was rich with extraordinary stories and extraordinary lives.

In the case of the Boulevard, I was interested in two of those lives in particular: Madame Saqui and Antonio Franconi. Saqui was a fiery rope-walker who rose to become one of the biggest stars in Europe, and in the process catapulted her disciplines to new dramatic heights. Franconi was an aristocrat–turned–animal trainer, France's original circus mogul, and creator of some of the biggest and strangest circuses in history. I brought Tina to listen to the stories.

"Sure, I get it," she said, as we traversed the southern rim of the Place de la République and arrived at the top of the boulevard, a wide, nondescript street branching off the southwest corner. "You want to make sure the graves don't disappear."

THEY CALLED HER the "Queen of the Boulevard," but she was an unlikely queen. Endowed with features that one critic described as "so misshapen as to seem deformed," Madame Saqui (née Marguerite-

Antoinette Lalanne) captivated Paris's popular imagination for an astonishing fifty years. She was by no means destined for such notoriety. Born poor and far from Paris, Saqui grew up traveling with her family. Her father, Jean-Baptiste Lalanne (a.k.a. Navarin the Famous), was a tooth-puller and a potion salesman. Her mother, Hélène, came from the Masgomieri clan, a dynasty of ropewalkers.

Historically, ropewalking is one of the oldest of the circus arts. Numerous ancient societies practiced a version of the discipline. In A.D. 333 the Roman playwright Terence famously complained about ropewalkers distracting from a public performance of his play *Hecyria*. (*"Ita populus studio stupidus, in funambulo animum occuparat."*) In Greece, where ropewalkers wore white, like the members of the Senate, there developed a whole ropewalking vocabulary to designate different categories of performance. *Oribates* danced and played the flute on horizontal ropes. *Schoenobates* dangled by their feet. Most of these performers worked on ropes made of hemp or hardened animal guts, which, when twisted like taffy, became almost magically thin.

By Saqui's time, the discipline remained popular, but the form had narrowed slightly. Now there were two main types: the *funambules* and the *fils-de-féristes*. The *funambules* were the high-wire specialists. Traveling from town to town, they fastened their ropes between the cathedral towers or the gables of tall houses. The acts were simple; the main appeal was danger. Inching onto the rope, outlined against the sky, they would execute a series of ordinary feats—pivoting on the rope, sitting down, making the rope sway to elicit a gasp. Occasionally more daring fare was added to spice up the act. During one seventeenth-century London performance, a certain Mr. Barnes traversed a rope with a pair of children dangling from the spurs of his riding boots like Christmas ornaments. A century later, Blondin (né Gravelet) made headlines around the world by cooking himself an omelet on a rope over Niagara Falls.

The *fils-de-fériste*, the second type of rope performer, weren't so daring. Also known as "ropedancers," they strung their cords closer to the ground, in plazas or on the fairgrounds, where audiences paid to slip behind a curtain and watch them perform their impressive, precarious stunts—dangling, flipping, dancing popular dances, like the waltz and the gavotte. Since the discipline required minimum upper-body strength and maximum grace, many of the earliest stars were women. Sex appeal also played a role. In an age when an ankle was considered revealing, it could be downright scandalous to watch a woman in a billowing skirt and a bust-enhancing bodice bounce energetically while waving her shapely calves. After a visit to the Bartholomew Fair in 1669, Ned Ward, the "London Spy," remarked of an agile German: "If she be just as nimble between the sheets as she is upon a rope, she must needs be one of the best bed-fellows in England."

In part because of men like Ned Ward, Saqui's father, Navarin, initially forbade his daughter to take up the family discipline. He also knew firsthand the craft's inherent danger; while working in Paris, he had fallen from his rope and injured his leg, casting the family again onto the road. But Saqui was an energetic child, and, during a stop in Tours, she found a way.

On the fairgrounds, Saqui's family happened to park their wagon next to a legendary family of acrobats, the Bénéfands. The daughter of the family, Françoise, a.k.a. Mademoiselle Malaga, was a ropedancing star, famous for working on a silver stage. After a few days of star-struck hesitation, Saqui asked her for a lesson. Malaga agreed, and the girls began training in secret. Given her years of observation, Saqui picked up the basic maneuvers quickly—how to walk and fall, how to gauge the rope's rhythms and sways. Inspired, the girls decided to mount a small show. They posted bills announcing the spectacle on wagons around the lot. To avoid the attention of Saqui's parents, they gave her a stage-name: "Young Nini."

On the day of the show, a surprisingly sizable crowd formed at the foot of the makeshift wooden stage, curious to see the skills of the mysterious new performer. Backstage, Saqui listened nervously to the building murmur as she slipped on her supple deerskin slippers. At the appointed hour, she assumed her position by the rope that ran across the stage. Her heart pounding in her chest, nodding absentmindedly at Malaga's final instructions, she stepped onto the rope and inched her way into the view of the crowd.

Instantly a cry erupted in the gallery. Saqui looked out from the stage to see her mother collapsing into the dirt. Her father was already dashing toward the stage.

She continued with the routine, executing each move with pointed-toe poise, her father poised beneath her, waiting in case she fell. Afterward, Navarin delivered her a proper scolding, but he couldn't deny the raucous applause from the crowd: his daughter was a natural.

Madame Saqui first took to the rope in Tours in 1778. Meanwhile, in Paris, the Boulevard du Temple was erupting as the new commercial theaters made it the nucleus of acrobatic action. Noted an observer, "With their high facades, their large windows framed by columns and marquees, most of these theaters make you forget their fairground pasts."

But not everyone approved of the boulevard's success. Besides the commercial theaters, Paris also featured a number of so-called legitimate theaters, state-sponsored venues that featured more highbrow fare, works of what Charles Dickens once called "poetic quality or superior literary worth," such as Molière or Racine. The venues were supposed to pull the public into higher work, to introduce them into art. But with the rise of the boulevard, their popularity had suffered.

The city decided to crack down. Beginning in 1807, the Paris *conseil* passed a series of draconian laws that choked theatrical action. Only eight Parisian theaters remained open, each with a specific license dictating the right to work in a particular genre. Nicolet's Théâtre de la Gaîté was restricted to mime shows and harlequinades (acrobatic pantomimes). Circuses could only feature "horses and related attractions."

Collectively known as the "patent laws," the injunctions would prove a defining force in the development of the circus over the next century. In the long term, they served their intended function by stifling venues into limited theatrical boxes. In the short term the effort backfired. Restricted to their genres, venue directors innovated to expand the range of their offerings as far as lawfully possible. The result was a proliferation of curious forms. At the Théâtre des Funambules, where the laws forbid performers from talking, actors expressed themselves in gestures and acrobatics. In theaters where dialogue was forbidden, venues would have their audience sing the exchanges or make their protagonists speak while balancing on a rope.

Much to the city's chagrin, the public loved the hybrid shows, and the boulevard boomed to even greater heights. Jean-Baptiste Deburau, an acrobat and mime, whom Baudelaire described as "mysterious as silence, supple and mute as the serpent, thin and long as a gibbet," became a darling of the Parisian literati, lauded by Nodier, Nerval, Balzac, and George Sand. King Louis XV summoned Nicolet's ropewalkers for a royal performance, and afterward allowed the company to rename itself the Grands-Danseurs du Roi, the Great Dancers to the King. For a summer in Versailles, two of Nicolet's most famous acrobats, Placide and Le Petit Diable, even gave the young Count of Artois (later King Charles X) secret ropewalking lessons at Versailles. For the *saltimbanques,* the attention was unprecedented. After nearly a thousand years on the periphery of society, they had finally penetrated the mainstream.

Such, then, was the state of things in Paris, when, in 1804, at the age of eighteen, Madame Saqui came strutting into town. Slim and strikingly featured, with piercing gray-brown eyes, she was by then a star of the fairground circuit and looking to make her name on a larger stage. After the death of her father, she had written to Daneaux, the director of the Tivoli, a variety venue like Nicolet's. He had promised her a leading role, but she arrived to find the marquee occupied by an even bigger name: Forioso, one of the great stars of Europe, famous for his luxurious costumes and brazen stunts, such as his midair walk from the Pont de la Concorde to the Pont des Tuileries. Saqui resigned herself to working under her master.

She didn't have to wait long. On her very first night, Forioso, ever his reckless self, and perhaps distracted by the young star waiting to assume his position, botched the landing of a leap and crashed to the stage, snapping his ankle like a twig. Saqui made her Parisian premiere the following night.* Dressed in a garland of roses and a white tulle skirt spangled with blue stars, she launched herself through a display of unexpected prowess—bounding, spinning, and twisting on her wire. Daneaux, fearful of losing another star, was irate. But as Saqui's memoirist Paul Ginisty writes in *Memoirs of a Ropedancer,* the young ropedancer "was destined to conquer the capital in a night."

And conquer she did. Over the next decade, Saqui would go on to become one of Europe's biggest stars and a staple of Parisian entertainment. Endowed with a will and a fearlessness forged on the road, she had an incandescent charisma. A journalist who met her in 1852 for the French weekly *L'Éclair* called it an uncommon "vivacity, a fire." Whereas other dancers dressed as ballerinas, Saqui wore silver sequins and scan-

* The event gets a mention in the first paragraph of Victor Hugo's *Les Misérables*: "In 1817 . . . Madame Saqui had succeeded Forioso."

dalous flesh-colored leggings. Alone on her rope, she enacted full dramas, complete with characters and plot twists woven around a central theme. Accoutered like a Spartan warrior—in a golden helmet, a golden chest-plate, and, on special occasions, a golden beard—she reenacted Napoleon's glories abroad: the "Siege of Saragossa," the "Passage over Saint-Bernard Mountain." Men flocked to ogle her bravery and catch a glimpse of her thigh. Women copied her style. Within months of her premiere, confection shops had stocked their shelves with candy boxes featuring her angular face. When she adopted a headpiece made of colorful ostrich plumes, milliners suffered a rush of orders for identical hats.

In 1810, at the height of Saqui's Parisian fame, word of the feisty young starlet reached Napoleon, who invited her to perform for his Imperial Guard in the Beaujon Gardens. It was a warm summer night when she stepped onto the rope before the emperor and his watchful soldiers. As per Saqui's custom, a barrage of sparks and smoke met her arrival on high. But that night the timing was off, and as she hoisted her arm for her final salute, a rocket scorched her shoulder.

Saqui screamed and tumbled from the rope. With her undamaged arm, she managed to catch herself, and she slid to the ground, white as a specter.

Napoleon rushed over to receive her. "Madame!" he implored. "I beg you not to continue." But Saqui would hear nothing of it. To the horror and titallation of the crowd, she climbed again onto the rope and ascended into the now silent night. She executed her routine as intended, then descended. Again, the emperor was waiting at the bottom of the rope, baffled.

He began to interrogate her in his usual aggressive way: Who was she? Where did she come from? How did she learn her art? "One does not learn this art, Sire," Saqui replied coolly. "One discovers it. If, that is, one is bestowed the sacred fire."

In Ginisty's memoir, the badinage continues for two pages. Afterward, other scholars note, more intimate contact ensued, primarily in Napoleon's secret apartment in the Tuileries Gardens. Ultimately, Saqui became a staple performer at royal ceremonies (including Napoleon's second marriage, to Marie-Louise), and also at the battlefront, where she buoyed the weary troops with sassy reenactments of their triumphs. In private, Napoleon called her *"mon enragée"* (my little lunatic). In public, she proclaimed herself "First Acrobat of His Majesty the Emperor and King." She painted the imperial eagle onto her bags and hired a team of Turks to serve as her cavaliers and, with them, paraded through the French countryside in a carriage painted gold.

IN 1814, at the height of her Parisian fame, Madame Saqui purchased the Spectacle des Acrobates, a five-hundred-seat theater on the boulevard. The address of the place was number 62, and Tina and I tracked down the site. A four-story neoclassical apartment building now loomed in place of the old theater. It had stone doorways and iron flower boxes. A plump white cat lounged in the second-story window.

I told Tina about Saqui and the site. Saqui performed on and off on the boulevard until she was well into her sixties. After her reign, theatrical ropedancing had faded. The sorts of theaters that could support such acts had disappeared, especially after the rise of the cinema, and circuses weren't equipped for (or interested in) all the dramatic scenery. Today, however, the dramatic shows are coming back. Working under the Soviet state, the Voljansky troupe, a group of wire-walkers, choreographed a number based on the myth of Prometheus that won the coveted Silver Clown at the Monte Carlo Circus Festival. Cirque Baroque, one of France's earliest and most respected modern companies, created *Ningen*, an account of the life and works of Japanese author Yukio Mishima. The modern era parallels the historical moment of the boulevard in other ways as well. Over the last thirty years, theater practitioners have increasingly adopted the circus and variety arts. Acrobatics, mime, puppetry, music—all have been integrated into what critics call "physical theater" or "total theater."

Tina had studied at a physical-theater school, and I asked her what she thought explained the shift.

"On the surface, I think there's respect for the technique," she said, looking out over the churning rush-hour traffic. "The amount of time and dedication is obvious, certainly more obvious than in something like theater, and theater artists know this." More persuasively, perhaps, she added that actors had come to understand the potential value of the circus arts in their own work. "Theater got kind of staid for a while there. Physical performance is engaging. It's dynamic. The skills bring a live element that people can relate to." She paused to watch an ambulance roar up the boulevard, siren whooping, blue lights ablaze.

ON THE NIGHT of March 14, 1826, Philip Astley's circus on Rue du Faubourg du Temple caught on fire. An errant firework had whizzed into the drapery during the aptly titled *Fire of Salins*, and now the whole building was engulfed in flames. A fire brigade rushed to the scene, but they arrived too late. Though the spectators had escaped, and so had the horses, the building itself was beyond repair. Paris's first circus was gone. Astley was long dead by then, so the burden of recovery fell to the building's director, the noted equestrian and France's first circus mogul, Antonio Franconi.

In the story of the circus, Franconi is a figure as big as Astley and as dynamic as Saqui. A striking physical presence, with a broad chest and a booming voice that made the timid shrink, he is credited with founding the first French circus, the Cirque Olympique, and deepening the genre confusion in the hybrid of circus and theater. More specifically, his specialty was theatrical zoology: vast animal pantomimes, or "mimodramas," written by noted local playwrights and starring everything from hundreds of horses to domesticated stags.

Unlike Saqui, Franconi hadn't seemed destined for such idiosyncratic greatness. Born to a pair of Italian aristocrats in 1738, he spent his youth hobnobbing not with Gypsies and bearwards but with the courtesans of Venice at palace balls. When Franconi was a teenager, however, his father killed a senator in a duel and was condemned to death. Antonio, his own life threatened by the prospect of revenge, fled to the road, where, among the ruffian company of merchants and vagabonds, he turned to animal training to survive.

Such animal acts have a long history. There are two types of acts: animal showing and animal training. Animal showing was the easier of the two. Returning from conquests abroad, soldiers or entrepreneurial explorers would pack exotic animals into their hulls to display upon their return. In 1749, an intrepid Dutch sea captain boasted Europe's first rhinoceros. "It runs with an astonishing lightness," bragged an advertisement. "It knows how to swim and likes to dive in the water like a duck."

Animal training required less money but more skill. Performers taught small domestic animals—dogs, monkeys, pigs, mules, and occasionally bears—how to dance, tumble, count, and perform imitations. Today these displays seem trite and, according to some, morally dubious. But they nevertheless require great ability and, when practiced correctly, an intimacy between the trainer and his charges.

Hundreds of years ago, the feats could be astounding. The British Museum has an Arundel manuscript showing an ox riding a horse. In 1660, after a trip to the Saint Margaret's Fair, the famous diarist John Evelyn noted seeing monkeys and apes dancing on the high-rope, saluting, bowing, pulling off their hats, all "with as good a grace as if instructed by a dancing master."

On the road, Franconi became a master of such precise animal control. After briefly tending lions for a zoo in Lyon, he developed a canary act that was revered. Later, during a stop in Spain, the Duke of Duras introduced him to bullfighting, a Moorish practice newly popular among the Spanish elite. Franconi convinced a few of the matadors to join him on the road. According to legend, when they refused to perform one afternoon in Toulouse, he stepped in and tamed the bulls himself.

In 1783, Franconi (who was now in his forties) came to Paris. He arrived at an electric time. In the hectic prelude to the revolution, commercial theaters were sprouting up around the city, including Nicolet's Théâtre de la Gaîté on the boulevard, and Astley's first circus on the Rue du Faubourg du Temple. Eager to participate, Franconi made his way to Astley, who hired him on the spot. The men worked together for three years, Franconi running his canary act while Astley captained the horses. In time, Franconi learned the rudiments of *voltige*. (His sons would become some of the finest riders in Europe.) He also studied the peculiar genre of spectacle that Astley had begun cultivating, a curious mix of horsemanship and theater known as "hippodrama."

Today hippodramas are forgotten. The word itself sounds like a Disney cartoon. In the nineteenth century, however, the shows were all the rage, and the epitome of this fluid period in circus history. Loosely speaking, the term refers to "horse plays," melodramas staged on horseback. Nobody knows how the genre started. Theaters had long imported equestrians to work on their stages; as early as 1668, Samuel Pepys noted the use of horses during a revival of Shirley's *Hyde Park* at the King's Playhouse. With the rise of the circus, the overlap between horsemanship and drama deepened. Lacking proper venues, early circus entrepreneurs rented theaters for their tours, incorporating the orchestra pits as rings. In 1782, Astley's rival Charles Hughes joined forces with librettist Charles Dibdin to construct the "Royal Circus" in London, a dual-purpose theater, with both a ring and a stage, the latter hidden by a curtain.* Similar hybrid venues followed, and by the turn of the century they littered England. The venues featured a cornucopia of acts: circus acts, pantomimes, melodramas, staged hunts, plus what hippodrama specialist A. H. Saxon calls "sub-dramatic entertainments"—burlettas, dances, fireworks, farragos, and *ballets d'action*—all performed in rotation.

Naturally, the forms began to fuse. As Saxon notes, "A grace equestrienne might interpret the role of a young prince in the opening stage spectacle, while a featured ropedancer or strongman might appear as Harlequin or a bereaved father in an afterpiece." Soon full hybrid shows emerged. In 1789, the Royal Circus staged a piece called *The Bastille*, by John Dent. In 1807, Astley produced *The Brave Cossack*, a military drama that concluded with a cavalry battle. As the genre grew more popular, the shows grew more spectacular and complex, with hundreds of equestrians, charging over mountain peaks and bridges, capturing châteaux designed by the finest decorators of the period. Astley's stage was the biggest in London. Circus owners contracted local writers to pen scripts, often drawing on myth and literature. A show that proved popular would be remounted in various venues. *Marzeppa and the Wild Horse of Tartary*, based on Byron's poetic account of a youth lashed naked to a horse roaming the steppes of the Ukraine, made a splash at Astley's in 1831. Its sets featured spectacular mountain views, moving panoramas, and a mechanical vulture. It was restaged around the world. Shakespeare was an equally frequent choice, especially the horse-laden *Richard III*. Equestrians and their mounts always were the heroes of the show, galloping through cannon smoke, rearing up, swooping in to save children in peril.

Hippodramas signify for us the essentially limitless potential of the circus as a dramatic medium and its inherent lack of clear boundaries. Like pure circuses, hippodramas aspired to baffle and amuse; like plays, they had themes, morals, and plots. The shows weren't just demonstra-

* Hughes chose the word "circus" for its neoclassical associations. Astley referred to his venues as "amphitheaters" for his whole life.

tions of prowess. The audience derived meaning from the shows, from their dramatic elements and contextualization of the skills. They weren't "flat" performances. "The action is simple and moves quickly toward the goal," a government censor wrote of one piece, *Le Drapeau ou Le Grenadier français*, staged in Paris in 1827. "The feelings expressed by the various characters are honest and generous."

The shows inspired Antonio Franconi. At Astley's theater in Paris, he spent three years studying the genre and then galloped off to Lyon to create spectacles of his own. With the outbreak of the revolution, Astley was forced to flee to England, abandoning his beloved Parisian venue. Franconi, now a successful circus director in his own right, returned to the capital and claimed Astley's building, still the only circus in Paris. He renamed the venue the Cirque Olympique. Scholars consider it the first native circus in French history (and the first use of the word *cirque*).

Two decades of creative circus followed, as Franconi, now aided by his two sons, Laurent and Henri, worked to expand and refine the fusion of circus and theater. At first they stuck to Astley's military model. During Robespierre's Reign of Terror, Franconi staged adaptations of *The Death of General of Marlborough* and *The Adventures of Don Quixote de la Mancha*, featuring heroic charges and countercharges, exploding ammunition wagons, and crackling musketry. "We forget the theatre!" proclaimed an adoring observer of one such show. "We're watching a battle!"

As his directorial talents blossomed, Franconi incorporated a wider variety of fauna into his shows: dogs, pigs, bears. On stages around the world, producers had similar ideas; in 1808, the prestigious Park Theater in New York rented an elephant for their production of *Blue Beard*. But whereas most shows incorporated animals for simple stunts or set pieces, Franconi was an innovator. Every season he premiered a new hybrid: animal operas, animal melodramas, Easter pantomimes. For each, he would train a beast for the starring role and incorporate it seamlessly into the action. The 1812 production of *Le Pont infernal*, for example, starred a stag named Coco who wandered through the audience, presenting flowers to ladies and nibbling from their palms, and in a climactic final scene escaped a bawling cohort of dogs and men by triumphantly leaping over a mountain chasm.

For *The Elephant of the King of Siam*, staged in 1829, an elephant named Mademoiselle Djeck carried the Prince of Siam into battle, sprung him from prison, and, in the final scene, indulged in a celebratory banquet with an enormous napkin tied around her neck, summoning slaves and courtiers with a bell. Franconi's animals were the stars of Paris.

The Franconi reign would last for decades. Between 1807 and 1848, the Olympique staged 260 pieces, premiering five or six new scripts a year, including pantomimes, mimodramas, and melodramas. In England, his shows incited a rage for elephant drama, leading theater managers to reinforce their stages and playwrights to revise their old plays for pachyderm actors. In Paris, the Franconis became royal favorites: regal theaters recruited them to perform in shows, and Napoleon's grandson hired them as equestrian coaches. In 1826, when those fireworks set the theater ablaze, King Charles X himself created a royal fund to have the circus rebuilt. Dukes, generals, and judges all contributed to give the circus a new home at 66 Boulevard du Temple, in the center of the action, and just a few doors down from Madame Saqui.

The new circus, the boulevard's first, opened on March 31, 1827. Enormous and intricately constructed, with a cast-iron roof, the biggest ring in Europe, and a stage hidden by a gold-fringed crimson velvet curtain, the building marked the apex of the age of theatrical circus. It became, in the words of one critic, the "people's theatre par excellence."

Ultimately, Franconi's love of excess drove him into ruin: swimming in debt, facing state repossession, he sold the building and the company to a butcher turned real-estate developer, Louis Dejean. (About this epic character, more later.) Historical forces were also at play. The popularity of the Franconi brand of circus, that of intellectual "meaning," started to wane, supplanted by a new type of show, more spectacular and dangerous, full of flying men and women with beards. Officially, this form wouldn't fully emerge until the 1860s, with the arrival of a certain celebrated gymnast in Paris. Harbingers of its birth, however, could be felt decades before. Ironically, the earliest signs appeared at Franconi's circus itself.

Arriving for the show on April 21, 1831, spectators at the Olympique found the circus in an agitated state. Armed policemen lingered at the heads of aisles. On the stage, half of the scenery had been obscured by a sturdy wire net masked with jungle foliage. To the side, a series of vertical bars leaned against the wall.

According to the program, the star of the performance, a mimodrama

A wooden Chinese sculpture dating from approximately 200 B.C.

*A*n illustration of the Franconis, France's first native circus family and some of Europe's most famous nineteenth-century equestrians

*F*or hundreds of years rope dancers performed in fairgrounds and public gardens. This image was painted in France around 1820.

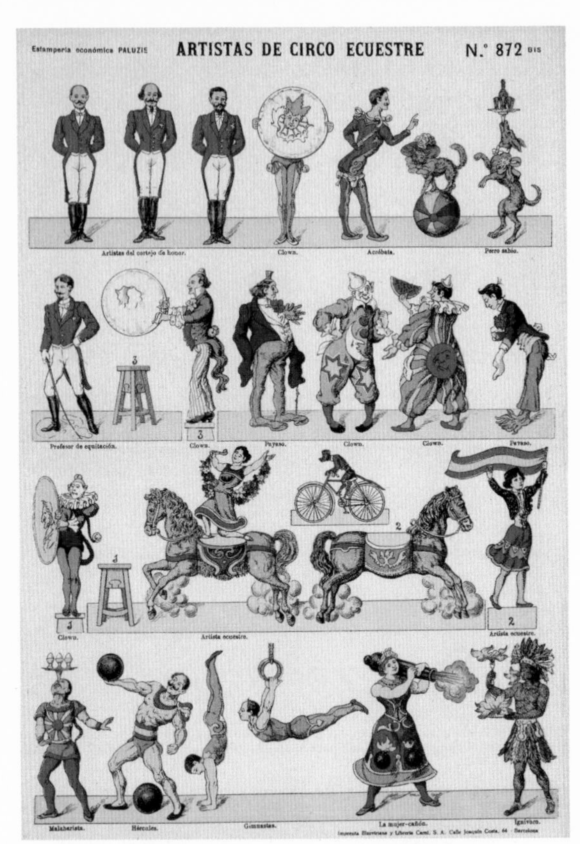

A Spanish lithograph from 1880

An 1860 French chromolithograph. In Paris, female riders borrowed heavily from the ballet tradition for their movements and costuming.

Jules Léotard, originator of the flying trapeze, in 1860

A pair of unidentified nineteenth-century clowns. White makeup and such "sack" outfits were common in both circus and pantomime shows.

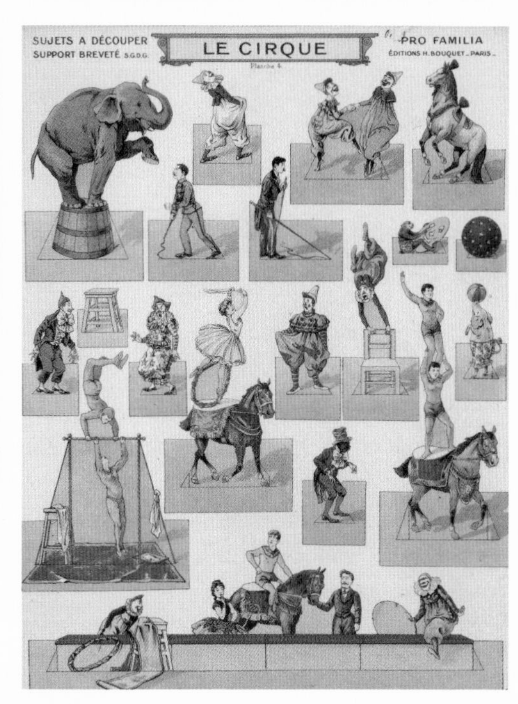

A French lithograph from the turn of the century, the end of the elegant period of French circus. The horse remained the driving force of the art.

*A*n advertising card for the Rainats, a troupe of nineteenth-century French trapezists, or "gymnasts," as they were called

*P*hineas Taylor Barnum, creator of the American Museum in New York and, with W. C. Coup and Dan Castello, of America's first three-ring circus in 1871

*T*he Ringling Bros. and Barnum & Bailey combined circus lot in Cleveland in 1921. The Ringling brothers purchased the Barnum & Bailey circus in 1907 but ran the circuses separately until 1919.

*P*aul Cinquevalli, a Polish-born juggler and an international vaudeville star during the 1880s and the 1890s

A pantomime starring Chocolat (Rafael Padilla) at the Nouveau Cirque in Paris in 1890

A 1907 courier centerfold from the Sun Bros. Circus "Grand Imperial Program." Circus images were often recycled from previous shows, and this one possibly came from George W. DeHaven's Grand Imperial Circus of 1868.

For 150 years, circus artists served as commercial spokespeople, like movie stars or athletes today. When "Fratellinimania" swept through Paris, the clowns appeared on countless products—candies, jewelry, fabrics, even radiator caps.

According to the show program, the 1934 Ringling Bros. and Barnum & Bailey combined show included 800 artists, 800 crew, 735 horses, 100 clowns, and 8 elephants.

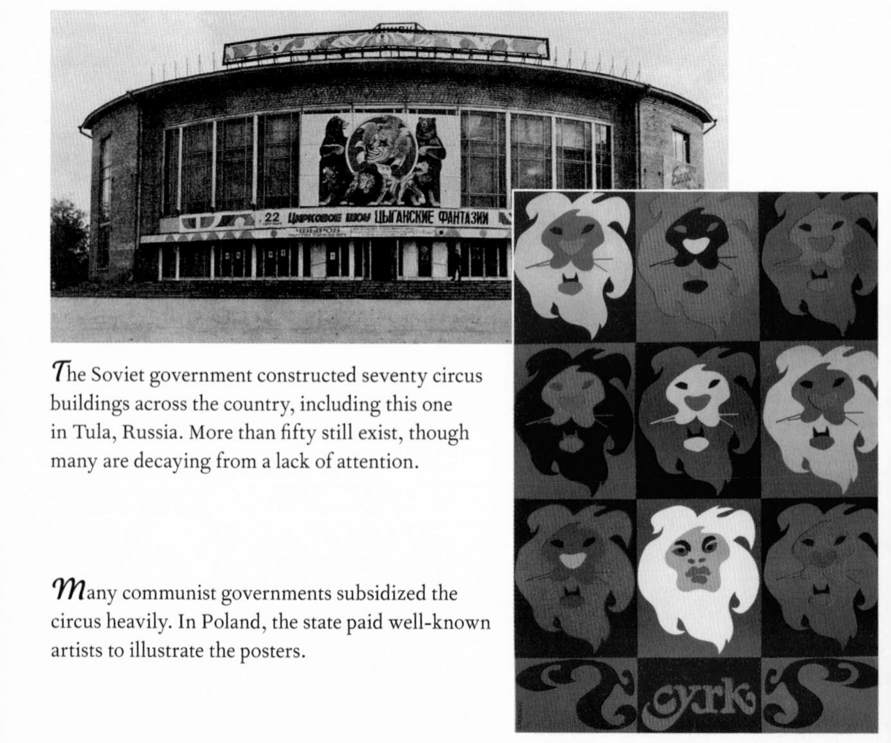

The Soviet government constructed seventy circus buildings across the country, including this one in Tula, Russia. More than fifty still exist, though many are decaying from a lack of attention.

Many communist governments subsidized the circus heavily. In Poland, the state paid well-known artists to illustrate the posters.

Les Arts Sauts, a contemporary French company, practices strictly trapeze. For their third show, *Ola Kala*, they performed in a cone-shaped tent until it was destroyed.

Jérôme Thomas, the French juggler, performing in *Ici* in 2010

Les 7 Doigts de la Main (the seven fingers of the hand), a contemporary company based in Montreal, performing *Traces* in 2011

The Nouveaux Nez (Roseline Guinet, Raquel Esteve Mora, Alain Reynaud, Nicolas Bernard) performing in *Cirque en Cascade* in 2012. In 2004, Mora replaced Roger Bories, one of the founding members.

Les NoNo Font Leur Cirque, directed by Serge Noyelle, director of the Théâtre NoNo, a company of actors and musicians, in 2011

In 1998, Cirque du Soleil premiered *O*, a resident water circus, at the Bellagio in Las Vegas. Franco Dragone directed. Since the premiere, *O* has grossed over a billion dollars and remains one of the company's most popular shows.

entitled *The Lions of Mysore,* was a reknowned "zoo-gymnast" named Henri Martin. When the curtain rose, animals—a veritable zoo of pelicans, llamas, elephants, even a kangaroo—invaded the stage behind the wire netting. For two acts, Martin stalked among the animals, dressed in the white robes of the Indian nabob, cast into the jungle for his sins. Then, before the third act, the bars were installed across the front of the stage. When the audience had returned to their seats, Martin strode on, dressed as a gladiator. A moment later, a lion lumbered into the cage with him. To the astonishment of the slack-jawed, formally dressed crowd, he "tamed" the beast into submission.

It was the first time a man entered a cage with a lion onstage. Antonio Franconi was in his nineties then, and almost completely blind. But, according to legend, he would ask to be carried to the circus every night anyway, to sit in the balcony listening to the cries of the performers and the gasps of the crowd.

FOR A LONG TIME, circus historians talked about the hippodramas and mimodramas and their spirit of fusion as an anomaly, an errant period of experimentation before the circus settled into its true form. In the half-century that followed, the circus locked itself down, adhering more and more strictly to the codes we associate with it today, settling into the circus as the classically practiced "pure" form: equestrian acts, as I've said, interspersed with physical feats of agility, staged in a ring. Anthony Hippisley-Coxe, a British historian, went so far as to describe the hippodrama as a "bastard entertainment" that "actually inhibited the development of the circus."

This distinction remains fuzzy today. Aside from the single-skill shows mentioned earlier, there has also emerged a wave of modern hippodramas. Zingaro, a French "equestrian theater" company, stages *voltige* and exhibitions inspired by diverse cultures. Another group, Theatre Centaur, creates equestrian renditions of classic dramatic works, including a version of *Macbeth* that I saw in a stunning and ominous black tent pitched in the garden of a seventeenth-century château.

The similarity between these new shows and the shows of the past forces an obvious conclusion: the new isn't as new as it seems. But it also calls into question the conventional understanding of the past. What if the "true" circus was actually the anomaly? What if it was just a fad, a time when the art unnecessarily reduced itself to an arbitrary and restrictive combination of elements? What if the circus properly defined was actually what came before, a show of fusion, of spectacular and dramatic arts commingling?

It wasn't an unreasonable idea. The first "circus" building, Hughes's Royal Circus, was designed for such entertainments. Astley spent his life staging circodramas and was charging headlong into their exploration when he died. And even after the true circus imposed itself, the fusion circus recurred, as in *Le Noce de chocolat*, a lavish pantomime featuring acrobats and actors at the Nouveau Cirque in Paris.

Of course, what really matters is how you define the circus, how you distinguish it from the theater. Purists define the art practically, as a genre of performance. Others emphasize the thematic focus of the form. David Hammarstrom points out several distinguishing features in *Circus Rings Around Russia*, his book about Soviet circus. Whereas the theater is mental, he notes, the circus is physical. Theater treats conflict between humans; the circus treats a human's struggle with himself or the environment. Theater is imaginative, "a display of what is unreal," but circus is real, what is "actual and without pretense."

Personally, I found such distinctions useful but easily transcended, as the boulevard's history showed. As Tina said as we walked along, "It's funny, but I always saw this mix of theater and circus as kind of a highly evolved creature—the way of the future. But maybe they are the way of the past, too."

12

What Grace, What Hardiness

JANUARY BROUGHT a brisk wind, a new semester, and changes at the National School. After four months of slogging through acrobatic basics, the freshmen set about selecting their new disciplines, a process the school referred to as the *découverts* (the "discoveries"). Each week, the *découverts* introduced students to a new piece of exotic equipment: a Russian swing, a Chinese pole. A few of the students had used them before, but most were newbies. "It looks like a medieval torture device," a freshman named Sebastian said of the Korean cradle. Nearby, Frédéric, the equanimous administrator, smiled over his paperwork. "That's why we call them 'discoveries.' "

And then there were the skills that needed no introduction. Stepping from the biting chill into the hall's warmth one January morning, I found myself staring up at a monstrous web woven laterally across the air. On a table-sized platform bolted to the ceiling, a pair of bulky sophomores peered down into the hall. One was beating chalk into his hands and muscular forearms. The other fished at a limp trapeze with a long, surgical-looking hook. At a barked signal from a coach down below, the chalk-laden flyer, an Austrian, laid one hand on the bar, then the other, and, with another bark, hopped into space, his taut body rising, lingering, then rushing out over the net.

I had been attending classes for four months, but the trapeze still intimidated me. My own traumatic first flight had scarred me. My reading hadn't helped. One author refers to the history of the trapeze as a "history of death." Since the discipline's invention by a French gymnast in the 1850s, dozens of trapeze artists have died while performing or training. Hundreds more have been seriously injured.

Watching the students, however, gave me hope. A few were obvious experts—crawling onto the rafters like spider monkeys—but most seemed as frightened as I was. Odilon, a stud on the trampoline, approached the wire ladder as if it were a wild animal: inching forward, poking at it, retreating, approaching again, tugging to see if it would hold his weight. Another big freshman, Baptiste, who rumbled the spring-loaded floor when he tumbled, got halfway up the ladder before freezing like a cartoon elephant on a chair above a mouse. *"Oh non!"* he bellowed, his thighs clamped to the rungs. *"C'est pas possible!"*

Though mortifying for poor Baptiste, the display inspired me. The freshmen showed me that my fears were rational, and that, with work, I could overcome them. Learning the trapeze was a process of technical acquisition like any other.

And so, the following Monday, I visited Anny in her trailer. She was hunched wearily over a stack of papers, but when I told her to enroll me in the flying-trapeze class, her eyes sparked. *"Enfin!"* she said. Finally!

THE CLASS WOULD START in a month. In the meantime, to glean some insight into the craft, I arranged a visit with France's most famous company of flyers, Les Arts Sauts. Over forty strong, including trapezists, administrators, technicians, and children, the company travels the world performing what they refer to as "aerial ballets"—poetic, open-air spectacles staged above an audience and consisting almost entirely of trapeze.

I caught up with the company on a brisk and overcast afternoon in Lannion, a cobblestoned coastal village in Brittany. The company had pitched their tent in a field on the edge of town for a weekend of shows. The tent, affectionately known as "the Bubble," cut an otherworldly vision. Bulbous and white, it rose from the field like an alien moon. A single line of trailers snaked off it like the tail of a mouse, toward a forest in the distance. I approached the first trailer, which turned out to be the troupe's office, or the "red wagon," and there found Laurence de Magalhaes, the company administrator, with her boots propped on the desk.

"You picked a hell of a night to visit!" she said. Her hair was as black as her skintight leather pants. Her eyes were only slightly lighter, and she spoke quickly in a husky smoker's rasp. "It's not usually like this," she said, waving a hand at the room, which buzzed with an election-day fervor. At desks piled with printers and paper debris, assistants prattled loudly into phones. The door banged with a constant flow of visitors.

"Seriously," Laurence said, "trapezists are usually pretty relaxed people."

The energy spoke to the significance of the night. After four years of touring, the company would give the final performance of *Kayassine*, their second show, and the product of ten years of work. The company had been founded in 1993 as an attempt to rewrite the rules of the trapeze. At the time, the founders, six French trapezists, were working for other circuses, including Cirque du Soleil and New York's Big Apple Circus. But even in "modern" companies such as those, the trapeze was employed in a fairly conventional fashion. Routines rarely lasted more than a few minutes. Most were structured around a repetitive rhythm, in which the flyers, usually men clad in colorful singlets, took turns throwing flips and twists, landing in the arms of a partner.

The founders of Les Arts Sauts set out to break these codes by approaching the trapeze as a medium for expression. They contracted a group of Parisian engineering students to construct a "flying machine," a mobile trapeze, for which they choreographed a show combining traditional tricks—flips, pirouettes, layouts—with more theatrical features: characters, scenes, mime techniques.

Like Jérôme Thomas, Les Arts Sauts developed a full performance from a single circus discipline. The performers were costumed in sprightly white loincloths. A cellist and a soprano performed what one critic described as a "nonstop medley" of everything from "Bulgarian-style vocal harmonies to baroque opera." The company aimed for something simpler than their technically advanced Russian and Mexican counterparts were producing, if also more difficult. They aspired to create works of trapeze that were "more like a film or a work of art." They aimed to invoke a feeling. "We would like you to see the show and, afterward, to feel as though you have flown," Laurence told me.

The company toured all over the world, from Korea to Norway. At each stop, they unfolded their rigging in a town plaza or an open field, like latter-day *saltimbanques*. Because the shows were outdoors and free, with local governments picking up the tab, the crowds could be enormous. In Laos, twenty thousand people pressed into a plaza to watch them fly. In Cambodia, where they set up at the bottom of a hill, estimates topped forty thousand.

After almost five years of touring, the company retired the flying machine, took a short break, and started work on *Kayassine*, named after the Laotian word for "circus." They expanded the dramaturgy of the first show with the help of a theater director, Hervé Lelardoux, and developed the themes of their inspiration, the story of Daedalus from Ovid's *Metamorphoses*. Under the guidance of German architect Hans-Werner Müller, they designed the Bubble.

Like the first show, *Kayassine* spent extensive time on the road—five years, 543 performances, mostly in Europe, South America, and Asia, but with stops in North America as well. The show created a minor frenzy wherever it went. Nobody had ever seen anything like it. In New York, where the company pitched their tent in the tamped earth of Damrosch Park, *The New York Times* called it "richly thoughtful and highly skilled entertainment." *The Washington Post* said the show was "of overwhelming beauty and humanity" and "a great leap forward in the performing arts."

And tonight the journey would end. After the show, there would be a party. Tomorrow the Bubble would be disassembled and packed off to Belgium, where, according to Laurence, it would serve as "some sort of exhibition space for modern art." The company would begin work the following month on their third show, to be staged in an enormous cone.* First, though, the whole crew would take a break, which Laurence admitted she was looking forward to.

"Don't get me wrong, touring is the most amazing experience in the world," she said, gazing at the tent through the dirt-caked window of the trailer. "But it's also stressful, all the logistics. And of course the shows."

I asked her what she meant by this last comment.

"We had an accident just the other day," she said. One of the flyers had recently come back from an injury. "He was rusty, and his timing was off, and he crashed against his partner's head."

She fell silent. I asked her if the flyer was okay.

"Oh sure, he's fine. He wanted to go right back up again, though of course I wouldn't let him." She thought. "It's just an important reminder." She noted that her own husband was a trapezist with the company. "We don't talk about it. But it's there every night, underneath the art. It's the risk we have to live with."

IN EARLY 1859, Jules Léotard, eighteen years old, was lounging in the pool in a gymnasium in Toulouse, France, when a simple discovery altered the trajectory of his life forever. Gazing at the skylights above him, he noticed a series of ropes dangling from each window. The shape and position of the ropes reminded him of the old trapezes in the workout hall, the "moving triangles" that gymnasts like himself had employed for decades as equipment for pull-ups and sit-ups. He wondered: What if he attached a trapeze to each skylight over the pool? What if he swung between them? He gave it a shot. After mounting a bar to each of the three skylights, he built a small pile of mats at the edge of the pool. Climbing onto the mats, he gripped the first trapeze and, with a hop, swung out over the pool—once, twice, then released, shooting forward almost horizontally over the water, snagging the second bar in his hands. After a pause, he kicked himself into a swing again and repeated the flight, swinging, releasing, catching the third bar, this time landing exhilarated

* The show, *Ola Kala*, toured in the cone until the cone was destroyed in a storm. Fortunately, they were able to buy back the Bubble.

on cold tile. According to his memoirs, Léotard glanced back at the distance covered and felt a burst of pride. "Eureka!" he cried.

Less than six months later, he was on his way to the Cirque des Champs-Élysées in Paris. His father, an old gymnast himself, had encouraged his son to work up an act with the trapeze, which he premiered in his hometown, Toulouse, soaring over mattresses stuffed with straw. Immediately word spread of the daring young man. The crowds flocked. The critics fawned.

Louis Dejean, the circus mogul of the boulevard, dispatched a scout to confirm the rumors, and then raced down himself. While auditioning Léotard, Dejean told him that "the race of the trapezes," as Léotard called it, was unquestionably magnificent. But was it safe? How did he know the boy wonder wouldn't make headlines for the wrong reasons, by breaking his neck within a week? To prove the act's safety, Léotard released into the mattresses mid-flight, producing only a puff of dust. Dejean signed Léotard on the spot.

Yet, as Léotard describes in his memoirs, his own doubts festered. Now, on the train to Paris, he wondered what his on-purpose fall had proved. What if he suffered an unplanned fall? What if sweat slicked his fingers and his grip slipped? What if he lost his bearings in the air and landed upside down? These and similar questions clouded Léotard's thoughts as his train hissed to a stop. Out the window, he spotted Dejean waiting for him on the platform. Léotard wondered if he wasn't being escorted to his death.

His arrival in Paris corresponded with a turning point in circus history. In the beginning, there had been Astley and his equestrian stunts. Then came the "theatrical period" of acrobats and dramatic fusion, epitomized by Madame Saqui. Now the circus was entering the age of romance. In Paris, circuses had begun to rise in stature, to become refined entertainments on the order of the ballet or the opera. In America, shows had begun to morph into the lavish, magical pageants that we know today. It was also an age of death.

In the early days of the circus, during Astley's reign and later on the boulevard, the circus's emphasis had been straightforward. In early posters, Astley billed his shows as "displays" or "exercises." He aimed to impress people with his skill and savoir-faire. Danger was present, but it wasn't central to the work. Injuries, when they occurred, were minimal.

Death at the circus required an almost freakish confluence of events—such as when the dainty Parisian equestrienne Émilie Loisset fell beneath her horse during rehearsal and punctured her lung on the horn of the saddle. Audiences didn't attend shows hoping to experience what Pascal once called "that pit-of-your-stomach feeling."

But in the years leading up to Léotard's emergence, circumstances had started to change. Around mid-century, circuses witnessed an uptick in the number of dangerous acts and a corresponding increase in bloodshed. In the wake of Henri Martin's shiver-inducing big-cat triumph at the Cirque Olympique, circuses around the world rushed to include wild-animal trainers in their programs. At the Bowery Theatre in New York, a toga-wearing Isaac Van Amburgh* starred in *The Lion Lord,* a stage play written for him, two tigers, two leopards, and a pack of hyenas. At Astley's in London, another American, John Carter, wrestled a live jaguar inside a steel cage. The acts were extraordinary, but they were also hellaciously dangerous. Van Amburgh was the first man to put his head in a lion's mouth. Almost every trainer suffered some kind of terrible injury. Van Amburgh broke his back twice. Others had their arms and scalps ripped off.

Also during this time, acrobats started experimenting with technologies allowing for more dangerous flight. They created the *batoude,* a downward-sloping runway that terminated in a stiff hickory springboard. Not long after, a pair of German acrobats, Walpert and Paulan, created the first teeterboard, a flexible teeter-totter used for vaulting.

These devices had a tremendous impact. Using a *batoude,* Jean-Baptiste Auriol, star of the Cirque Olympique, could clear twenty-four soldiers standing upright with their bayonets drawn. Among acrobats, the possibility of landing the triple flip sparked a public competition that was also a bloodbath. Johnny Aymar shattered the bridge of his nose. William J. Hobbes snapped his neck. In 1869, during a performance with George W. DeHaven's Circus, a railroad-and-steamboat show, Warren Hoyt overrotated his second somersault on a vault over twelve horses and smashed into the clay ring with his chest. Although he managed to drag himself out of the ring, complications from the blow killed him shortly

* Apparently, lions have bad breath; they can also have bad gas, but this is a good thing. "As I often say: a lion who farts, it's absolutely *insupportable!*" wrote a lion-tamer from the Rubba family. "But that also means he's well fed. Which for us, the tamers, is also reassuring."

thereafter. At Hoyt's funeral, his brother Joe threw a backward somersault over his grave.

As a burgeoning acrobat and the son of a gymnast, Léotard had of course heard such stories, and as he roamed the bustling streets of Paris, he struggled to strike them from his thoughts. "The thought of my debut haunted me constantly," he writes in his memoirs. Stopping by the circus one afternoon, he found the technicians installing his rigging. "I had the sense of watching them erect my catafalque." After a few weeks, the stress had made him ill, and his inaugural flight—the official world premiere of the flying trapeze—had to be postponed until the autumn.

Finally, on November 12, 1859, he appeared at Dejean's Cirque d'Hiver (called Cirque Napoléon at the time). By modern standards his routine was surprisingly simple. In leather boots and a black singlet, to a popular waltz played by an orchestra, Léotard flew horizontally between trapezes, always rushing in the same direction, like Tarzan on his vines. His flight covered a span of roughly ten feet, and his most complicated trick was a flip. For the Parisian crowd, however, the performance was a revelation. Critics hailed him as a god. Wrote a critic from Toulouse, "The Marvelous Gymnastics executed by Monsieur Léotard have proved that a rationally and gradually exercised human body might manage to evade our ancient gravity." Within weeks, stores were stocking Léotard canes and pastries, Léotard bowler hats and neckties. Women literally fought for a glimpse of his body in action. "They stopped his car," wrote Signor Saltarino (a.k.a. Waldemar Otto), "beautiful women dropping to their knees in front of him in the street, duchesses and working-class girls." (Léotard's memoirs, published when he was just twenty-two, are largely a collection of love letters from female admirers. "I should have called this book *My Temptations*," he writes at the beginning.)

For the next ten years, Léotard swooped across Europe, playing to princes and tsars at the world's most prestigious venues. Then, in 1870, at the age of twenty-eight, he died from smallpox. Although Léotard managed to avoid an accident, the dozens of flyers who rushed to imitate him would legitimize his concerns. Like Léotard, most early flyers used minimal safety equipment: mattresses, canvas stretched by stagehands, or nothing at all. Under such perilous circumstances, a single mistake meant injury or death, and statistics from the period are gruesome. According to one study, at least sixty-five trapezists died in Europe alone between 1860 and 1970. At the Hippodrome on the Rue de l'Alma, one of the Silbons missed his catch and crashed into the crowd. At the Academy of Music in New York, William Hanlon fell sixty-five feet and glanced off the side of the net. According to a witness, "His head had struck against the iron back of a chair, tearing the scalp away between the eyebrows and the back of the crown." The list goes on: Emma Rafaelli, 1908; Fefe Gavazza, 1910; Eva Metzler, 1954. Writing in the forties, Pierre Guillon noted the surprise that struck him every time he completed a successful turn. He called it the *"On est encore là!"* ("I'm still here!") feeling.

In spite of such carnage (and perhaps because of it), the circus officially entered its next phase. Managers constructed buildings with higher ceilings to accommodate bigger riggings and more spectacular acts. They pressured their animal trainers to introduce sensationalist touches—cracking whips, loaded pistols—and in their advertising emphasized their stars' risks. Acts were no longer billed as "skillful" or "graceful." They were "dreadful" or "stomach churning."

This macabre tone crept into the work itself, a shift epitomized by another act that gained popularity in the period: the "dare-devils," or what the French call *"casse-cous,"* the broken-necks. Guillermo Antonio Farini (a.k.a. William Leonard Hunt) built an early version of the human cannon in 1877. The spring-loaded catapult propelled a fourteen-year-old named Zazel across the Royal London Aquarium. Similarly risky acts followed: women jumping off of platforms on horses, bicyclists looping-the-loop.

A performer's skill sometimes mattered less than his mettle. Appeal resided in seeing another human being risk his life. Many acts assumed appropriately gruesome nicknames. The Salagurs called themselves the Amants de la Mort, the Lovers of Death. Aloys Peters, a popular performer from the 1930s, billed himself as "The Man with the Iron Neck." From an elevated platform, he dived, headfirst, with a noose around his neck. As Roland Auguet notes in his excellent *Histoire et légende du cirque*, "Circus isn't a show about death, but death is its permanent guest."

There are multiple theories about what provoked this shift. Steve Gossard, the trapeze historian, suggested it was a consequence of "the age of daring." "There was an obsession with courage at the time," he told me. "People going up in hot air balloons, people traveling to the farthest parts of the world." In an intriguing 1905 essay entitled "The Limits of

Human Daring," stuntwoman Octavie Latour offers a related theory. As the world evolved, Latour writes, men were deprived of the opportunity to prove themselves with "wars, jousts, and crusades." To compensate, they invented new outlets for what Latour calls "their craving for courage." "They drive racing autos. They launch forth in airships." And they came to the circus, where they could "satisfy their natural inclinations with the admiration of another's thrilling feat."

Pascal had a simpler answer: "It was the Industrial Revolution," he said. With the rise of liberalism and capitalism, the audience changed. Until then, in refined cities like Paris, the art remained an aristocratic affair. Now working-class viewers arrived. True popular culture—based on emotional and visceral appeal—emerged for the first time. The new audiences worked for a living, and they saw risk differently. "A capitalist appreciates achievement," Pascal noted. "To be the best, to be the most profitable. He understands risk—in his actions, in his investments." The new audience also lived in a different world—faster, harder, and more violent. "The lion-tamer in the cage, the trapezist, the *funambule* on his wire: they bring that violence to the circus."

I told him his words reminded me of Rome, of the Colosseum and the bloodthirsty hordes.

"Yes, it really was that," he replied, "a return to the ferocious energy of the past. In the opera, there is a metaphorical violence. You die among the décor. In the circus, you die and it's for real."

OUTSIDE LAURENCE'S TRAILER, the sun was tucking itself into the woods to the west, bronzing the horizon. At the bottom of the iron steps I paused to let my eyes adjust to the dusk. According to Laurence, more than a hundred friends had been invited to that night's show, and I noticed a row of cars starting to form in the company lot. Opening curtain was still four hours away.

Laurence had suggested I could find some of the trapezists in the company dining trailer, also known as the "cookhouse." In the old tenting circuses, the cookhouse was the troupe's hub, the first tent to go up in the morning and the last to come down at night. To judge by the cookhouse of Les Arts Sauts, not much had changed. As I slipped into the trailer, I felt as though I had wandered into a Greek wedding. Dozens of people sat at long, cafeteria-style tables, chatting loudly over paper plates of rich-smelling food—lasagna, French bread, salad. Wool sweaters and work pants abounded, but the diversity was otherwise impressive: acrobats talked with the elderly, hippies spoke with children. At the rear of the room, an enormous sheet of butcher paper covered the wall. Words were scribbled all over it. At the top, in big letters, it read, "IDEAS."

Flagging down a cook in a saucy apron, I asked if he could direct me to a trapezist. He used a ladle smeared in tomato sauce to indicate an enormous man hunched in the back of the trailer.

"Him?" I said skeptically. It was hard to imagine a man of his size on high.

The cook smiled, understanding the implication. "His name's Frank. He's a catcher."

Ah yes, the catchers. In a trapeze act, there are two species: flyers and catchers. Flyers are what we imagine trapezists to be: nimble and slight, they fly through the air and grab the spotlight. Catchers are twice as big but half as prominent. Dangling by their legs instead of their arms, catchers are the unseen heroes of the discipline, like offensive linemen in football—always in the play, but almost never touching the ball.

The distinction didn't always exist. Léotard never had a catcher, and neither did his slew of imitators, all of whom flew between two bars—releasing, throwing a trick, then grabbing. But the routine was repetitive, and audiences soon lost interest. Flying this way was also difficult, not to mention dangerous. Grabbing the bar at high speeds put tremendous pressure on a flyer's shoulders. A miss of even a few inches could ruin the trick and possibly the performer's teeth; getting cracked in the face during a trapeze move is like getting hit with a crowbar. It looked for a while as though the act might disappear.

Fortunately, catchers appeared. Technically, catching began with an act called the "leap for life." Hurling himself from his trapeze, a flyer would land in the arms of a partner hanging by his knees. But the act was jarringly brief. After being caught, the flyer would grab a rope and shimmy to the ground.

In England in 1873, Azella and her partner, Gonza, came up with a better system. The gist of the act was the same: one flyer, one catcher. Only instead of hanging static, as in the leap for life, Gonza swung in rhythm with Azella's flight, allowing him to catch her while maintaining her motion. Meanwhile, an assistant on Azella's board caught her bar and delayed it long enough for her to come swinging back.

The duo called this the "flying return act," and it revolutionized the trapeze. With a partner to account for minor errors, flyers could attempt bigger tricks—triple somersaults and double layouts. What had been brave now became dramatic, as one man reached into the open air to haul his comrade to safety. In effect, the innovation marked the beginning of the act as we know it today, a display of rhythm and flow and majestic sweeps. The trapeze never again lacked for popularity.

For obvious reasons, catchers tend to be husky, with bulky torsos and powerful arms. Frank was no exception. He had mailbox shoulders and a fire-hydrant neck. His forearms were like lamb shanks. One lay on the table while the other shoveled heaps of lasagna under his handlebar mustache with a comically small fork. A single word was printed on his T-shirt: "Acrobat." At first I took it for an ironic statement about his craft. Later, Frank informed me that it was the name of an Australian company. "They do pure acrobatics," he said. "They're fucking raw, man. Raw."

We talked about catching. I had no sense of the practicalities involved. To maximize the chances for a successful "pass," Frank explained, a catcher has to optimize his "catch point"—the point where his swing brings him closest to the flyer. But this is complex. Different tricks have different catch points, and it's the catcher's responsibility to adjust to variations in his partner's flight, which is difficult because flyers and catchers hang on trapezes of different lengths (eight feet and eleven feet, respectively), which means they swing at different rates (longer pendumlums have slower swings). Also, a flyer's weight changes the velocity of the swing. Also, a catcher is hanging upside down, which is disorienting. And since human beings are unpredictable, even if you manage to organize all these variables in your head and arrive in the right place at the right time, you might find that your flyer has botched the trick entirely, and is hurtling toward your face.

Needless to say, the pressure is tremendous. Any catcher will tell you he bears the ultimate responsibility for his partner's safety. Collisions can be catastrophic. An approaching flyer is like a buzz saw of knees and elbows. Broken cheekbones are common, as are broken necks, even cracked skulls. There is ultimately very, very little margin for error. Alfredo Codona, the great Mexican flyer, once alluded to this in an essay for *The Saturday Evening Post*. He described a collision between himself and his brother, Lalo. Alfredo was attempting a triple somersault, a move he had completed hundreds of times. Only this time his takeoff was wonky, and a collision ensued that put Alfredo in the hospital with five cracked ribs. As Codona writes, "The accident resulted from the fact that I had misgauged my time in leaving the bar by less than a hundredth of a second."

As we were finishing dinner, I asked Frank if he ever dreamed about being on the other side. Given the difficulties of being a catcher, and the obscurity in which he worked, did he ever wish he were the one soaring through the air?

He let out a deep chuckle. "Rich man, poor man, fat man, thin man—everybody wants to fly. I think that's true. And I don't think catchers are any different." He was sopping at the remnants of his lasagna with a crust of bread. "You know, they say flying is the universal dream."

IN THE TRADITIONAL FAMILY CIRCUS, performers had a special term for the lot where they ate, slept, and trained: "the backyard." In circus lore, the backyard looms almost as large as the performance itself. This was especially true in the circuses of the late nineteenth and early twentieth centuries, when massive shows traveled by railroad, and big tenting circuses were the rule. To stroll across the lot then was to peek behind the curtain, to glimpse the incomprehensible lives of the performers and crew. Witnessing the arrival of a show was observing the creation of an entire village, a dreamscape erected in an empty field.

This greater show started as early as four in the morning, when curious locals would ride down to the railyards and wait in the hazy half-light for the long trains to arrive and disgorge their wonders—the big cats, the grizzled roustabouts who would raise the big top, what historian Dominique Jando once called "that great lake of canvas." Some of these fans were true circophiles. Most came out of curiosity. "And everywhere, as light came, there would be a scene of magic, order, and of violence," wrote Thomas Wolfe, remembering the circuses of his youth. Even by modern standards, the logistics of these circus operations were stunningly complex: Thousands of performers and crew. Hundreds of cars. Six tents. Five rings.

After unloading, many circuses organized a parade through town. In an age of television and Internet, it's hard for us to imagine how magnificent these parades might have seemed, how alien and grand. Imagine yourself a teenager in the middle of America. Your whole life is prairie, work, and church. You've only ever seen a painting of an elephant or a giraffe, only ever heard stories about jugglers. And then, one afternoon, here they are, parading down your dusty main street—a line of gilded chariots pulled by horses bedecked with feathers, carrying Egyptian queens; a brass band playing an English march; an elephant lumbering on a chain, its enormous ears flapping against its gleaming tusks.

It must have felt like another world descending, another culture, which—in an anthropological sense—it was. The circus had its own language (a "clem" was a fight, "bunce" was profit), its own holidays ("Christmas in the summer" celebrated every July 4), and its own values (physicality, diversity, worldliness, an affinity for nature). It had rituals and practices that dated back thousands of years, a series of unwritten codes dictating everything from what people ate, to what they wore, to whom they courted. "Their morals are, in fact, almost thoroughly Victorian," Morris Markey wrote in *The New Yorker.* "In the case of marriages that seem to go awry (although these are singularly few) there are no sudden bursts of passion or violence, but earnest family conferences—and the family includes nearly every performer on the lot."

I thought of these old circuses on my visit to Les Arts Sauts. I had never seen a proper backyard. I had even come to wonder whether they still existed. Touring without a tent is 30 percent cheaper and logistically simpler, without worries of lights, heating, housing, and food. The troupes that continue to use tents are often small, and so their lots have a different feel, more like that of a family on vacation. Even Cirque du Soleil, a tenting operation that takes seven days to set up a lot and three to dismantle it, fails to evoke the old wonder. The performers fly in on airplanes and sleep in high-priced hotels. The troupe's village is organized and secure.

Yet something about the atmosphere at Les Arts Sauts that night recaptured a lost world for me. Exiting from the cookhouse, I found the lot buzzing. The sun had set completely. A set of floodlights illuminated the bulbous tent from below, causing it to glow ethereally. The parking lot was full. Groups of people drifted around the tent, down the line of trailers, toward the dark forest.

The lot felt like the genuine article, like the lots I had read about. I wandered among the trailers. There were at least thirty of them, of various shapes and sizes. They reminded me of the wagons in the old photos and films. I could see into their windows, which glowed with shadow plays of domesticity: a woman feeding a child with a spoon; a sturdy man hunched on his elbows over a newspaper. There was nothing extraordinary about the scene—it was what I had expected in many ways—but I was moved. The tent had a lot to do with my response. Although many modern companies tour in theaters, a tent evokes the mythic circus, the mystery and romance of swooping into one town after another, assembling a world and then tearing it down. When Jeff Jenkins got a tent for his Midnight Circus in Chicago, his phone immediately started ringing off the hook. High-level performers offered their services for next to nothing, simply for the experience. "Every performer we know wants to do a little one-ring tenting show," he told me. "Putting up a real tent—that's a circus!"

But it wasn't just the tent. The circus has changed; elephants and freaks no longer hold the same attraction. But what I felt in the lot that night was that some essential part of the old culture remained. I felt I was observing people outside the mainstream. There were echoes of the old values. It was an elemental life. These were traveling people who had chosen to work with their bodies and in relation to nature. And they were a family.

At the National School, students were drawn into the place's culture. Everybody gained ten pounds of bulk. They all became a little freer. They let their hair grow long and spent more time with their shirts off. During breaks in class, they wandered out into the grass, the girls in their sports bras, the young men with their sunburned backs, to lounge or train barefoot. But there was something suspect about their behavior. Because the transformation was so uniform among the students, it felt forced, even disingenuous, more like a style than a lifestyle. (I wasn't the only one who thought this. My trampoline teacher, Gabby, thought the "hippy" vibe distracted the students from the discipline and physical rigor they would need to be strong performers.)

With Les Arts Sauts I observed none of that. The life felt genuine, the sense of community real. "It's almost incomprehensible how well they get along," Roger Le Roux, director of the Cirque-Théâtre d'Elbeuf and a longtime collaborator with the company, told me later. "One could almost claim that their lifestyle, their way of living, is more important than their artistic productions. It's as if their lives were themselves a work of art."

Where did this closeness come from? In part it was a result of the way the company organized itself. From the outset, Les Arts Sauts had been established as a "pure collective." Every member—the cooks, the performers, the crew, and the musicians—contributed equally to its finances and had an equal voice in company operations. But I suspect the communal sense also originated in the idea of the circus itself. Both historically and by definition, the circus is inclusive and collaborative, a form that brings people together. Because of the way shows operated—the travel, the sheer physical proximity of the performers to one another—the circus provides a life in which community plays a central role. "It's the opposite of my friends in the dance community," Gypsy Snider, director of the Canadian circus company Les 7 Doigts de la Main, told me. "In dance, everyone is hypercompetitive—every man for himself. That's the last thing you feel in the circus."

I was halfway through the year. As I reflected on my first semester, it occurred to me that, because of my interest in the circus as an art form, as an evolution of performance, I had ignored the circus as a life. Now I was starting to get it.

"AYEEEEEEEEEEEE."

Inside the tent, Patrice Wojciechowski, one of the company flyers, watched a little girl zip above him. She streaked through the dome's open expanse, arms and legs churning the air. Cast against the tent's luminescent black interior, she looked like a pale spider swinging by its thread.

"They've been doing this all day," Patrice said. He kept his blue eyes pinned on the girl. "We call it the pendulum. On most days we don't let the kids near it, or any of the rigging. But, you know, it's a special night."

It's been said that flyers are the "aristocracy of the circus," and there's some truth to this. There's unquestionably something elegant, even graceful about the way they drift and plummet. Like the higher rungs of society, flyers are also uniquely distinguished, both within the circus and without. Gossard likes to call them "the greatest performing athletes in history." "Of all the great athletes, how many would have the courage to even climb a rope ladder?" he told me. "Of those that do, how many have the ability to swing off? How many have the timing to make a hand-catch? How many have the personal ability to do any kind of trick? That's a really unique person who can pull that off, one in millions."

There's also something dynastic about the history of the craft. Since the beginning, a rotating roster of nations have produced the discipline's greatest stars. First came the French, then the British; in 1897, Lew Jordan, an American, discovered and trained Lena Jordan to throw the world's first triple somersault. Other triple somersaults followed: Ernie Clarke in 1909; Ernie Lane, in 1921. There was a hub for American aerial royalty in Bloomington, Illinois, and another in Saginaw, Michigan. Neither city seems especially regal, but they were milling towns and so produced sawdust, whole barns of it, which was useful in an age before nets.

Since then, the reign has shifted several times: to the South Africans, the North Koreans, and especially the Mexicans, who are power specialists. Their technical feats are astounding. Tito Gaona estimates that he had thrown more than twenty thousand triples by the age of forty-three, including several dozen blindfolded. He tried to become the first flyer to throw a quadruple, but never managed it in performance. Instead, the honor went to Miguel Vasquez, who, as a sixteen-year-old, first threw a quadruple somersault to his brother during a practice for Ringling in August 1981, and then during a performance in Tucson the following July. (News of the stunt was featured on the front page of *The New York Times*.)

In the history of flyers, however, one Mexican stands out: Alfredo Codona (he of the cracked ribs). Born in Hermosillo, Sonora, in 1893, he was the son of a circus manager and a former flyer. After starting as a solo trapezist for Barnum & Bailey in 1909, he switched to the flying trapeze in 1913, recruited by his father for an act with his brother, Lalo.

Technically, Codona was top-shelf: he was one of the first flyers in history to throw a triple consistently, a stunt he learned without the use of a safety belt. His fame, however, was also due to his grace. "He couldn't look bad," Art Concello, another flyer, once said. "If Alfredo had been run over by a truck he'd have done it so gracefully that your first instinct might have been to applaud."

I was hoping to talk to Patrice about some of the great flyers; jugglers loved to chat about the old masters, from Brunn to Rastelli. But Patrice was distracted. Melancholy tinged his voice. His answers meandered.

When I asked him about the joy of flying, he talked about work. "People compare us to birds," he said, watching another child get buckled into the pendulum above us. "Unfortunately, we're not birds. A bird flaps its wings—*flap, flap*—and up he goes. For us it's incredibly hard."

After a few minutes, the problem dawned on me: I had interrupted Patrice's pre-show routine. The clowns of Cirque d'Hiver were notorious for drinking until showtime, then sprinting back to the bar during intermission, but few acrobats are so cavalier. They take this time seriously. (The backstages of Cirque du Soleil, I'm told, can be as tense as the locker room of a professional football team before a playoff game.)

I reflected on this in silence next to Patrice, watching the kids whiz by above. For all my dabbling—all the books, conversations, and classes—here was something I would never comprehend: how it must feel to be a circus *performer*, to experience the pressure and the pleasure of executing a dangerous feat with hundreds of people watching, to gaze down on all those faces, grip the bar, and swing.

13

Catch

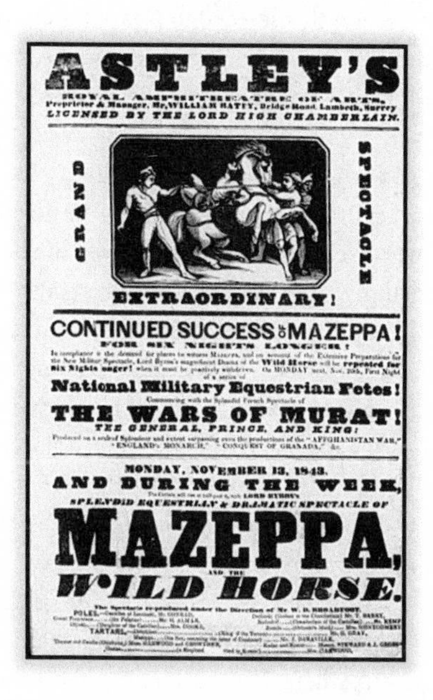

THE FOLLOWING FRIDAY, I returned to the Great Hall for my reintroduction to the flying trapeze. As I arrived, another student, an obvious amateur, was breezing through her final flight—swinging out, her knees draped over the bar, ejecting into the arms of a stocky catcher in leopard-print leggings. I felt my heart pound. I had been hoping the conversations with Les Arts Sauts would have worked some osmotic magic on me. Clearly, this wasn't the case.

"Who's next?"

Stripping off a pair of work gloves, a coach came striding toward me under the net. He was in his forties, with tousled blond hair, an unseasonable orange pallor, and the saunter of a cowboy president. When we shook hands, I could feel the calluses on his palms, stiff sheets on top of muscle. He introduced himself as François, but said that everybody called him Tiger. Later, I would find that his type was common among flyers. As Laurence said, they tend toward casual cool.

Tiger briefed me on the trapeze. When he asked me about my previous experience, I told him I was a rookie, not feeling the need to rehash unpleasant memories, and this seemed to please him. Grunting in a satisfied way, he clapped me on the shoulder and said, "All right!" And then, "Don't worry, we'll make sure you won't die! You're gonna live!" Which I appreciated.

We walked to a box of harnesses. In circus lingo, the rigging acrobats use to train or as a security precaution during performances is called a safety belt. (Codona referred to the device as the "life belt of the circus.") Safety belts, surprisingly, are the object of some controversy among circus professionals. The pro-belt camp points, of course, to the increased safety that belts bring, and also to their effectiveness in training: learning with a belt allows an acrobat to focus on technique without thinking about danger. Those against belts claim the devices interrupt the learning process by providing a false crutch and detract from how acts look in performance. They also lower the appeal: wearing a belt for a high-wire walk, they say, is false, dramatic, and sometimes just unimpressive, like putting a helmet on before banging yourself in the head with hammer.

"You want some help with that?" said the catcher in the leopard leggings, ambling over to where I stood holding the harness. We chatted as he set to work untangling the mess I had made trying to put it on. His name was Claude, and he was actually an amateur himself. Five years ago, he told me, he had discovered the discipline at Club Med. This was not uncommon. In the eighties, as other circus arts were catching on as recreational pursuits, Club Med had the brilliant idea of slipping the trapeze into their usual resort smorgasbord.

Claude handed me the harness, and I wiggled into it as if it were a diaper. He cinched the buckles on my hips and took a step back, looking at me as if fitting me for a pair of trousers.

"How's that feel?"

I did a couple of deep knee-bends. "It kind of pinches."

He nodded. "That means it's tight enough."

I waddled after Claude to the base of the ladder, which resembled a series of metal chopsticks strung between two wire fishing lines. He reiterated the correct climbing procedure: use your heels, one rung at a time, alternating feet—like climbing a rope. I was barely two meters up before the adrenaline rushed in. The room swooned. Details became crystal clear—the shine of the metal rungs, the sweat on my palms, the sharp wires bumping my crotch. Below there was only a single mat. Its width and thickness struck me as laughably inadequate to the task of saving a life.

I groped my way toward the feet of the women on the platform, then lunged at them. "Wow," came a voice from above. "Very brave!"

Meet Claudette. In the argot of the biz, Claudette was my "board muffin," the assistant who helps the flyer find his way safely off the perch, as well as prepping trapezes and securing the lines. Usually board muffins are experienced flyers themselves, and this was obviously the case with Claudette: her shoulders bulged, and her torso cut the telltale V.

"So," she said, once I'd hauled myself to my feet and established a white-knuckled grip on one of the bars running up to the ceiling. "I take it this is your first time?"

I inhaled a pungent odor, a mix of chalk and sweat, and nodded in reply.

Claudette laughed. "I'm jealous!" And she set to fastening me into the ropes, handling me like a rag doll, jostling against my back, making the perch sway unnervingly. Trying to maintain focus, I leveled my gaze out over the net. The *mécanique* might be a subject of debate, but the net was universally agreed upon. Everybody, from Cirque du Soleil to impoverished trapezists in the most reckless circuses of Brazil, flies with nets.

This hadn't always been the case. As with much of circus history, the exact origins of the device are murky. According to legend, a pair of American flyers, Charles Noble and Fred Milmore, saw a group of fishermen hauling a catch out of the Illinois River and had a flash of insight. But their net was slow to catch on. Theater directors balked at the cost of installation. Flyers worried about the loss of excitement. "With the net, where's the thrill?" Louisa Cristiani, an Italian flyer, once quipped (before shattering her spine and four ribs at Madison Square Garden). But in the twenties, Parisian music halls moved to ban "flying open," and the city followed suit. (This wasn't the first such law. In ancient Rome, Marcus Aurelius mandated safety mattresses after a tightrope walker fell to his death.) It was an enormously important step, but, as flyers like to point out, nets aren't marshmallows. They are rope—rigid, taut, prickly rope. It won't hurt you if you land correctly—on your butt or your back—but this isn't always possible, and so nets regularly snap wrists, legs, even necks. Codona, a man comfortable in a net if there ever was one, once called the device a "lurking enemy." The knots, he noted, possess a "satanic joy in gouging the flesh."

I happened to read these lines two days before my trip to the workshop. I gazed out over my own "lurking enemy" with the words echoing in my head—"satanic joy in gouging the flesh"—and was grateful to hear Claudette's carabiner click behind me, alerting me that I was officially locked in.

"So." Claudette's shining eyes emerged around my hip. "What are you doing?"

The question struck me as a riddle. I told her I was waiting for her to finish whatever she was doing.

Her eyes narrowed. "I mean, what trick?"

In fact, Tiger had decided that I should begin with a knee-hang. I related this to Claudette and in the process realized what I was about to attempt—hanging from my knees upside down—and immediately felt another jolt of adrenaline rip through me. Meanwhile, Claudette explained the move: At Tiger's command ("Hep!") I would spring from the board and swing, hanging below the trapeze, until I heard his next command ("Legs up!"), at which point I would heave my legs up to my chest, pass them through my arms, and drape them back over the bar. In this tucked, inverted position, I would then swing until Tiger yelled, "Hands off!" whereupon I would let go of the bar and dangle from my knees.

While Claudette was describing this, I rehearsed the move in my head. Most acrobats, like most athletes, have gimmicks they employ to steel themselves. Christine Van Loo, a professional acrobat and former gymnastics champion, told me that as a girl she used to imagine Mikhail Baryshnikov in the room with her. "If I was really scared of something, I would imagine he was in the room watching me, and everything would be fine." Tumbling, I had learned to visualize tricks in my head while executing a series of gestures: rotating my wrists, cracking my fingers, pointing each toe. In an interview with Marc Moreigne for the book *Avant-garde cirque*, one of the flyers for Les Arts Sauts claimed to use chalk for a similar purpose, to create "a space of calm before the moment of action." With this in mind, I dug out a handful of chalk from the bag attached to the pole and slathered it on my palms and my wrists. I didn't feel any stillness or clarity, only a small moment of feeling manly.

"Think you've got enough there?"

I looked up. Claudette was gazing at my arms bemusedly. They appeared to have been dipped in flour. I had also managed to get chalk on the backs of my knees and kneecaps. The manly feeling lessened before dissipating completely as Claudette drew the trapeze bar toward me with a long hooked spear (a "noodle") and told me to take it with my left hand. I hesitated. Claudette repeated herself slowly: "Take . . . the . . . bar. . . ." I followed her instructions.

Watching Les Arts Sauts, I'd assumed the bar was made of wood, but in fact it was quite heavy, metal wrapped in grip tape and now, thanks to me, covered in chalk. I felt the weight of the bar pulling me out into the void, and at the same time noticed that Claudette had at some point taken hold of my harness and was tugging me backward by the diaper.

"Take the bar with your second hand."

This seemed like an impossible command. I was sure I would tumble forward.

"Take . . . the . . . bar. . . ."

I took the bar. Magically, my position held, thanks to Claudette, who was now leaning backward.

For a moment, Tiger futzed with his gloves. We waited, a tableau of anticipation. It was easily the most emasculating moment of the year thus far: watching my arms wobble while a woman whom I knew to be of significantly greater fitness than myself kept me from plunging to my death by giving me an aggressive wedgie.

"Got it!" Tiger's voice rang out, his vexing glove issue resolved. He reached up and took hold of the ropes.

I felt Claudette increase the pressure on my wedgie. Voices became inchoate. Tiger yelled something. Claudette yelled something. Again Tiger's voice:

"Hep!"

I jumped. As I rushed downward, the wind pushing against my body, gravity pulling me toward the ground, the adrenaline flooded in. Again, I became hyperconscious of certain minute details—the pull of the bar on my armpits, the rough, stringy texture of the grip tape in my palms—and not at all of others. There was no sound, not even my breathing. It was as if I was underwater. Just a vast cloud of silence, occasionally shot through with voices.

"Knees up!" Tiger bellowed from below. I had arrived at the far side of the swing. I tried to heave my knees toward my chest, but gravity prevented it. I felt my stomach muscles clench.

"KNEES UP! KNEES UP!"

I hauled my knees toward my chest. My feet wouldn't fit under the bar. I clawed at it with my toes. *Get through! Get through!*

They broke through. I pulled my thighs against my chest and draped my knees over the trapeze so that I was tucked into a ball, the steel of the bar in the soft crevice of my calves, my hands gripped on the bar, my thighs tight against my chest.

"The bar!" Tiger shouted. "The bar!"

My mind raced. *The bar? What bar?* I felt a half-second behind every move.

By now my swing had brought me back to the perch. I saw it and momentarily considered grabbing it.

"Not that bar!" Tiger screamed. "Your bar! Let go of your bar!"

I did.

Later, when we were settled on the ground after the flight, laughing about the warbling sound I had made upside down, about the way I had uncontrollably waved my arms and clawed nonsensically for the ground, I asked Tiger how he would describe his first flight on the trapeze, what he would compare it to.

Immediately the laughter died down. Tiger shook his head with gravitas. "No, man," he mumbled. "There's nothing like it, nothing like it in the world." And Claude added: "Except maybe an orgasm!"

ALL TOLD, I made seven flights that day. The experience of each was roughly identical to the first. Climbing the ladder, I would get fired up.

On the perch, Claudette would give me feedback about the previous flight. In one instance, she pointed out that I was unconsciously tensing my arms, leaving me less room to push my legs through. "Just let them go loose," she coached, extending a pair of limp arms in front of her. "You don't want any unnecessary tension." Each time, I tried desperately to focus on her words before hurling myself again into the void and immediately forgetting them all. This was normal, I was told.

Afterward, with my hands still raw from the bar and my muscles still charged, the memory of the rush was very strong: the chemicals of peril charging through you, the swish of your body racing through the air, the feeling of gravity seizing at your arms. The activity was more physically challenging than I remembered, more extreme and difficult than the exercises at school. The next morning, I awoke to find every muscle in my torso was sore.

Oddly, though, it hadn't felt like exercise, not in the way tumbling could. I was too much in the moment to notice the effort, too distracted by the rush. It reminded me of a full-body sport like rock-climbing or skiing. There was no heaviness to it, no sense of purposely expending force or power, as in many other acrobatic activities. What I actually felt was a tremendous sense of lightness. I didn't really appreciate this right away; I had to burrow through layers of fear and learn to work with the forces of motion. But once I did, there was a feeling of covering a lot of ground quickly. In an age of increased awareness and creative engagement with the body (yoga, break-dancing, Zumba, and all the rest), it was a near-perfect workout.

Over the next two months, I went back every Friday for more of the same. I would love to say I made huge strides, but this was not the case—once a week wasn't enough for mastery. I did see some small improvements, though. I learned the correct swing, which was surprisingly complex and involved pumping your legs to an odd rhythm and holding a pike position on the backswing—hell on the abdominals. I mastered the knee-hang and tried a few swings without a harness, a breathtaking experience, and even threw a few moves to a catcher.

The first time didn't go well. From a knee-hang, I was supposed to arch backward with my arms extended, such that Claude, also hanging by his knees, could reach out, grab my wrists, and drag me from the fly bar. Unfortunately, on seeing Claude in my peripheral vision, dangling upside down, my head full of blood, my instinct was to lunge for him aggressively, the way you would reach for a branch if you were falling through a tree. That not only ruined the rhythm, but actually made the transfer more difficult, since Claude had no idea where I would be. ("Don't grab him. He'll grab you.")

We tried the move twice. Both times I made the same mistake, and after each received the appropriate dressing down from Tiger. ("Just don't do anything! Just put your freaking arms out!") Finally, on the third attempt, we connected. Claude's printed leopard tights rushed toward me. I extended my arms. I was sure the move wouldn't work, but at the last instant, I felt his wrists smack mine. Then I felt the hard fly bar pull away from my knees. Suddenly I was rushing forward as if on a zip line, my hands locked into Claude's.

The accomplishment of the feat provided two notable lessons. The catch itself was thrilling. I experienced a euphoria unlike anything I had felt in other disciplines—the rush of being airborne, even for a moment. But there was also the pleasure of accomplishment in the slap of Claude's arms against my own. It was a big achievement.

I had a totally different kind of breakthrough on the ground afterward. Since the beginning of the year, I had struggled to make sense of the amateur circus movement. I mentioned this earlier as it relates to juggling, but it applied to every discipline. Circus schools and "youth circuses" targeting kids were rampant. In France, every little town had at least one program. America had almost two hundred, with ten new chapters added every year. Among adults, classes and what are known as "community circuses," like the Stone Soup Circus in Princeton, New Jersey, were also booming. Like community theaters, community circuses served as a way to bring people of different ages and backgrounds together.

Easily the most intriguing and potentially groundbreaking aspect of the movement, however, is what's known as social circus. The concept dates from the seventies. Reg Bolton, an Australian educator and clown, is largely considered the father of the movement. As part of the effort to take circus beyond its usual confines, he taught circus skills to underserved populations around the world, from the Aborigines of the outback to refugees in Palestine, not for performance purposes but in the hope of motivating social change. In 1995, Cirque du Soleil, noticing a strong response to their art from young people, picked up on Bolton's idea and began organizing international programs through a branch called Cirque du Monde. Today Soleil is involved with over eighty communities, from some on the steppes of Mongolia to African villages that have never seen a touring circus. Other programs operate just as broadly, with a variety of aims. Some are pure service organizations, hoping to spread joy. Clowns Without Borders dispatches clowns to troubled parts of the globe—refugee camps, war zones, countries ravaged by famine or disease—to entertain the struggling populations.

Others work more locally, using circus as a tool for outreach. In Australia, the Women's Circus works to teach circus skills to women who have suffered domestic or sexual abuse, empowering them by helping them connect with and be proud of their bodies in a noncompetitive environment. In Hillsborough, New Jersey, Craig Quat, a juggler, created a circus school with classes for children across the autistic spectrum, using adapted circus props to help them learn fine motor skills such as coordination, balance, and flexibility. CircEsteem, a Chicago-based group, focuses on urban youth and refugees.

"Instead of punching people, they are doing back flips," Amy Cohen, the executive director of the American Youth Circus Organization, told me. "You're teaching them life lessons, about work and teamwork, but you're also teaching them a profession they can use to support themselves." The veneer of danger in the circus presented an outlet for what she called the "risk-seeking curiosities" that most young people have. "The curiosities can be sexual," Cohen said. "They can be physical. The circus translates that into a context: Doing a back flip. Throwing a knife. It's a risk, not to mention a challenge, but practical in the sense that it's for an end: performing in front of a public."

Why do these organizations work? One reason is the circus's inherent inclusivity and diversity. Historically, the circus was the place that welcomed everyone, from the tallest to the smallest, from the most skilled acrobat to the least educated roustabout. As a discipline, it offers diverse opportunities for participation, what practitioners call "access points." Ed LeClair is the executive director of Circus Smirkus, a youth circus based in Vermont, which trains, and tours with, over thirty kids every summer. "Not everyone has to be the high-school quarterback," he told me. "But if you want to be in the circus, there's room for you. You can juggle, you can work the trapeze, you can be a clown." As a mix of art and sport, the circus is attractive to both males and females. As students grow, their roles in the circus can change. "Maybe you get tired of juggling scarves and want to learn how to do a back flip," Cohen suggested. "In a circus program that kind of extreme diversity is possible."

The result, according to Cohen, was an "amazing space where all different activities and all different people can coexist." In a traditionally structured show, every person is responsible for her particular act, and yet everyone also contributes to the whole. And because the roles are so different, participants judge each other less. As LeClair noted, "In the circus world, it's not your last name or your skin color or your religion that matters. You're accepted for what you bring to the show."

Another important explanation for these organizations' success was the feelings circus engendered, and particularly the form's ability to bond participants. As with Les Arts Sauts, this quality emerged as a regular theme in my conversations about social circus. The circus, I was told, creates a natural camaraderie, a physical, even existential connection. Aloysia Gavre, the director of Cirque School in Los Angeles, described the phenomenon as "quick bonding," an accelerated version of the team-building exercises that companies foist on their employees. "In almost every circus act," she told me, "you are being asked to trust people quickly, whether you're being thrown, pitched, or caught, whether somebody is holding your line or not offstage." Our brains respond by forging a kind of biological bond born of extreme circumstances, a "very deep and profound" connection to other people. "It really is a fight-or-flight sort of thing," Gavre speculated. "You know these people are going to have your back."

This connection had largely been missing from my own experience in acrobatics class, mostly because I trained around others but not with them. And so my full realization of this power came only after my first catch on the trapeze. On the ground, I felt an outsized affection for both Claude and Tiger. I had probably spent a total of ten hours with them, but they felt like old friends. I found myself slapping Claude on the back and gripping his shoulder. I had the sense that they were people I could trust.

"It's really this amazing thing," Jonathon Conant once told me. Conant runs the Trapeze School New York, which has branches in Chicago; Washington, D.C.; and Los Angeles. Like Claude, he was a trapeze addict who had discovered the dragon during a trip to Club Med. "Something went off in me," he said. "Watching how other people reacted, feeling my own reaction, it was clear there was something amazing going on."

After returning to upstate New York, where he was a counselor working with abused spouses and children, he shopped around for a place to train. When he couldn't find one, he decided to start a school of his own. By the end of the first month, he was turning a profit. By the second, he noticed that people were driving as many as four hours to attend classes. Later, he expanded to the other cities, becoming, after Club Med, the single biggest force in the propagation of trapeze in America, with a mailing list that includes over sixty-five thousand people around the country.

He described the trapeze as a "machine for helping people re-evaluate what they are capable of." "Before a flight, people are invariably uncomfortable. They're pissed off, they're scared, they're sad. There's a real fear of getting hurt." Behind these feelings are the preconceived, romanticized notions, often dating from childhood, that they have about trapeze: "It's magical. It's unattainable. It's hugely difficult. It's completely out of the realm of possibility for most people's minds. They're standing on the edge of the platform going 'yes or no.' "

But the minute they jump off, everything changes. "I experienced it," Conant said; "everybody experiences it. There's an evolution, an acceptance of what's possible. The trapeze is so built up in people's heads. And then somebody says, '*You* can actually do this, too.' That totally shifts the realm of what's possible."

The experience, he said, mirrored the breakthroughs he used to see in his counseling and organizing work. Adding other people to the mix widens and enhances the experience. Flyers come to realize the importance of other people to their success. A mutual trust develops. The bonding aspects of the trapeze are so strong, Conant said, that urban planners had started contacting him about incorporating the trapeze into attempts to rejuvenate impoverished neighborhoods. Shortly before we spoke, he had received a call from a developer in Puerto Rico, looking to enliven a dead zone in Old San Juan. "It brings families in. It builds community. It has a magical, mystical vibe."

I asked Conant when he realized that this power existed.

"From the beginning," he said. The first school, he explained, was founded in New York City in 2000. On September 11, 2001, Conant was in a meeting in the South Street Seaport and personally saw the planes fly into the buildings and workers jumping to their deaths afterward. When the one-year anniversary of the attack arrived, dozens of people showed up at the trapeze school in TriBeCa, uncalled, unorganized, all wanting to lay flowers and candles at the base of the rigging.

"People like to say the trapeze is a metaphor for overcoming your fears. But this is wrong. A metaphor is just a symbol. The trapeze actually works."

14

Opera for the Eye

EXTERIOR OF THE CIRCUS OF THE CHAMPS ELYSEES.

OUT WALKING one early spring afternoon, I found myself admiring a circus poster tacked to a pillar on the Champs-Élysées. It was Sunday, and the crowd was thick. After a moment I felt a presence at my side. I looked to discover a girl gazing up at the poster. She must have been seven or eight, with big hazel eyes and a wide forehead curtained behind blond curls. I looked around for her parents and spotted them on a bench, indulging in ice cream.

I'd had almost no contact with children since the beginning of the year. There were none at the school, and few at the shows I attended. But on the Champs-Élysées, inspired by the girl's obvious adoration for the poster, I asked her if she'd ever seen a circus. She responded with a detailed description of one she had attended recently, followed by several past experiences, eventually tracing her passion all the way back to her original encounter with a tenting in the Bois de Vincennes. She talked about the circus the way old authors wrote about it: a grand spectacle, a "happy dream" of fantasy made flesh. She had strong feelings about the acts, about those she preferred (the "big parade of lions") and those she didn't (the "gentleman who threw the balls in the air"). The details of the experiences seemed seared into her memory, down to the cap the clown wore and the words the tamer shouted to the tiger.

After a few minutes, her parents summoned her back to the bench. Before departing, though, she turned the question back to me. *"Et toi?"* She squinted up into the midday sun. "Have you been to the circus?"

Smiling, I told her that I had, many times. In fact, I said, I was going to visit a circus right then.

It was actually the ghost of one.

Before coming to France, I had assumed that all circuses traveled in tents. As should be evident by now, I was wrong. In reality, for the first seventy-five years, circuses took place in buildings, what were known as hard circuses, or *cirques en dur*. I've mentioned several of these buildings already: Astley's circus near Westminster Bridge; Franconi's Cirque Olympique on the boulevard. What's astonishing is their ubiquity. France alone had thirty-three hard circuses at one point. Between 1769, the year Astley built his riding school in Westminster, and 1900, the opening of the Hippodrome, London saw twenty-five circuses come and go. During roughly the same period, New York had twenty—on Canal, Broadway, 42nd, Greenwich.

To be sure, many of these buildings were shoddy affairs, with tin roofs and wooden walls. But others were quite magnificent, stone structures as luxurious and durable as a city's finest opera houses, with hand-carved friezes and sculptures ornamenting their exteriors. This was especially the case in the capitals, and each great European city had its version—the Cirque Royal in Brussels; the Tivoli in Copenhagen; in Budapest, the Orpheus. The biggest cities had several, and they dueled for audiences. Circuses were simply part of the urban landscape, as accepted as banks, post offices, and schoolhouses.

The more I read about hard circuses, the more they captivated me.

It was fascinating that the circus, so derided in my youth, had once been considered a part of every urban experience. I was also intrigued by the hard-circus period in the art's history. For a brief but beautiful time, from the middle of the nineteenth century to the turn of the twentieth, the circus witnessed a period of artistic perfection and critical appreciation unlike anything before or since. In tuxedos and gowns, aristocrats bantered, cheered, and scoffed as clowns capered and equestriennes in tutus struck refined poses on horseback.

Today this age of highbrow circus is almost completely forgotten, but I wanted to explore it more fully. Luckily, it was easy to trace it back to its roots. Though highbrow circus had spread around the world from Moscow to Buenos Aires, the form originated and, according to many, reached its apex in Paris, as indicated by the movement's name: *l'élégance française*, the period of French elegance. I knew the style had peaked in the second half of the nineteenth century, but I wondered if there was a single circus that stood above the rest, an epitome of the time. During one of our café appointments, I put the question to Pascal.

"The Champs-Élysées," he said. "Without question, the Cirque des Champs-Élysées."

ON A BITTERLY COLD AFTERNOON in 1840, almost two decades before his discovery of Léotard in Toulouse, Louis Dejean summoned architect Jacques Hittorff to his office for a meeting. Dejean wanted to build a circus. At the time the mogul already had one venue up and running, the Cirque Olympique, purchased from the financially inept Franconis in 1836, but a new opportunity had presented itself. To the west of the city, a long-neglected tangle of bushes and weeds had been under renovation. Informally known as the Elysian Fields, or the Champs-Élysées, the untamed glade was becoming a bastion of aristocratic leisure, a highbrow equivalent to the boulevard across town, complete with planked footpaths, gurgling fountains, and bustling, gaslit cafés.

Now Dejean wanted to add a circus to the Champs-Élysées, and not just any circus. Hittorff was a royal favorite, responsible for the Place de la Concorde and the resurrection of the Gare du Nord. At their meeting, Dejean indicated that he wanted a circus on the order of the architect's previous constructions, a circus to attract the denizens of the *quartier* and rival any theater in town.

Inspired, Hittorff set to work. He drew up plans and dispatched a crew to undertake construction. Within a year, Dejean found himself gazing up at his dream.

And it was magnificent. Round like the ring inside, the building looked less like a circus than like a Greek temple. Corinthian columns framed the gilded doorway, each surmounted by an equestrian statue crafted by James Pradier, a noted sculptor.* Higher up, more equestrians charged along a stone frieze that wrapped the building like a ribbon. At the top was a glass cupola that glowed like a lantern when the circus was in session. As an audience member would later comment, "Viewed across the darkened greenery with its interior ablaze, the building's effect was marvelous."

On May 6, 1843, Dejean opened his regal circus to the public. Within a matter of weeks, Paris's patrician class had flooded the building, lured by the stately horses and secluded location. Within a season, the circus became their regular meeting ground, a place to gather to converse and conduct business, as regular a part of the social calendar as the ballet or the opera. It was, in the words of *L'Artiste*, a publication of the period, *"le rendez-vous de toutes les élégances."*

Reading about this elegant circus, I found myself longing to have been around during its height, to experience a circus in such an elegant venue. I settled for the next best thing. I went to Pascal.

"Well, your evening would begin at home obviously," he said. We were in a cab on a rainy night. Stars of light sparked on the window. I had asked him to talk me through an evening at the Cirque des Champs-Élysées. "It was a *soirée mondaine*," he said, "a night of high society. Women wore gowns. Since you're a man, you would put on your tuxedo, then leave with your wife."

In the street, he continued, carriages line the block. If you are rich, you might have your own horse. More likely, the recent rise in stable prices (a product of the migrant flood into the city) has forced you to sell, and so you hire one of the drivers. It's a warm and cloudless night, as you make your way to the circus. On quiet afternoons, you sometimes come

* According to one report, Pradier carved the statues in exchange for lifetime admission to the circus.

across the building while strolling along the Champs. In such moments, it lingers apart from the action of the main thoroughfare, dim and quiet. But tonight the circus is bustling! Light from the cupola washes the glade in a buttery yellow. Carriages line up against the curb in front of the doorway.

You assume your place in line. As you wait, you listen to the locusts buzzing in the fields, to the clop of hooves on cobblestones. After a few minutes, the valet arrives. He's tall and dressed in livery and a powdered wig. Taking your ticket, he helps you from the carriage and guides you under the chandelier hanging above the doorway. Inside, the men sport brushed horsehair top hats, the women pink or blue taffeta dresses. You attend the circus to see and be seen, and tonight all the regulars are there, connoisseurs such as yourself—barons, judges, officers. Drifting through the crowd, you might recall that Henry James attended as a child. So did the Shah of Persia, more recently, before his visit to the Louvre.

You find your seat. As one critic wrote, the interior of the building looks "less a circus than a boudoir," and you would agree. The seats are velvet, the railings brass. An enormous, four-thousand-candle chandelier hangs like a piece of dazzling fruit above the ring.

Now the sound of a violin rises from the orchestra pit. The tremelo fills the hall.

But the lights don't dim. Unlike in the theater, Pascal explains, the lights never go off at the circus. "That's why we call it the space of truth," he says.

The reign of the Champs-Élysées lasted for more than three decades, through a variety of regimes and name changes (Cirque d'Été, Cirque des Champs-Élysées, Cirque Impératrice). As astonishing as it seems in retrospect, in reality, it was very much in keeping with its time. The Industrial Revolution had given the working class more income and a new status. A new class emerged: the haute bourgeoisie. Eager to assume the cultural place of the retreating aristocrats, the *nouveaux riches* naturally gravitated to a spectacle that was refined but also spectacular enough for them to comprehend.

Dejean understood this and deliberately aspired to create a circus for this clientele. There was the luxurious building, of course, an advertisement unto itself. More instrumental was his choice of acts, which were among the finest in Europe. He hired Richard Risley, the foot juggler, and George and Sam Lockhart, Europe's most celebrated elephant trainers. During the 1840s, he featured the Hanlon Brothers, creators of macabre acrobat pantomimes. (In his treatise *Le naturalisme au théâtre,* Émile Zola noted that the brothers "laid bare, with a gesture, a wink, the entire human beast.")

Dejean's most critical decision had to do with the circus's central element: horses. In the seventy years since Astley's first canter around his London ring, equestrian exhibitions, and trick riding in particular, had remained the sturdy backbone of the circus program. Directors fought to hire the most spectacular riding acts. In the 1820s, *acrobats à cheval* emerged. Unlike *voltige* performers, who mostly remained fixed to the horse, these acrobats used the horse's back as a sort of moving floor. Performers struggled to top one another. Didier Gautier became the first man to throw a somersault on the back of a horse.

At the Champs-Élysées, Dejean also featured trick riding acts; Paul Cuzent, one of his stars, taught himself to ride four horses without a saddle, an act known as the "Roman games." But he also leaned on a more refined form of horse training known as *haute école.* Like trick riding, *haute école,* or classical dressage, dates from martial practices of the Middle Ages, when military trainers taught their "war moves" for the battlefield, such as how to turn (*volte*), kick (*capriole*), and rise up on their hind legs (*levade*). During the Renaissance, the moves were codified, first as training exercises to build a horse's strength, later as displays for military ceremonies and jousting tournaments. In the seventeenth century, the displays made their way into the palaces of Europe. Companies including the famous (and misleadingly named) "Spanish Riding School" of Vienna developed routines to showcase an equestrian's mastery of his horse and his grace of movement. Performers were judged not on their spectacularity but on their refinement, on the appearance of "total unity" with their mount. Often riders would perform at the same time, in a practice sometimes known as "horse ballet." "They turn and turn again," wrote *L'Éstoile* of a Spanish horse exhibit in 1581, "to the sound and cadence of trumpets, oboes, and bugles."

After the French Revolution, *haute école* had fallen from favor, but there remained a fondness among the aristocrats, passed down from their ancestors who had fled the châteaux for the city. Recognizing this latent love, Dejean resurrected the practice and built his shows around it. He hired François Baucher, France's most famous trainer and a "Galileo of the hippic sciences," to be his equestrian director. He recruited Antonio Franconi's son, who a writer of the period called one of "the most complete circus equestrians of all time."

Dejean's female riders, the *équestriennes,* were especially renowned. They cames in two forms. The *équestriennes du panier* were ballerinas on horseback. In tutus and bodices, they worked atop a large pad strapped to the horse (the eponymous *panier,* or basket), striking poses and daintily hopping over colorful ribbons held taut by clowns. The second type of female rider—queens to the *panier* princesses—worked in pure classical dressage. Known as Dejean's "divas of the whip" (*divas de la cravache*), they worked from the saddle or in "liberty," directing the horses from the ground. The women were revered for their inventiveness and strength. Caroline Loyo, a student of Baucher's, trained her own horses, a rarity at the time. She was relentlessly exacting. As she once told Dejean, "I will wear out any horse that defies me."

By emphasizing *haute école*, Dejean gave the upper classes a circus that fit their world. As French circus scholar Roland Auguet has noted, the practice was a "visual projection" of the values of refined French culture—a love of forms, of grace through work, of ease in unnatural movement. In return, aristocrats celebrated Dejean's performers as serious artists. The Count of Daru courted Loyo. Empress Elizabeth of Austria proclaimed Émilie Loisset, another Dejean rider, "the most ladylike person" in Paris. "For me," Balzac wrote, "the *équestrienne* in the fullness of her powers is superior to all the glories of song, of dance, and of dramatic art."

THE CIRQUE DES CHAMPS-ÉLYSÉES was torn down in 1902, eventually replaced by a quiet glade of flowers and winding paths, which I found after a bit of searching. Tucked behind high, thick bushes, the spot retained vestiges of romance. Sprinkled across the grass were an old theater and a mansion with a high veranda and vines spilling down the sides. A narrow street curved around the knoll, blocked that day for a small market. A dozen or so merchants had laid out their wares on collapsible tables under white awnings. It was a pleasant legacy, on the whole.

I poked around. After taking some pictures of the daffodils in bloom, I investigated the market, where I found a few pictures of hard circuses from Amiens and Elbeuf, though none of the circus on the Champs-Élysées. One of the vendors, a cheery old Normand in a faded blue cardigan, reminded me of a curious fact. At the destruction of the circus, the city bureaucrats, showing a surprising (and unprecedented) sympathy for circus-lovers, had renamed the street in honor of the lost building. And sure enough, bolted to a corner was a sign: "Rue du Cirque." I had retreated to the sidewalk and was snapping pictures when I heard a chirpy voice behind me:

"Looks like we have a circus fan!"

I turned. Two elderly women stood eyeing me. They looked like a pair of cartoon birds, a stork and a barn owl. In addition to a pair of oversized Gucci sunglasses, the stork wore a conspicuously white pantsuit, the sort of outfit I had only ever seen in catalogues and movies featuring polo matches. The owl, who came up to the stork's shoulder, was dressed in equal luxury, with a blue pastel jacket over a pink blouse spun of what appeared to be cotton candy.

Addressing the owl, I confirmed her suspicions: yes, I was indeed a circus fan, come to pay homage. To my surprise, this quickly led to a conversation about the site and the great circus. Both women had lived in the neighborhood their whole lives and had grown up hearing stories about the magical old building. Neither could remember any specifics, but the stork recalled her grandmother saying she had attended a show there.

"I mean, it really is a beautiful building," the owl added wistfully. "One rather hopes they'll make it a circus again one day."

I felt myself straighten in curiosity. I asked her what she meant. "Well, the building," she said flatly, as if I was being silly. "The circus." She raised a bony finger and indicated the theater in the lawn.

This was one of the more startling moments in my year. Every source I read indicated that the circus had been destroyed. But the women made me wonder. And so did the theater building, once I examined it more closely. Like the famous circus, the theater was round. What's more, though I didn't know enough about architecture to identify the specifics, the building seemed vaguely of France's neoclassical era. Was it possible this was the circus building?

Eagerly, I pressed the women for details. What else did they know about the building?

The stork answered first. "Well, I believe it was constructed by Napoleon. He built it for *sa favorite.*" She turned to face the owl, the sunlight glinting off her glasses. "Isn't that right?" Now I knew it could not have been *my* circus, but I listened just the same.

The smaller woman nodded. "Mmm-hmm. Josephine it must have been." Now they were both nodding.

"That's right, Josephine," the stork repeated. "She lived in that building over there." She pointed to the nearby mansion. "Josephine wanted a circus next door, so Napoleon built her a circus. She must have walked over at night." Then she added, in a softer voice, "Can you imagine?"

Trying not to sound presumptuous, I asked the stork where she had heard all this. From her grandmother?

She shrugged. *"Oui, j'imagine."* Her tone said the question wasn't important. "Mostly, they're stories you hear growing up in the neighborhood, *des histoires de quartier.* People talk about the buildings, you know. I've always known the stories. They're part of the collective memory."

Later that week, I stopped by the circus library to verify truth about the circus's destruction. Sure enough, in 1880s, after the Parisian elite had flitted on to new pleasures, Dejean was forced to sell. The circus became a skating rink, with ice spread over the ring. In 1899, Charles Franconi, great-grandson to Antonio, abandoned the building completely, claiming irreparable damage to the walls. The new owners dispatched a wrecking crew to destroy it, but the company went bankrupt, and for several years the building rotted ignominiously in a state of half-destruction. Finally, in 1902, the city took pity on the ruins and razed them. According to one report, the stables beneath the building survive; street cleaners use them to store their brushes.

Meanwhile, hard circuses across Europe were suffering similar fates. A few were converted to theaters or boxing halls. Most were torn down. In America, every last circus was destroyed. Out of the hundreds of circuses that once dotted the Continent, fewer than twenty remain. Amsterdam has one. Munich has one. In London, all that remains is a façade, the front of the Palladium, once the entrance to the Corinthian Bazaar.

What was causing this scourge? In a word: America.

WHEN THE *Delaware Gazette* hit newsstands on November 15, 1825, it contained a curious notice: One week hence Wilmington would host a circus under the direction of a fledgling producer, Joshua Purdy Brown. The show itself was nothing new. At the time, circuses were common in the New World. More than thirty years earlier, on April 3, 1793, John Bill Ricketts, the English rider educated by Astley's nemesis Charles Hughes, had opened America's first venue. In the one-ring amphitheater in the center of Philadelphia, he performed for, among others, the young country's first president, George Washington. Other circus proprietors quickly followed. In 1808, Victor Pépin, one of Ricketts's students, brought the circus to New York, setting up shop at the corner of Broadway and Magazine. Before long, families were flooding over from France, Spain, and Italy, lured by the dearth of competition. By the 1820s, America had more than twenty shows and was in the middle of what could rightly be considered its first circus boom.

What made Brown unique was his venue. Like the European circus producers, early American entrepreneurs staged their circuses in one of two ways: in buildings or in open-air arenas, often appropriated horse pens or village greens. Brown invented a new, in-between model. He assembled what his advertisements called a "pavilion," a thirty-six-foot, umbrella-shaped sailcloth tent. (Technically, he wasn't the first to have done this. Astley had experimented with a tent during a visit to Liverpool in 1788, but almost immediately abandoned the idea.) Brown took his show from town to town, but, rather than staying for weeks, as was the custom, he would offer his show for a limited time, as little as a night or two, and then push on. "If the weather should prove favorable," his notice stated, "there will be a performance tomorrow evening; otherwise this evening will be the last."

No innovation would have a greater impact on the shape and nature of the circus than Brown's tent. In the decades to come, his circus would become the model for circuses first in America and then around the world, and in the process change everything from how the art was marketed, to where it played, to the type of acts it featured. Economically, the tent opened up new markets. Previously limited to long runs in cities big enough to support a permanent building, circuses were now able to appear in smaller towns. The tent brought the circus west, which made it aesthetically rougher, ruddier, and more rural. It also made the circus more spectacular. Free of the logistical constraints of a building, circus producers could analyze their earnings from the year before and adjust the size of their show accordingly. By the turn of the century, the circus boomed in a way that would have been incomprehensible to Brown: hundreds of performers and thousands of staff all chugged across the continent with a logistical complexity that even the military admired. As Pascal once put it, "You can literally watch the circus grow with America."

Not that Brown himself was expecting any of this.

"I'm sure that Brown's sole thought was, 'How can I take my show to the settlers out west?'" Fred Dahlinger, Jr., curator of circus history at the John and Mable Ringling Museum of Art in Sarasota, Florida, told me. Dahlinger is widely considered one of America's most knowledgeable circophiles and an expert on the growth of the American circus in the nineteenth century. "Brown came from a region populated by traveling menagerie proprietors," he said. "He realized that the canvas pavilion could enable a circus to tour the hinterlands."

Brown wanted to go to the hinterlands because that's where everyone else was going; his arrival on the scene corresponded not just to the explosion of the American circus but also to the explosion of America as a whole. Every week, many thousands of immigrants poured through America's ports and headed west in the hope of forging a life in the wilderness. Unprotected by justice, unencumbered by the rules of the past, these American dreamers forged a new society: free, landed, self-sustaining—and looking for a good time. "They were desperate for entertainment!" Dahlinger said. "Their lives consisted almost exclusively of work and church. They celebrated any excuse for respite."

The circus trouped out to find them. After his tour through Delaware, Brown pushed south to Virginia in 1826, then into the Mississippi valley, where he played Natchez and New Orleans. That same year, Nathan Howes, a New York farm boy turned showman, lit out with Aron Turner, a Connecticut shoemaker, playing in New England under a tent stitched of Russian duck, a white linen canvas.

Most of these early shows were small, almost ramshackle affairs. Creaking into town with a canvas tent rolled into a pair of covered wagons, the team of performers and crew, usually fewer than a dozen men, would divvy up the work and set up camp. One group would knock on doors to scrounge up an extra horse for the show, while another dispatched themselves to the forest to cut down a tent pole. The tents were small and often umbrella-shaped, with room around the outside for people to stand or set up chairs. Since lighting was expensive and a fire hazard, performances were often scheduled for the afternoon. Horses were the main attraction; "grand and brilliant" stunts of trick riding were interspersed with other easily transportable acts: leapers, clowns, a perch-pole act, a trained mule.

The shows were simple but popular; within a decade after Brown's first tented circus premiered, other entrepreneurs had pushed across much of the country. As the art spread across the plains, it evolved. Like Dejean, who had adapted the circus for his high-class clientele, the circus entrepreneurs of America recast their shows to fit the demands of frontiersmen and farmers, rough-and-tumble men with rough-and-tumble tastes. Equestrians performed cowboy stunts in spurs and britches. Clowns in beat-up knickers swilled moonshine from barrels and told dirty jokes.

With time, the circus troupes became rough-and-tumble themselves. "The manager of a circus is hard because the business makes him," Glenn H. Wakefield, a well-known circus con man, once noted. In the lawless and fierce environment, circuses sabotaged one another by slashing tents and stealing horses. They shortchanged ticket-buyers and openly supported what was known as "grift," sanctioned criminal activity, from pickpocketing to con games. If locals found out and came looking for a fight, the circus crew would shout "Hey, rube!" and dive into a "clem," a raucous brawl involving dozens of men wielding sledgehammers and chains.

Towns rebelled. Spurred on by the puritanical fervor sweeping the country, towns passed anti-circus legislation similar to the vagabond decrees of the fifteenth and sixteenth centuries. Connecticut banned circuses outright. Sunsbury, Pennsylvania, prosecuted six acrobats for witchcraft in 1829, for "having private conferences with the spirit of darkness," as well as exposing their populace to such "performances of magic" as "leaping over a horse through hoops."

Some stars fought religious prejudice by cultivating acts specifically engineered for a Christian crowd. Van Amburgh, one of the great early lion-tamers, trained his lion to lie down with a lamb, and later a child. Others were less accommodating. Regardless, the circus continued to boom. By 1852, over thirty circuses were trudging across America. In cities, circuses had ballooned into immense and spectacular pageants, usually accompanied by menageries of imported exotic animals—lions and pythons and camels. By 1868, the centennial of Astley's first circus in the Thames, the circus was easily the most popular entertainment in the American West, and maybe in all of the country. Circus performers were household stars. Dan Rice, sometimes referred to as "President Lincoln's Court Jester," became so famous that he ran for president in 1868. Circus producers such as Seth Howes, who retired in 1870 with a fortune of more than $70 million (almost $1 billion in today's money), ranked among America's richest men. All because of the tent.

Why hadn't other forms of performance also adopted tenting—the theater, or even the ballet or the opera? Dahlinger speculated that the difference between the circus and other forms was partly practical. Because the circus appeal was primarily visual, it could play through conditions that would have quashed other shows—winds whipping the canvas, a driving rain clattering the roof. The circus also appealed to a wide variety of cultures speaking a wide variety of languages, essential in an America made up of immigrants.

The most critical aspect, however, was what you might call the circus's "constitution." Life on the road brought a host of challenges: bandits and belligerent natives, prairie fires and disease. As circus manager and then owner W. C. Coup wrote in *Sawdust & Spangles*, "No other human being can realize like the showman the volume of dread hardship and disaster held by those two small words, 'bad roads.'" The other arts weren't equipped to handle these challenges. "Think of an actor on a stage," Dahlinger suggested. "He goes to the theater every night, then goes home. That's a nice clean life." The circus wasn't so proper. It took place not on a stage but with horses in a circle of dirt. The cacophonous fairgrounds were woven into its DNA. Pioneering, spectacular, adventuresome, resourceful—the *saltimbanques* of the Middle Ages were quintessentially American before America ever existed. How interesting, then, that it would take another quintessential American to push the form to a whole new level.

IN 1860, at the height of his European fame, Jules Léotard passed a poster on the way home from his performance at London's Alhambra Theatre. As he recounts in his memoirs, the poster had bright-red letters on a blue background. It read:

> Barnum has the honor of alerting his English brothers that in a public lecture next Monday he will teach them the honest and natural way to make 30,000 pounds by profiting from the idiocy of his contemporaries.

Like practically everyone in the Western world, Léotard knew the legend of P. T. Barnum. Merchant, journalist, banker, showman, the garrulous New Englander had elevated himself, through abiding industry and a genius for self-promotion, into a captain of American entertainment, the father of what writers had taken to calling "popular culture." Curious, Léotard decided to investigate, and on the day of Barnum's lecture, made his way to Cheapside Road, where he pressed into the theater with a garrulous crowd.

When Barnum appeared, he looked every bit the legend. Almost fifty, with curly black hair slicked back and energetic hazel eyes, he was corpulent, with what the actor Otis Skinner would later call "an air of having lunched heartily." Arranging himself behind the podium, he eyed the multitude for a long moment, as a sly smile pressed into the corners of his lips.

"Ladies and gentlemen," he began in his New England twang, "your total number here today is three thousand. Each of you has paid a shilling. Imagine, then, this session reproduced ten times. Do the math." He paused and studied the crowd, imperious yet benevolent. Another satisfied grin spread across his face. "I have nothing else to teach you."

In the history of the circus there are countless stars: Astley, Hughes, Franconi, Saqui. But P. T. Barnum is the name most Americans offer when asked about the circus. As Hugues Le Roux notes in his 1890 study *Acrobats and Mountebanks,* "To write a book about the traveling class and omit to celebrate Barnum would be equivalent to erasing the venerated name of the Prophet from a commentary on the Koran."

Before Barnum, the circus of the American West remained an Astleyesque affair, with horses galloping around a single ring. Barnum, in combination with a fine team, refashioned the form through marketing, promotion, and logistical genius, creating the circus as it exists in our collective imagination: colossal, crassly commercial, bamboozling, inspiring, populous, simplistic, joyful—a three-ring show of spectacular overabundance that dominated the American entertainment landscape.

Surprisingly, these changes came late in his career, in 1871, when he was sixty-five years old. Their roots, however, lay in his experience decades before.

Phineas Taylor Barnum was born in Bethel, Connecticut, in 1810, the son of "a tailor, a farmer, and sometimes a tavern-keeper." His youth was marked by the now familiar hallmarks of circus greatness: energy, ambition, thirst for adventure. His father passed away when Barnum was just fifteen, leaving the son to support his mother and four younger brothers and sisters, which he did first by founding a fruit-and-confectionery shop and then, at the age of twenty, a newspaper, the *Herald of Freedom*.

Quickly, however, Barnum found himself tiring of what he would later denounce as "the ordinary trade." Just across the state line, a town called Somers, New York, had become an epicenter of early circus action. The town was home to the Zoological Institute, a trust of thirteen menageries and three circuses, and the old showmen liked to visit Barnum's shop and regale him with stories. Captivated, Barnum decided to join them on the road. Bidding farewell to his mother, he hitched on as secretary and treasurer to Aron Turner, one of America's earliest circus entrepreneurs, heading south as part of the country's first circus boom.

The experience proved a disaster. Turner was a roughneck, morally dubious, and unremittingly cheap. Within a year the show had folded. Barnum persevered, marshaling a four-horse company of his own, "Barnum's Grand Scientific and Musical Theatre." This, too, proved a mess. "We were not successful," Barnum later wrote. "One of our small company was incompetent; another was intemperate—both were dismissed; and our negro-singer was drowned in the river at Frankfort."

Disgusted with the traveling showman's life, Barnum retreated. "When I consider the kinds of company into which for a number of years I was thrown, . . . I am astonished as well as grateful that I was not utterly ruined." In 1841, with a wife and an infant daughter to support, he migrated to New York City to seek his fortune. His arrival corresponded with a period of explosive growth. With the machine age came a boom in business, fueled by the emigrants arriving from Europe by the boatload every day. "What a vast emporium of wholesale commerce, of retail business, of universal bustle!" wrote theater manager Alfred Bunn upon first visiting New York in 1853.

Unsure how best to profit from the action, Barnum spent several months experimenting with various entertainment endeavors. At the

Vauxhall Gardens, a pleasure garden and theater near Lafayette Street, he staged three months of unsuccessful variety shows. Later, he penned a series of articles titled "The Adventures of an Adventurer: Being Some Passages in the Life of Barnaby Diddledum," which drew from his experiences on the road and were published in the *New York Atlas*.

Finally, he struck upon an endeavor worthy of his energy: Scudder's American Museum, a five-story "commercial" museum at the corner of Broadway and Ann. In young America, before state-supported cultural institutions came into being, such commercial or "proprietary" museums were common. Like most, Scudder's featured a diverse collection, everything from paintings by famous artists to wax depictions of notorious crimes, displayed alongside ethnological and scientific exhibitions, such as two-headed calves and mummified rodents. Weary of caring for the eccentric collection after Scudder's death, the trustees had put it up for sale along with the building. Barnum sniffed an opportunity: every week, tens of thousands of immigrants landed at the southern tip of the island and washed up Broadway; to pull the museum into profit, it would suffice, simply, to capture the horde's attention.

So that's what Barnum did. Through a bit of nimble financing, he acquired control of the building and immediately launched into a wholesale renovation. Dropping "Scudder" from its name, he rebranded the building "The American Museum" and festooned the exterior with brightly colored banners, fluttering flags, and huge oval paintings depicting "nearly every important animal known in zoology."

During the day, he hired the worst brass band he could find to play above his doorway, a racket of trombones, drums, and tubas luring people in. At night, he illuminated the whole façade with Drummond lights, the first case of outdoor limelight being used for advertising. "It was my monomania to make the museum the town wonder and town talk," he wrote in one of the numerous versions of his memoir, *The Life of P. T. Barnum*.

At the same time, he expanded aggressively. He bought neighboring buildings and smashed through walls. He acquired any collection he could, and combined it with his own. He made no distinction between high and low. In 1861, he imported America's first hippo; a giraffe, which he promoted as a "camelopard"; and a beluga whale, which he installed in a tank full of seaweed and saltwater pumped from New York Bay and kept alive via a full-time attendant paid to dab the whale's mouth and spout with a sponge. Other hired hands included a magician, a ventriloquist, and Indians imported from the West for tomahawk demonstrations and canoe races. A resident taxidermist was on hand, receiving deceased pets from the public in the morning and returning them stuffed at night.

In his museum, Barnum was basically duplicating Astley's vision for the codified fairground. Both were meant to be venues where a person could experience in a day all the wonders of the world—animals, spectacle, and adventure. This similarity to the fairgrounds is particularly evident in Barnum's relationship with "freaks" (a.k.a. human oddities, living curiosities). As a concept, "freaks" date back to the ancient period. African Pygmies entertained the royals of Egypt, and Roman emperors delighted themselves with midgets dueling obese women. There were self-made and congenital or natural "freaks." Those self-made altered themselves through body modification—most frequently tattooing or piercing—but also through weight gain or starvation, such as the Fat Boy of Peckham and Giuseppe Sacco-Homann, the famous World Champion Fasting Man, both celebrities on the English fairgrounds. Natural "freaks" were usually born with some kind of deformity or genetic condition—dwarfs, conjoined twins, and people with secondary sexual characteristics of the opposite gender (e.g., bearded women). Often they had a skill to complement their abnormality. Matthias Buchinger was born on June 3, 1674, in Nuremberg without arms or legs, but later learned to play a half-dozen instruments and perform calligraphy displays, which he did for the kings and queens of Europe.

The first "freak" display in the United States occurred in 1771, when Emma Leach, a dwarf, was shown in Boston. Around 1840, full "freak shows" began to emerge, traveling with menageries or in the company of "handlers" who managed the promotion and exhibition of the stars, enhancing their natural deformities with a story or an exotic medical explanation. (As Tom Norman, Barnum's English equivalent and the handler of the Elephant Man, wrote in his autobiography, "It was not the show, it was the tale that you told.")

Barnum was in this tradition, and he excelled at it. According to his biographer, A. H. Saxon, nearly every famous freak of the period spent a few weeks in the showman's employ: R. O. Wickward, the skeleton man; Jane Campbell, "the largest Mountain of Human Flesh ever seen in the form of a woman"; S. K. G. Nellis, the armless wonder, who could shoot a bow and arrow with his toes. Many of the freaks appeared as stars in his museum, either as roving attractions, as part of special exhibitions, or as spectacles in the theater in back. Sometimes Barnum toured with them as well. General Tom Thumb (Charles Stratton) was a twenty-five-inch-tall four-year-old midget, who Barnum claimed was eleven. Barnum coached the boy to perform impersonations of various heads of state, including Queen Victoria, whom he visited on three separate occasions. In Paris, the duo played to Napoleon III and in a series of shows at the Salle Musard that sold out months in advance. "The French are exceedingly impressible," Barnum wrote of the visit in his 1896 autobiography *Struggles and Triumphs*, "and what in London is only excitement in Paris becomes furor."

Given our modern mores and science, most people—circus historians included—lament these displays. At best they were grossly lowbrow, at worst debauched. Russian circus-historian Yuri Dimitriev once called them "a disgrace to human dignity." "They were an insult to the very essence of the circus where the skill and beauty of the human body are celebrated," he alleged, "playing on the basest instincts of the gawking crowd." But it's also important to consider the context. Though much of the interest in "freaks" indeed derived from inconsiderate or malicious instincts, the 1850s were an age before photographs, cultural museums, or widespread literacy. Audiences were curious about the world, and Barnum played to this curiosity in his exhibits. He advertised his museum as an "encyclopedic synopsis of everything worth seeing in this curious world." He presented his artifacts, however strange, as part of the scientific revolution sweeping the globe. For example, he called his ape-man the "missing link" in Darwin's theories of evolution. Barnum succeeded in this presentation because the museum's atmosphere was consistently middlebrow. A lifelong teetotaler, he prohibited profanity, sexuality, and liquor. In letters he referred to himself as the "Director of Moral and Refined Exhibitions for the Amusement and Instruction of the Public." "Barnum's genius was in developing popular potential," Bluford Adams, a Barnum scholar, told me. "He would take an idea, make it safe for the middle classes, and then commercialize it to the hilt."

Between 1842 and 1865, Barnum's American Museum, his Boulevard du Temple in a building, was the single greatest attraction in America.

Approximately thirty-eight million paying visitors passed through Barnum's doors in that time span. This figure is particularly astounding given America's population at the time: thirty-two million just before the Civil War.

The American Museum made P. T. Barnum rich. In combination with his autobiographies, which sold over a million copies, the museum also made him an international celebrity. In America, his name was as well known as the president's. Abroad, he came to symbolize America itself, and everything that was big, rash, and brash about the place. In 1871, Barnum brought this wealth and fame to the circus.

Now sixty-one years old, he had settled into retirement in Bridgeport, Connecticut, following a fire at the museum. He was eager to dedicate his days to "serious reflections on the ends and aims of human existence"—but then he was approached by two men, William Cameron Coup and Dan Castello. Barnum knew them both to be capital showmen: Coup had worked in Barnum's Asiatic Caravan as a teenager; Castello had starred as an acrobat and later run several successful shows himself. The men had an idea for a circus that required Barnum's help.

American proprietors had long been seeking an easier way than wagon travel to bring their acts west. In the beginning, many thought the future lay in waterways. In 1851, Gilbert Spaulding, a former pharmacist from New York, had partnered with English equestrian Charles Rogers to launch a two-hundred-foot "Floating Circus Palace," a white-and-gold bargelike contraption rigged with a thousand-seat amphitheater on the main deck, two hundred gas jets for lighting, three enormous flags, and a steam-calliope whistle that could be heard for miles. But, more recently, hopes had turned to the railroads.

Coup and Castello wanted to exploit this new technology on a grand scale. Even with a strong team of stock horses, they argued, the most you could move a show was fifteen, maybe twenty miles a night. On a train, a circus could travel ten times as far. Practically speaking, this meant a show could bypass small markets in favor of the large ones: Pittsburgh, Cleveland, Chicago, Saint Louis, Kansas City. And with a train there were no more worries about weight limits. Bigger tents, bigger crews, bigger menageries—the possibilities were enormous. For the first time, companies could play a big show to a big town, then push on after a single night—and it made both fiscal and logistical sense.

But to create a truly monumental circus—the biggest the world had ever seen—Coup and Castello would need an equally impressive backer. They would need somebody who knew how to promote ambitiously, somebody with business acumen and a golden touch. Who better than the man responsible for the most eccentric, most eclectic, most popular, and best-known entertainment venue in the world? Though much of his museum had been destroyed in the fire, much also survived, and Barnum could bring to their circus a collection of oddities the likes of which the circus had never seen. It could be an American museum on wheels, the world's first true colossal circus for the masses.

Presented with Coup and Castello's offer, Barnum hesitated, haunted by the itinerant experiences of his youth. Then, on October 8, 1870, he wrote to Coup: "I will join you in a show for next Spring. . . . We can make a stunning museum department."

The April after Barnum sent his letter to Coup, the men opened operations in Brooklyn. In honor of Barnum's contribution (and in exploitation of his name), they called the show "P. T. Barnum's Grand Traveling Museum, Menagerie, Caravan, and Circus." The ten thousand visitors who took the ferry from Manhattan that first week found the action divided into three tents: the big top, the animal tent, and the sideshow tent, a standard organization for years to come. During the subsequent tour of the Eastern Seaboard, hordes gathering outside the ticket booths became so massive and so raucous that Coup, who ran operations, decided to add a third daily show. A month later, they began running what amounted to a continuous spectacle, with attractions open from noon until night. The following season, Coup abandoned all precedent and added a second ring to the main tent. (The circus considered widening the ring, but the equestrians had trained their horses to the smaller size.)

By now the profits were astronomical. The tour grossed over $1 million, the first show in history to do so. This, of course, inspired other circuses to adopt the model, taking to the rails and enlarging their shows. Rivalries quickly ensued. In 1882, Barnum, now associated with the nervous young circus genius James A. Bailey, added a third ring. Adam Forepaugh, an old horse dealer turned circus entrepreneur, followed suit. ("I have a boy and Mr. Barnum has none," Forepaugh once claimed. "My show will outlast his.")

Meanwhile, on a warm afternoon in 1884, a group of brothers were standing on the banks of the Mississippi River in McGregor, Iowa, when the Great Pavilion Circus docked for a day of shows. Al, the eldest, turned to one of his brothers with a twinkle in his eye. "What would you say if we had a show like that?" he said, to which his sibling replied, "You know I was just thinking the same thing." Thus was born the Ringling Brothers Circus. Like Barnum and Forepaugh, the five Ringling brothers—Al, Otto, Alf, Charles, and John—saw success in size. After learning the business from a man named Yankee Robinson, they struck out on their own, purchasing their first elephant in 1888. When Forepaugh retired in 1889, they bought his railroad cars to transport their stable of one hundred horses.

Their growth continued through the turn of the century, eventually reaching heights that are hard to fathom today. The Ringling lot was fourteen acres across, double the size of Chicago's Soldier Field, the biggest football stadium in the world. Their big top, which featured three rings and two stages, sat fourteen thousand people, over three times the number in a full house at the Metropolitan Opera.* The logistical demands alone were amazing. One thousand people occupied a ninety-two-car train. Their parade through New York lasted five hours. And yet the whole operation could be packed up in an afternoon.

Today, American scholars often refer to this time, from Barnum's arrival to the beginning of World War I, as the "golden age" of the circus. "Like the golden age of Hollywood," writes historian John Culhane in the *The American Circus*, these years were "a brief, sunny period when there could never be too many circuses." At the period's high point in 1902, ninety-eight circuses and menageries operated throughout the country, more than ever before or since. The largest—Ringling Brothers, Barnum & Bailey, Forepaugh—were household brands, as Disney is today. The performers were celebrities. When May Wirth, a famous Barnum & Bailey equestrian, fell off her horse, the news made the front page of *The New York Times*.

In 1897, Bailey, the sole director of the Barnum & Bailey Circus after Barnum's death in 1891, brought the American model to Europe, shipping his entire fourteen-thousand-ton operation across the Atlantic on a

* Each stage was roughly the same size as a ring. At any given moment, nine acts would be going on at the same time.

pair of steamships. The show spent five years abroad, inciting mayhem wherever it went—in London, the circus's arrival nearly shut down the city. In its wake, certain European producers moved to adopt what the French call *le gigantisme américain*. In 1901, the clown Hans Stosch, son of a wealthy Prussian family, founded the Sarrasani circus in Dresden, Germany. By 1908, his circus was trouping with three rings, and eventually boasted upward of four hundred animals. At the same time, former fairground families, especially animal trainers, flocked to the circus game. Today many of the biggest names in European circus come from this migration: the Amars and Bougliones in France, the Chipperfields in England, the Kreisers and Busches in Germany, the Kludskys in what would become the Czech Republic.

And yet, for all these inroads, the American model never quite caught on in Europe. The big menageries or sideshows remained largely elements of the fairground, unassociated with the circus. Historical forces played a role in this failure. With the approach of World War I, countries stiffened their borders, and touring a big circus became more difficult. But there were also cultural reasons. The European experience of the circus, dating back almost 150 years, gave both performers and audiences different expectations for the sort of pleasure it could provide. The performers, used to working in hard circuses in cities, found touring in the American fashion distasteful. The logistical demands of setting up, taking down, and traveling left almost no time for rehearsal, and much less time to create new work.

European audiences settled down after their initial fascination with Barnum & Bailey, returning to the form of circus with which they were comfortable. In the hard circuses, there was a closeness that humanized the performers and created an almost physical intimacy. "There is something especially attractive in the coziness of these one-ring circuses of Paris," Frank Berkeley Smith wrote in his 1903 guide to Paris, *How Paris Amuses Itself*. Audiences had a relationship with their performers. They watched their acts grow and appreciated new material. At close range, an audience could appreciate the subtlety and refinement of a strong performance.

In the big American circuses, all this familiarity and precision was gone, sacrificed for other pleasures: spectacle, pageantry, sensory stimulation, what Barnum called in advertisements his "avalanche of attractions." For American audiences, where the circus tradition was less entrenched and rougher, this trade was clearly worth it: why not take three rings for the price of one? Europeans felt the performers were too far away, the peripheral action too distracting. Writing in 1904, French historian Georges Strehly noted that in a Barnum show "the merit of a work, as perfect as it is, disappears, lost in the crowd of numbers presented simultaneously." In the American willingness to play to the lowest common denominator, Europeans felt there was something pejorative and possibly selfish, a sacrifice of the art's artistic sensibility for commercial gain. "[Barnum] piles on crowds on crowds, throws in a dozen of elephants here, a hundred ballet girls there," observed a critic during the circus's first appearance in London. "The audience does not matter, nor the stage, nor the expense."

Today this divide remains. Most Americans feel that both forms are valid. "It's a matter of apples and oranges," Dahlinger told me. What is clear from a historical perspective, however, is that the American-style shows were a devil's bargain. In the short term, the expansion allowed the circus to become the single most profitable entertainment in the world; in exchange, the circus nearly sacrificed its own future.

The shift had an effect on creativity. In a hard circus, performers, who often lived in the neighborhood, came to the circus during the day to rehearse or develop new material. Audiences expected ongoing improvement and innovation, since they attended the circus every month or even every week. But a performer in a traveling circus felt no pressure to improve. Hopping from town to town, he could perform the same routine for years. (As Pascal noted, "They found it easier to change the audience than change the acts.") Over time, as more and more shows took up the grand tenting model, there was less innovation in the art as a whole.

The American model also engendered a different commercial approach. Astley was closer to a businessman than an artist, but money did not *define* the circus. In England and later on the boulevard, circus owners had artistic reputations to maintain. The same applied for the performers. In the gigantic traveling circuses, by contrast, the circus became a business, plain and simple. Success was measured by profit, with performers there to serve the bottom line. But by diminishing the emphasis on individual acts, by promising "the Greatest Show on Earth," circus owners walked themselves onto an existential tightrope. Every year, the circus would have to be bigger, more impressive, more extravagant than the year before—and not just bigger than other circuses, bigger than anything, a dangerous game at the dawn of twentieth century.

"It's as if," Pascal once told me, "the form anticipated its own destruction."

15

Clown Equals Funny

A PARISIAN WINTER FEELS LIKE a wet blanket, spring like a relief. The scarves get put away. The skirts come out. Migratory species return: birds, tourists, clowns.

My first sighting occurred in late March. Crossing the cobblestone plaza in front of the Centre Georges Pompidou, Paris's modern-art museum, I stumbled on a crowd gathered around a man in a black porkpie hat and a soiled black suit, a taller, huskier Chaplin. He was improvising a scene you might find in a silent film, dragging audience members up to play characters (the scandalous wife, her dashing lover, the frumpy cuckold). They ran through the scene a few times: the doting husband arrives to find his wife with a lover, goes ballistic, pulls out a gun and shoots them both. But with every take something went wrong. The first time around, the husband forgot to knock on the imaginary door. The second time, the lover failed to kiss the woman with enough ardor. With each mistake, the clown, who played the film's domineering director, launched into a mock frenzy, spiking his hat to the ground, stomping around, collapsing to his knees, and pleading with his amateur charges to get the scene right, just this once.

I knew next to nothing about clowns. The school offered no regular clown training and even subtly discouraged students from specializing in the discipline. ("There are more effective venues to learn how to be a clown," Anny told me during my first week.) In shows, there were comedic characters, goofy everyman types, but actual clowns—or what I thought of as clowns—were a rarity.

I didn't get clowns, found them silly and trite. But the Pompidou clown seemed a breed apart. The bit was simple, but there was something raw, almost belligerent about him. Also, it was spring, and the sun was out, and I was feeling ebullient. And so, once the crowd had deposited their fistfuls of coins into his pillowcase, I approached him for a chat.

He was kneeling on the cobblestones, stuffing props into a black leather suitcase. The back of his neck was glazed in sweat, the collar of his shirt stained yellow. I began asking him a few questions about his background, but he didn't seem interested in sharing and mostly ignored me. Yet, when I asked him where he trained, he responded, "Training?," as if the word tasted bad in his mouth. "What the hell do I need training for?" He stood and marched over to retrieve from the sidewalk a scuffed plastic pistol, which he chucked into the suitcase along with a pink scarf. "This is how you learn. You fucking do it."

As he said this, a little boy walked shyly up. He had a round face and a mushroom cap of black hair, and his little fist was raised in front of him with a late offering for the clown. The clown didn't even acknowledge him, and instead went about lashing his suitcases onto a dolly with bungee cords. The boy in turn hesitated, uncertain how to proceed. Obviously, he was looking for some small acknowledgment.

After what felt like minutes, the clown caved. Grumbling unintelligibly, he gestured with his head toward the pillowcase lying on the ground. Disappointed, but relieved to be free of the stalemate, the boy lifted the opening, chucked the coin inside, and scurried back to his parents.

The clown meanwhile clipped the last bungee cord in place, double-checked it roughly, and then slumped past me, dragging his dolly like an unwanted pet.

Later, I found that his silent-film bit was actually stolen from another clown, David Shiner, an early star with Cirque du Soleil. He'd created it while working the exact same plaza almost two decades before.

It would be another month before I revisited the subject of clowns.

POOR CLOWNS. If jugglers have it bad ("Hey, juggler!"), clowns have it awful. The word "clown" for most people evokes the images of paunchy men sucking on cigarettes behind big tops, of rubber poultry, and lonely bachelors who live with their mothers.

It's hard to say exactly where this scorn comes from. Some of it is inherent in the job: after all, the clown's function is to be mocked. And even in the circus, among the dog-faced boys and the flying transvestites, clowns are conspicuous. They're the only performers who fail, who disguise themselves in outlandish costumes and makeup, who flaunt their emotions—laughing, crying, shouting, pouting. Still, it seems like our feelings have slipped beyond ridicule into something closer to suspicion. While I was surfing the Internet one evening, a picture of a maniacal knife-wielding clown popped up on my screen under the words "Shoot the clown and win a free laser pointer!" The game was a joke, but its tone struck me as representative.

I'm sad to say that when I came to France my own attitude wasn't much different. My experiences with clowns as a boy had been fleeting and unsatisfying. I remember seeing a few at parades, looking burdened under the hot sun. On television, they cropped up annoyingly in shows and commercials (e.g., Ronald McDonald, Bozo). My only direct encounter came at a pool party when I was six or seven. We were having cake and ice cream when a clown came striding through the backyard gate, throwing his hands in the air like a rock star.

I remember feeling put off by the chafe and stink of his rainbow-striped jumpsuit as he hugged me, by his forced enthusiasm. He was a walking cliché. Having plopped down in a deck chair, he knotted us a malformed balloon animal. Later, he tried and failed to pedal his unicycle through the grass. He struck my young self as more pathetic than joyful. I wondered who would choose to live such a life.

Six months at circus school had done little to change my attitude. To the contrary, my distaste for clowns only deepened as my respect for the circus grew. I came to see them as a sign of the circus's decline. In the past, I learned, clowns were important figures, satirical spokesmen who railed against cruelty and injustice. "Centuries ago, the clown was an obscene, diabolic figure," Nobel Prize–winning playwright Dario Fo writes in *The Tricks of the Trade*. "In the cathedrals of the middle ages, on the capitals and the friezes above the entrances, there can still be seen representations of comic buffoons in provocative couplings with animals, mermaids, harpies, grinning broadly as they show off their organs."

But the character has become, as Fo notes, "a figure whose job is to keep the children happy. He is synonymous with puerile simple-mindedness, with picture-postcard ingenuousness, and with sheer sentimentality." Since a clown is now mostly defined by his costume, circus producers will hire anybody to play one. I once observed this firsthand at a Shriners Circus in Montana. The show, a traditional three-ring extravaganza, took place in the university basketball arena. Outside, a gaggle of clowns leered at the children as they arrived, welcoming them in overly enthusiastic voices. I talked with one of them afterward.

Her name was Freckles. She wore a yellow polka-dot jumpsuit suitable for someone twice her size. The paint on her face, a white base splotched with red dots that resembled sores, had smeared, leaving a streak of pink. I asked where her name came from.

"I'm Freckles because I'm all covered with freckles!" she sang.

I asked how she came to work for the circus.

"Oh no," she said jovially. "I'm just a volunteer!" In real life, Freckles explained, she was a "part-time claims adjuster, part-time mom."

The Shriners is a wonderful organization. Every year they put together circuses to help fund their hospitals. And what better way to add some inexpensive festivity than a few volunteers in face paint? But for clowning, and for the circus as a whole, Freckles was a problem. Every time she cooed at a burgeoning circus fan, the kid's response was fear rather than joy. Freckles, without knowing better, was the circus decline personified, all skill subsumed by clichés.

To understand the circus, though, I knew I would have to try to understand clowns, whom Barnum once called "the pegs used to hang circuses on." So I put out the word among the students at the school that

I wanted to talk to a modern clown, somebody articulate, energetic, and influential—Jérôme Thomas in a rubber nose.

One name kept coming back: André Riot-Sarcey. When I looked him up, I discovered he was the director, developer, and motivator of an important French clown posse called Les Nouveaux Nez. I got his number from Anny and gave him a call. His wife answered and took a message. An hour later, my phone rang.

"So I hear you want to meet a clown" was the first thing he said.

After a quick description of my project and my unfortunate clown-bias, he agreed to meet and set me straight. His company would be performing in Paris that weekend, he said. I should meet him beforehand for a chat.

"But just to be clear," he said as I was about to hang up, "you're a clown, *n'est-ce pas?*"

I hesitated. Clearly, something had been lost in translation. No, I explained, I was not a clown, just an interested party.

"But you know what a clown is?" he asked, after a long pause.

"Actually, that's what I was—"

"A clown is a poet in space," André interrupted. "Do you know who said that?"

"I don't."

"That was your compatriot, Henry Miller. A clown is *une bête de la scène*. He doesn't know the rules, so he makes them up as he goes. Every moment is an adventure, a new life—the present instant! Always the present! Like an animal."

I had found a pen and was scrambling to take notes. "The clown . . . is an animal," I said aloud.

"No, no! He's *like* an animal. Like a dog or a fish."

"Like a dog?"

"And do you know why?"

I checked my notes. "Because of the instant thing?"

"That's right! The clown lives in the present. Also, he has to have *la rage*." As he said this last word, he slipped into a growl. "All the best clowns have *la rage*. Rhum had it. Grock had it. David Shiner has a mountain of it. It's another way of talking about that *côté brut* that every clown has, that part of their spirit that's not entirely human."

I was silent.

"Anyway," André said, calmer now, "if you ever hope to be a clown, you'll have to get in touch with *la rage*."

I stopped writing. "You know, I'm really just curious. I don't plan on becoming a clown myself."

A chortle rose on the other end of the line.

"Right, well, okay," said the clown, chuckling. "We'll see about that."

THIS IS THE STORY of André Riot-Sarcey and Les Nouveaux Nez, France's most famous modern clown quartet. Like most circus icons today, André grew up outside the circus, although an interest in theater led him in 1972 to Paris and the acclaimed École Internationale de Théâtre Jacques Lecoq.

Then and today, the school, informally known simply as Lecoq, was a force in the modern theater scene, and arguably the single most important institution in defining modern clowning. ("Lecoq is where we begin developing the spirit of the modern clown," André states unequivocally.) Founded in 1956, the school was created and run for over thirty years by Jacques Lecoq, a former gymnast and physical-education teacher who had migrated into the theater. In the course of the two-year curriculum, students cycled through a wide variety of theatrical disciplines, or "territories": melodrama, commedia dell'arte, tragedy, *bouffons,* masks, comedy, acrobatics, even animal movements.

They also studied clowning. As a scholar, Lecoq investigated how clowns provoked laughter. But he wasn't interested in circus clowning, at least not as traditionally practiced. As he writes in *The Moving Body*, "As a child I had seen the Fratellinis, Grock, and the trio of Carioli, Portos, and Carletos at the Cirque Medrano in Montmartre, but this was not the sort of clown we were researching at the school." Rather, he wanted to understand clowns as historical figures of ridicule and shame. He investigated as far back as the Middle Ages, and, based on his studies, created a philosophy of the craft. Playing a clown, he noted, was different from most acting: the clown was less a role than a reflection of self, a comic doppelgänger. "One does not act to be a clown," he notes, "one is a clown, when one's deepest nature is revealed, in the first fears of one's youth." In his classes, Lecoq encouraged students to "find their clowns" through "the search for one's own ridiculousness." The goal was vulnerability onstage, the ability to work in a "state of openness without defense." "The less that he defends himself, the less that he attempts to play the role of a character, the more the actor allows himself to be surprised by his own weaknesses, the more forcefully his clown will appear."

André took to Lecoq's ideas with abandon, and in the school's mirror-lined classrooms he fell in love with clowning, so much so that upon graduation he decided to pursue a career in it. André joined one of the original companies of the modern circus, the German Circus Roncalli, a "neoclassical" single-ring show founded by Austrians Bernhard Paul and André Heller.

Riot-Sarcey spent three years with the company, working as principal clown and choreographer. Afterward, there followed a period of theatrical wandering in France, Switzerland, and Belgium. Other clowns were also in the process of "liberating" their discipline from the circus by creating acts for the stage. These were full plays instead of short bits, combining traditional clown techniques (e.g., physical comedy, slapstick, and pantomime) with more "theatrical" elements, such as text, plot, light, and sound.

Today critics call this genre "clown theater." In Europe, its proliferation was spearheaded by students of Lecoq and a few renegade mimes: in the Czech Republic, Ctibor Turba made macabre clown pantomimes; in Switzerland, Dimitri Jakob Müller (a.k.a. Dimitri) studied under Marcel Marceau and appeared with the Circus Knie before creating a theater company of his own.

In America, the movement started as avant-garde theater, progressing to the mainstream in the eighties. In 1984, Lecoq graduate Avner Eisenberg (a.k.a. Avner the Eccentric) premiered his one-man show on Broadway. (Television critic Joel Siegel called it "hurt-yourself, hysterically funny.")

A decade later, Bill Irwin, a founding member of the Pickle Family Circus in San Francisco, teamed up with David Shiner, who had been a street performer before being recruited by Cirque du Soleil, for an even bigger success in *Fool Moon*. Billed as an "evening of inspired lunacy," the two-hour show, which was derived largely from the clowns' previous material, featured the two men tumbling, bouncing, singing, and generally goofing through physical sketches, stunts, and gags, to the folk music of the Red Clay Ramblers. The show, which was a smash hit, ended up returning to Broadway three times, for some five hundred performances, eventually landing a Tony Award for Live Theatrical Presentation. For the clowns involved, it was a windfall: Shiner landed a deal with Paramount Pictures and went on to become a director for Cirque du Soleil; Irwin came away with a $500,000 MacArthur award—the first clown to win one.

In France, meanwhile, the movement floundered. Despite the presence of Lecoq, clowns were slow to emerge. Ironically, the one exception was an American: Howard Buten (a.k.a. Buffo), who had created a silent solo show that made him a local icon (along with a novel, *When I Was Five I Killed Myself,* which sold more than a million copies in France).

Hoping to change this, André went in search of collaborators. At the time, he was teaching acting at the nascent National Circus school in Châlons-en-Champagne (his official title: Professor of Circus Acting and Clownish Arts), and in the inaugural class four students caught his eye: Roseline Guinet, Nicolas Bernard, Roger Bories, and Alain Reynaud. They were all skilled musicians—Reynaud had studied accordion at the National Conservatory of Lyon—but André spotted something else. "It was as if they were already clowns," he told me.

In 1989, the four students graduated. André asked them if they would be interested in creating a company, a clown quartet specializing in shows for the stage. They would be the stars; André would direct and act as artistic guide, drawing on his diverse experience. When the young performers agreed, the group set up camp in Bourg-Saint-Andéol, where Reynaud's family ran a woodworking compound. André led the rehearsals, helping the four refine their clowns. In 1990, they premiered *Cinq Folies en cirque mineur* in Paris under the moniker Nouveaux Nez (meaning both "new noses" and also a wordplay on *nouveau-né,* "newborn"). The show looked a lot like others of the period: employing music, physical business, and banter, Nouveaux Nez wrapped a series of bits around a loose story to create something like a coherent tale. But the execution set the show apart. The product of André's knowledge and the broad training of its clowns, the show combined an almost virtuosic number of elements. A critic from *L'Express* called a later show a "delirium of intelligence, finesse, and Dadaist gymnastics." Each word, slap, and musical note was choreographed, imbuing the show as a whole with an almost musical rhythm.

Success came quickly. In Paris, *Libération* called Nouveaux Nez "the inheritors of France's mythic clown past." Afterward, the clowns found themselves jetting all over the world, as far as West Africa and Thailand. In the meantime, the company collected a mantel of trophies, including the Minister of Culture's Grand Prix and a Prix Raymond Devos, a prestigious French comedy award—making the group the first clowns to win one. Since then, the company has created five more shows and performed over eight hundred times, to some five hundred thousand people. At Lecoq, current students venerated Nouveaux Nez. "They were the original masters," one told me. Another called them "the Beatles of the clown world."

André really was the Jérôme Thomas of clowning. In interviews, he talked about his craft in inspired language. He referred to the clown's "presence before the world." "When we try to enclose clowns," he said, "they flee." In 2003, he helped create in Bourg-Saint-Andéol a "house of the clown and circus arts," a multipurpose center for classes, shows, and seminars on subjects like "the clown and transmission of knowledge." In short, André took clowning very seriously.

ANDRÉ HAD SENT ME the address of the theater where the company would be performing, a little converted venue on the eastern outskirts of the city. I got lost looking for the place, and ended up approaching a tall young man with a backpack and a vaguely circus air. His name was Georges. As luck would have it, he was a student at the National Center for the Circus Arts in Châlons-en-Champagne, and he was headed to the theater himself.

We chatted on the way, first about Georges's experience at the school, then about André and the company. "André's very good," Georges said in a serious tone. "He's a real clown."

I asked him what he meant. He smiled down through black bangs.

"I take it you're not a clown?"

I admitted I wasn't.

Georges nodded. "It's just that I have this little theory." He believed that each circus discipline attracts a certain type of personality. "Acrobats tend to be pretty easygoing, which is about right, since they have to take risks. Or think of contortionists. The ones I know all tend to be pretty hard on themselves, which in a way is good, since your success as a contortionist is totally determined by how hard you're willing to push yourself."

"So what are clowns?"

Georges mulled it over for a second and said, "I'm hesitating, because my instinct is to say that clowns are sensitive. But that's not quite right. Or it doesn't do them justice. 'Passionate' is probably a better word. Real clowns are passionate."

Out of curiosity, I asked Georges what he was studying.

"I'm a juggler," he replied, before adding wryly, "We tend to be heady."

Besides being a theater, Le Samovar, where Nouveaux Nez was performing, was also a clown school, Paris's largest and the only one offering a full three-year degree in the discipline. Inside, I made my way through a crowd gathered in the lobby, a low-ceilinged room lined with clown posters and black-and-white photos of famous graduates. At café tables, fans sipped Heinekens and chatted about the troupe. From behind a makeshift bar, a tall woman pointed me to the theater, and I went in.

"Okay, Rosaline—how'd that feel?" André was sitting in the front row, his fingers knitted over his knees, a derby cocked haphazardly on his brow. He spoke loudly toward the stage. "Rosaline? Do you hear me?"

Upstage, a woman poked out from behind a black curtain. "Yeah, I think it's fine," she said, drifting downstage. Tall and flamingo-thin, she looked like Audrey Hepburn dressed like Gilda Radner, with tortoiseshell glasses perched on a red rubber nose. I recognized her from photos: she was Rosaline Guinet, also known as Madame Françoise, the lone woman of the company, and a female icon in a discipline that favors men.

She came to a stop next to a steamer trunk mounted on wheels. "I mean, it's still a bit cramped. I feel a bit like I'm juggling in their laps, but I'm not sure we have a choice." I gathered that they were rehearsing for the evening show.

André hoisted himself to his feet and joined Rosaline onstage. He was smaller than I'd expected and dressed almost formally—in pleated khakis, brown loafers, and a navy sweater over a white-collar shirt.

"Remember, the audience is closer than normal," he said to Rosaline. "There's less room to play with, so everything needs to be even clearer, even more precise." He paced a small circle on the stage. "Here." He stopped and poked the ground with his toe. "When you do it again, try it here." Rosaline nodded and retreated behind the curtain, pushing the trunk like a mining cart.

Over the next ten minutes, I watched them repeat the twenty seconds of action fifteen different ways. Each time, Rosaline would burst onto the stage, riding a trunk like a steer, waving enthusiastically to the imaginary crowd. *"Salut, les filles!"* She leapt to the ground, hips first, her hands plunging into her dress coat for five balls, which she juggled easily.

After each iteration, André corrected a detail—her stance, her posture, her place on the stage. It was like watching a sculptor install an exhibit or a chef in a kitchen, zipping here for the sauce, bounding there with a dash of salt.

"Yes, yes. No, there. A few inches more. Perfect!"

Nouveaux Nez was known for rehearsing relentlessly. This particular show, I later found out, was more than two years old.

When they wrapped, Rosaline disappeared. André collapsed back into the front row. Peeling off his derby, he gave his hairline a good scratch.

"As they get older they get better," he said to me, dabbing his forehead with a white handkerchief. Without the hat, he looked ten years older. Wrinkles creased his forehead. His hair was matted by sweat. "Not just her," he clarified. "Most clowns. They get sadder, too, but that has to happen naturally, as the soul replaces the body." He looked at me squarely. "You came to talk about clowning. Well, that's the first lesson. A clown is like any artist, any real artist. The work comes from experience, experience of practice but also experience of life. This is especially true for clowns." He nodded in the direction of the stage. "They had amazing training, but in that way, they were almost at a disadvantage. They started younger than most."

In preparation for my meeting with André, I had watched a series of old clown films, including one of Grock, famous for his music-hall routine, and several classic "cinema clowns"—Chaplin, Keaton, Laurel and Hardy. Beyond a vague haplessness, it was hard to say what unified the men. There was no consistency to their appearance, for example. Some wore makeup, others didn't. None of them dressed like the deranged clowns of my imagination, with polka dots and swelled red noses. I found myself wondering who might count as a clown. Woody Allen? *Seinfeld*'s Kramer? The vocabulary of the circus tends to be straightforward: a wire-walker, a strongman. But what is a clown?

"There's no precise answer," André replied when I put the question to him. "If I'm going to be specific," he said, "I'd say a clown is a kind of improvisatory actor. He tends to be physical and multitalented. Often he plays music." He paused to swig from a bottle of water. Out in the hallway I could hear the gathering din of a crowd.

"But of course that's just on the surface. When we talk about clowning, what we're really talking about is a type of personality, possibly even a state of being. A clown is a searcher. He's lost. He's looking for something, but he doesn't know what. The audience becomes his radar—his guide for how to behave."

The last two sentences confused me.

"Here," André said, registering the response on my face, "let me give you an example." He stood and walked to the center of the stage. "Imagine I'm a clown. Let's say I do this. . . ."

Suddenly his entire physicality changed. He blew his eyes open and puffed out his chest and started strutting in tight circles, his backside jutting out behind him like that of a rooster. I laughed.

Immediately André stopped and sauntered back to his seat. *"Et voilà."*

"What?"

"What?" He seemed taken aback. "I made you laugh."

"And so?"

"And so?" He chuckled in mock disbelief. "That laugh, for a clown, that's magic. Suddenly I know I've done something right. I have *approval.*"

He jumped up and returned to the stage. It was clear he didn't like to sit still for long.

"That approval," he continued, pacing, "that's everything. And once I have it, I'm like anybody else: I want some more."

The rooster reappeared, only bigger this time, André's eyeballs bulging, his chest thrown so far back he was staring at the ceiling.

Again I laughed. Clearly, I was in the company of a pro. "You asked me what a clown is," André said, "and it's this." He waved a hand around him. "It's the reduction of ourselves into our purest desires, to our desperate hunger for approval. This is just a ridiculous little bit, but if it were part of an actual show, I might keep going. I know it works, so I do it again, hoping for the laugh. I would try to keep you laughing and grow despondent when you didn't. And it's that push and pull that makes a clown so endearing to us. We see him bumbling for our attention, desperate for a little love, and because we recognize ourselves in his fumbling, we want to give it to him. Because he is completely open about his intentions, completely vulnerable, we're on his team."

I was captivated by the clowning he was describing: a unique and powerful form of dramatic communication. It was not something I'd imagined previously. Was this the "modern clown" approach? Or had clowns always been this way? As I started to ask André, the house manager entered and told us she was opening the doors.

"Listen, we didn't have much time here," André said as we gathered our things. "Why don't we meet again?" He was doing a workshop in a week. It was for advanced clowns, so I couldn't participate, but I was more than welcome to attend. "We can chat more then. It'll also give you a practical sense of what I'm talking about."

We made our way toward the stage exit. At the door, André paused. "About your earlier question," he said. "To be honest, I don't know that much has changed between the old clowns and the new. We're going on here about clowns and animals and God knows what. But that's all extra dressing. That's all up here," and he waved his hand above his head. "More than any of this heady stuff, more than *anything*, a clown has to be funny."

I nodded, waiting for him to go on.

"Well, Jesus," he broke out, "write that down!"

On my notebook I wrote: "CLOWN = FUNNY."

André looked at what I had written and, clicking his tongue in dissatisfaction, plucked first the pen and then the notepad from my fingers. Propping the pad on his knee, he wrote something, then flipped it back to me. Next to my equation, he had added: "! ! !"

16

A Regal Past

WHILE RESEARCHING LES NOUVEAUX NEZ, I read a review referring to the company as "the inheritors of France's regal clown past." The reference is to a specific time, from the Belle Époque through the thirties, when Paris was the center of the clown world. During this period, clowns approached their work with unprecedented seriousness and earned unprecedented prestige. Clowns were some of the most popular celebrities. They traveled in the same circles as Stravinsky, Picasso, and Hemingway. It was a beautiful time, when a city and its circus complemented each other completely.

I decided to spend an afternoon connecting to this golden age. I boned up on clowns at the circus library and made a list of important sites. Coincidentally, as I was arranging my excursion, I received a call from Ernest

Albrecht, publisher of *Spectacle*, an American circus magazine. We had spoken before by e-mail. Now he was in town for a circus festival, the Festival Mondial du Cirque de Demain. He invited me to join him and some other circophiles—including a famous former clown—for dinner at an old circus haunt called the Clown Bar.

I decided to make a day of it: clown sites in the afternoon, Clown Bar in the evening. What better way to spend a Saturday.

AS WITH THE OTHER CIRCUS ARTS, the progenitors of clowning predate the circus by several thousand years. Most ancient societies had fools. As far back as 3000 B.C., midgets from African tribes dressed in leopard skins and masks to entertain royals in Egypt. On the stages of Rome, actors played stock characters defined by crass physical humor. Moriones, one such figure, had a hump on his back. Stupidus wore a pointed cap and a rainbow costume.

As their names suggest, the primary dramatic function of these Roman characters was to serve as a comic butt, to be, as one Roman writer put it, "slapped at the public's expense." But clowns had other roles as well. Through their failings and eccentricities, clowns provided audiences with the chance to reflect on their own lives, and perhaps not take themselves so seriously.

On an anthropological level, clowns offered implicit cultural commentary. In one sense, when they were mocked, they demonstrated the repercussions of acting outside societal rules and thereby reinforced those rules. But in another sense, clowns provided an outlet. As Dario Fo notes in *Tricks of the Trade*, clowns are natural rebels whose seemingly childish antics in fact display "an utter cynicism which undermines all the conventional values of the moral code—honesty, human respect, fidelity." This was especially true in cultures where strict social codes dictated behavior. As the lowest of the low, a clown had nothing to lose and so obeyed no rule. He could criticize local powers or serve as a proxy for those who lacked the agency to do so themselves. Clowns often suffered, but they were free.

In the Middle Ages, clowns, like other performers, took to the road, where they assumed a variety of guises. In castles and châteaux, kings, nobles, and sometimes clergymen employed jesters in colorful patchwork suits (possibly inherited from Stupidus) to "bring some merry." Even more numerous were "gleemen" or "minstrels" and *jongleurs*, who performed musical poetry and banter mixed with an impressive array of skills.

With the passage of time, clowns teamed up to offer more complicated comic fare. Some of the first proper duos consisted of a traveling quack doctor or potion salesman (a mountebank) and a "zany," who lured the crowd and entertained them during the pitch, an over-the-top monologue delivered in an unrecognizable slurry of Spanish, French, Italian, and Latin, and peppered with comic interjections. Mondor and Tabarin, who worked on Paris's Pont Neuf and then in the Place Dauphine, were especially famous. Beginning in 1618, the partners premiered a new show every Friday for nearly a decade. Their act tended toward the sexual and the scatological. Cross-dressing featured prominently. One writer of the period described them as a "constantly renewing celebration of asses, farts, and public toilets." In 1622, the duo published their farces to great success. Later, Molière borrowed from them heavily.

In Italy, the commedia dell'arte was being born. Today the form is considered the root of clowning as we know it. Commedia always featured a group of stock characters in familiar situations, although the shows were improvisational and physical. Each character was recognizable via traditional costumes and behavior. The gullible lover Pedrolino (origin of the Spanish word for clown, *payaso*) wore floppy white pants and a mask with a bulging nose. Harlequin capered around in a patchwork rainbow suit, waving a wooden bat called a *batte*. Later the bat would have another name: a "slapstick."

Commedia peaked at the beginning of the eighteenth century, roughly fifty years before the emergence of the circus as we know it. With the rise of the new genre, clowns would find what British historian George Speaight calls their "natural home." But not right away. The first circus clowns were rudimentary and, from a comedic standpoint, a regression. Astley himself played the first circus fool, a hapless tailor who tries and fails to ride his horse in a bit called "The Tailor of Brentford." Other performers burlesqued their own skills or served as maladroit assistants by helping out with an act (holding a ribbon for a rider, say) and bantering with the ringmaster. ("Ladies and gentlemen, Mr. Merryman has a great deal of wit!") The acts were simple, almost brainless, providing a point of comparison with the main acts. As Soviet scholar Victor Kalesh has noted, in their ineptitude the clowns "underscored the beauty of those who are really beautiful."

Across town, however, a more complex form of clowning was developing on the pantomime stages. Born from commedia, but silent in accordance with the theater laws, the pantomime shows also featured stock characters, including Harlequin and Pierrot, in raucous miming and acrobatics. With the migration to England, however, the character roles had shifted: Harlequin, once a beloved mischief-making servant, became a romantic lead. This left space at the bottom, to be filled by a new character: "clown."

Derived from the English words "clod" or "colonus," meaning "foolish rustic," the clown was an earthy, rural buffoon. Initially, his role in the show was minimal. Dressed in worn trousers and scuffed leather boots, he worked as a servant to the miserly old Pantaloon. As the character evolved, he insinuated himself more fully into action, largely thanks to the work of Joseph Grimaldi. Beginning in 1781, Grimaldi, the son of a ballet master, starred for decades as the lead clown at London's Sadler's Wells. He is responsible for many of the clown traits we know today. Dispatching with the bumpkin model, he wore a blue Mohawk wig and painted his face white with red streaks. Clever and physical, he was known for his intelligence and wit. Charles Dickens edited his memoirs. On stage, he recited parodies of *Macbeth*. "I never saw any one to equal him—there was such *mind* in everything he did," theater director Charles Dibdin wrote.

Thanks to Grimaldi's success, the clown became a totem in London society. After his death in 1837, the model spread to pantomime stages around the world, including New York, where George Fox clowned for twelve hundred performances. In the 1820s, John Ducrow brought the Grimaldi-style clown to the circus. Billed as "Prime Grinner, and Joculator General to the Ring," he appeared at Astley's, where he enacted elaborate tea scenes with his horses, Darby and Joan. In the 1830s, Grimaldi imitators surfaced on the boulevard in Paris, flipping, grimacing, and balancing on ladders. At first the French didn't know what to make of the character. "Clowning is a particularly English specialty," commented a Parisian writer of the period, "because it personifies the Englishman's extraordinary penchant for eccentricity, the dominant symptom of Anglo-Saxon melancholy."

But soon locals were adopting the act. At the Cirque Olympique, Jean-Baptiste Auriol, a Grimaldi impersonator, became Paris's first clown star. He was a *clown-sauteur,* an acrobatic clown, because his act was mostly physical. In the 1840s, another type of clown arrived from England, the *clown-parleur* or "talking clown." Attributed to William Wallett, a British actor turned "Shakespearian jester," the talking clowns improvised comic monologues based on verses cribbed from the Bard. ("Is this a beefsteak I see before me?") In Paris, where the linguistic barrier limited the effectiveness of such speeches, clowns compensated with absurd, often macabre surrealism. James Boswell, an artist as well as a clown, and a hero to French intellectuals, wrapped himself in a bloody bedsheet and ran around screaming lines from *Hamlet*. Billy Hayden, star of the Cirque des Champs-Élysées, trained a pair of mules to box and took as his assistant a small black pig, whom he dressed in boxer shorts, derbies, and summer dresses.

By the 1860s, clowns were a staple of European circuses. Their acts were somewhat limited, however, because of the patent laws, the city codes dictating the sort of performance each venue could produce. Circuses could only feature "horses and related acts." Anything encroaching on drama, including comedic dialogue, was forbidden. Clowns could speak to an audience or to an animal but never to each other.

Then, in 1864, Napoleon III changed all that. Bowing to democratic pressure, he struck down the patent laws and opened the city to unlimited theatrical action. Overnight, shows proliferated as itinerant performers flocked to the capital. In Parisian circuses, clowns began to develop new material. Their skits became more dramatically complex. "It's not enough to jump and bounce around," Hayden told an interviewer for the *Revue Bleue*. "You also must mock men, poor men, touch them with their own stupidity, and amuse them with their own ridiculousness."

In many ways, this new period marked a return to the past, to the situational comedy of the mountebanks and commedia. But clowning had also changed. Banned from speaking, clowns had perfected the art of physical expression—mime, acrobatics, grimacing. Now they would bring these skills to bear in developing their new comedy. Across Europe, clowns would set out to integrate these new skills with the old. And one pair of clowns would lead the way: Footit & Chocolat at the Nouveau Cirque.

THE DAY OF THE DINNER at the Clown Bar, I tracked down the former site of the Nouveau Cirque, 247–251 Faubourg Saint-Honoré. The building was long gone, closed on April 18, 1926. But, here again, the site was under construction. A scaffold covered the front of the building. Off to the side a construction permit was posted onto the brick. This was the heart of the city's haute couture district, and the street was luxurious. Gold logos emblazoned the shops: Gucci, Prada, Dior. Paragons of musculature and personal grooming packed the sidewalks. The scene was vaguely reminiscent of a Fellini movie. Everyone was tan.

Ironically, had it survived, the Nouveau Cirque wouldn't have been so out of place. Constructed by Joseph Oller in 1886, the peak of the city's fascination with haute couture, the circus was for the freewheeling champagne-and-fur crowd what the Cirque des Champs-Élysées had been for the aristocrats. The building itself was opulent, almost to the point of being gauche. Originally built as a Turkish bath, it had been converted to stage *pantomimes nautiques* at night, lavish water circuses conducted in a pool hidden beneath a retractable floor. The shows were impressive in their extravagance. One featured thirty polar bears on water slides. Contracts at the Nouveau Cirque required performers to maintain an "irreproachable freshness." What made the venue truly famous, however, were its star clowns: Footit & Chocolat.

They were an unlikely duo. Son of an equestrian, Footit had grown up as an equestrian in his father's circus in England. After losing his horse in a card game, he turned to clowning, and then quickly rose through the ranks as a *clown blanc*, a descendant of the Grimaldi model, with white makeup and a white sack for a costume. Chocolat (Raphael Padilla) came from the other side of the world. Born in Cuba to parents of African descent, he arrived in Europe as the servant to a rich businessman, before escaping to Bilbao, where Tony Grice, a clown star at the Nouveau Cirque, discovered him performing feats of strength at a café and took him as his assistant. At the Nouveau Cirque, Chocolat adopted the character of the auguste, a down-and-out bourgeois striver.* Compared to Footit, his look was relatively realistic. He wore little makeup, a tattered, ill-fitting suit, polished shoes, and a red satin jacket. He made a nice contrast.

In 1886, Grice fired Chocolat, and Footit, recognizing his poten-

* There are multiple stories about how the auguste character originated. The most common attributes the character to Tom Belling at the Circus Renz.

tial, took him as a partner. Their comedy was brutal and contemptuous. Grimacing and stern, Footit was the authoritarian master of the games. Stomping, sulking, scowling, he converted the ring into what Cocteau called a "devil's nursery," through a "malice that children can recognize." Chocolat was his punching bag. "You idiot! You fool!" Footit would rage, repeating his commands again and again, until Chocolat, ever staid, would finally turn to him and say with a smile, "I heard you the first time." The violence could be extraordinarily direct. "Chocolat, I'm going to have to hit you now," Footit might say, delivering a cuff to the temple. (In exchange for enduring this onslaught, it's said that Footit paid Padilla an extra 40 sous every night.)

The sketches sound horribly bigoted, of course, but circus historians contend that the act was less about race than about the shifting class standards of the period. "It was a typical master/servant relationship," Pascal said. What made the act effective was the dramatic complexity the duo brought to the work. Footit, who wrote and directed the pieces, which were known as "entrées," labored over the scripts and insisted on perfect execution. Star actors, including Sarah Bernhardt, came to see them perform and complimented them publicly.

By the 1890s, the clowns were a Parisian sensation. Hêve, a popular soap, hired them for advertisements. They hobnobbed with the city's elites and intellectuals. Footit was a drinking pal of Toulouse-Lautrec, who, years later, would paint a series of iconic images of the duo while a resident at the mental ward Folie-Saint-James. Largely because of this fame, their model would spread throughout Europe, and eventually the world. Before them, the white clown and the auguste had existed as separate entities. Now, every circus would have its duo: Ilès & Loyal, Dario & Bario, Antonet & Grock, Alex & Porto. One rule-maker, one rule-breaker. One clown, one auguste.

At the site of the old Nouveau Cirque, I felt a pang of disappointment that the clowns had been priced out of the neighborhood. Curious about what would replace the old circus, I approached a pair of tall stewards manning the door to the Brooks Brothers across the street. With their matching blazers and perfect hair, they were an entrée unto themselves.

"It's going to be a hotel *de luxe*," one of them said, barely looking at me.

"A Mandarin," the other corrected.

"That's right," the first said. "A Mandarin."

"Is it going to be a *Mandarine*?" I asked.

"That's right, a *Mandarine*."

We stood and stared back up at the building. I wondered, briefly, how the Mandarin would feel about a plaque.

BY THEN it was almost five. The sun was waning behind the Eiffel Tower. I had told Albrecht that I would meet the circophiles at seven, giving me just enough time to hit a second venue, the Cirque Medrano.

"Medrano! Medrano! Medrano!" wrote the French circus historian Adrian. "Each time we pronounce these three syllables . . . it's more than a circus show that's evoked—it's a swarm of memories." More than any other circus, the Medrano epitomizes the unique relationship between Paris and the art. Located in Montmartre, Paris's bohemian butte, it reigned for almost a hundred years as the city's artistic circus, a gathering ground for poets, painters, and intellectuals. For clowns the venue was a pinnacle. "To play at the Medrano was . . . a definitive ordination," wrote clown scholar Tristan Rémy.

Like most troupes, the Medrano began modestly. Originally known as Cirque Fernando, the circus was founded by Belgian equestrian Ferdinand Beert in 1873. First, he put a tent on the lot, then a small stone building. At the time, Montmartre still had the feel of a village, with cobblestone streets and cows lounging in the alleys, and the building captured the provincial atmosphere. Intimate, almost familial, it had 2,080 seats and a bar where regulars could mingle with the performers. The star was a doctor-turned-clown named Boum-Boum (a.k.a. Geronimo Medrano), who hosted shows with children from the neighborhood. Fernando advertised by letting his monkey caper through the streets with a sign.

This sense of authenticity was especially popular with the artists of the neighborhood. Lured by cheap rent, the ambitious aesthetic revolutionaries—Monet, Berlioz, van Gogh, Apollinaire, Toulouse-Lautrec—had installed their workshops in the quaint nearby streets of Montmartre, and they supported the circus by making it one of their main meeting points. At night, they would gather to watch a show before heading out for drinks at the Moulin Rouge or the Lapin Agile. During the day, Fernando's wife allowed them to watch the rehearsals, sketchbooks in hand, leading to such famous artworks as Seurat's *Le Cirque* (1891), and Edgar Degas's *Miss Lola*. "[Picasso] would stay there all night," said the artist's longtime girlfriend Fernande Olivier, "Braque sometimes with him, talking to the clowns."

In 1897, Beert sold the lease to Boum-Boum, now a star at the Nouveau Cirque. The clown changed the venue's name to Cirque Medrano, but he maintained the emphasis on his discipline, and, for a decade, the little circus was known across Europe as *the* venue for the clown, a temple of the craft. Rico and Alex packed the houses in 1910. In 1904, Brick and Grock made their appearance. In his memoirs, Grock described the time as the most joyful of his life.

Unfortunately, beyond the idyllic confines of Montmartre, all was not well in the circus. Unbeknownst to Boum-Boum, his arrival in Montmartre coincided with the beginning of the art's decline. In less than a decade, cars would flood the streets of Europe, displacing horses as the primary means of transportation, severing the circus's relevance to people's lives. Equally disabling were several new forms of entertainment. Music halls hired circus stars for more comfortable gigs with better pay. In America, the Chicago World's Fair ignited an explosion in traveling carnivals, amusement shows featuring rides, shows, and games of chance.

At the same time, motion pictures insinuated themselves into society with tremendous speed. In 1893, Thomas Edison introduced Americans to the first practical moving picture camera, the Kinetograph. In 1903, vaudeville managers had begun installing Vitascopes (early film projectors) in their theaters. Two years later, the first small movie houses, nickelodeons, appeared; two years after that, five thousand of them populated America alone. To the circus, the new media presented a mounting existential threat. Over the previous century, circuses had come to offer audiences a spectacle of fantasy and exoticism, presented with monumental visual appeal. Cinema could do the same, only more cheaply and efficiently. In 1898, the Cirque des Champs-Élysées bolted its doors. Cirque d'Hiver, Paris's oldest hard circus, was converted into a cinema. A new era of entertainment had begun.

Thanks to its loyal clientele, the Medrano was initially isolated from this competition. But debts soon began to mount. In 1912, Boum-Boum died, leaving the venue in the hands of his inexperienced widow and their five-year-old son, Jérôme. Two years later, France plunged into war. All horses and able-bodied men were summoned to the front. The Medrano closed. When it reopened the following year, the building was battered, the future bleak. Madame Medrano, not sure how to save her precious circus, turned to her marketing director, Rodolphe Bontem, who in turn enacted one of the great coups of circus history.

For some time, Bontem had been hearing reports of a trio of clowns drawing attention in the provinces. Born in Russia, sons of an Italian doctor-turned-equestrian, the Fratellini brothers—François, Albert, and Paul—had joined forces in 1909 at their mother's insistence after their brother Louis succumbed to smallpox. At the time, duos (one clown high, one low) were the conventional mode, but the brothers found a natural unity in three. François played the white clown. Suave and elegant, he warmed up the audience until the arrival of Paul, the auguste, dressed like a struggling banker of the petite bourgeoisie, in a scuffed charcoal top hat and a weathered tuxedo. Together, the duo would improvise based on a loose script, like their commedia dell'arte ancestors.

Then came Albert as a *contre-pitre*, or second auguste. The circus had never seen anything like him. As the writer and journalist Henri Béraud once observed, he looked like a "character from a cubist canvas, touched up by an alienated hairdresser with the help of a drunken stylist." He wore large pants that billowed around his ankles. His makeup was grotesque, his eyes enveloped by pools of white, his nose lost under a big red ball. He was a monster, but a monster with the soul of a child. As novelist and playwright J. B. Priestley wrote, Albert was so "filled with a wistful enthusiasm in his fantastic undertakings" "that he seemed like a pathetic parody of the whole race of men."

In 1915, Bontem brought the brothers to the Medrano. To tout their arrival, Bontem hit Paris with a marketing blitz worthy of Barnum, plastering taxis, billboards, even urinals with the clowns' faces. To attract the new crop of Montmartre artists—Dalí, Hemingway, Pound—Bontem kept the circus adult-oriented, even progressive. The evening shows didn't start until ten o'clock. The Fratellinis didn't go on until eleven-thirty. Many of their *entrées* were overtly surrealist. In one, François dressed up like an enormous butterfly. In another, Albert lumbered into the ring dragging a clanking mobile of metal tubes designed by the American sculptor Alexander Calder.

According to most historians, the appearance of the Fratellinis at the Medrano marked the high point of clowning as a cultural form. Within months of their arrival, "Fratellinimania" had swept the city. There were Fratellini combs and caramels, Fratellini shoe polish and perfume. To the artists, the clowns represented a unique and avant-garde vision of the theater—improvisational, physical, visual, musical, and popular. Jean Cocteau cast them in his plays. The Comédie-Française recruited them to its stage. *"Le clown,"* wrote theater director Jacques Copeau, *"voilà le vrai acteur."*

Suddenly, Paris was awash in circus all over again. Inspired by the Medrano's success, the Cirque d'Hiver reopened in 1923 and, the following year, poached the Fratellinis from the Medrano for a small fortune. Jérôme Medrano, Boum-Boum's only son, now in control of the Medrano, countered by recruiting some of the biggest stars in circus history: Enrico Rastelli, the flying Codonas, and Con Colleano, the Australian "Nijinsky of the wire." And, of course, nearly every great clown put in an appearance at the Medrano during this period, including several of the great clowns of cinema, Buster Keaton and Laurel and Hardy.

The renaissance carried on through the thirties—but not much longer.

IN MONTMARTRE, I made my way through streets, which were packed with tourists. I knew the Medrano had been on the corner of Boulevard Rochechouart and Rue des Martyrs, but I didn't know the exact address, and so I made my way over to a bookshop across the street. At my inquiry, the shopkeeper's face lit up.

"Oh yes, the circus was across the street," she said, and she led me to the window. She was a brittle woman in her seventies who wore a pair of orange pants that crinkled like paper. She pointed to a tall gray apartment building across the street. "There's a grocery store on the bottom floor. The ring used to be in the produce section, I've heard."

She seemed informed, and so we chatted for a few minutes about the Medrano and clowns. She indicated a shelf of circus books near where we were standing.

"We try to keep it stocked," she said. "It's our little tribute." She pulled a book down and began flipping through the pages. "There are some pictures of the Medrano in here somewhere. Ah, yes, here . . ." She fanned open the book and extended it to me. On the open page was a picture of a woman in an oversized black suit sitting on a pile of rubble. Below, the caption read, "Even Annie Fratellini couldn't save the Medrano."

The shopkeeper examined the photo for a long moment and then looked up at me. "I suppose you know the story. . . ."

In fact, I did.

By the late thirties, the circus industry had again fallen on hard times. In America, the Depression brought a rash of closures. Survivors were forced to cut costs drastically. In 1931, for example, the Ringling-owned Sparks Circus fired their famous circus band and replaced them with a record player, a drummer, and a calliope. In Europe, World War II fell like an anvil. Around the Continent, circus buildings were destroyed, their carcasses scavenged for firewood. Armies bought animals for labor and even food. They appropriated trucks and performers for battle. (Midgets were recruited for airplane assembly lines, to crawl inside the wingtips to buck rivets.)

With the armistice, circus owners hoped to rebound as they had after World War I. But the world had changed. The arrival of "personalized entertainment" in radio ate into the market share of more communal entertainments like fairs, festivals, and theatrical shows. Television would do the same. The rise of mass media also bolstered the prominence of professional sports. Athletes more easily challenged circus performers as celebrities. The proliferation of automobiles helped spawn suburbs, particularly in America. The new landscape rendered the traditional circus-marketing efforts (parades, posters, the tent) obsolete. "Last summer there were few circus parades," noted *The New Yorker* in 1929. "This year there will be none. . . . You can't have a circus parade of automobile trucks."

The circus industry entered a precipitous decline, what Pascal once described as a "guerrilla war" of survival. To cut costs, circus producers swapped their stars for inexpensive acts from abroad and abandoned their big tops to tour in sports arenas. (The last Ringling Bros. and Barnum & Bailey performance under canvas occurred on July 16, 1956.) Children became the target market. They were less demanding, willing to overlook a mangy tiger or an acrobat's frayed costume. Acts could be recycled ad infinitum, since children were always growing into and out of the circus.

The changes had lasting artistic consequences. Already, big American shows had forced clowns to adopt exaggerated costumes and makeup, to sacrifice their crafted *entrées* for cacophonous "production gags" like the clown wedding, the clown fire brigade, and the infamous clown car. Now every joke had to appeal to a five-year-old. Idiotic sight gags became the rule: violins with strings that pop off, exploding hammers. Today, the shift makes circophiles irate. "What a pathetic misinterpretation of the circus!" wrote Antony Hippisley Coxe. But the shift was widespread and accounts for many of our present stereotypes about the craft. "Why do you want to do a movie about clowns?" circus historian Tristan Rémy asked Federico Fellini in his 1970 film *The Clowns*. "All the real clowns have disappeared."

To be fair, not all shows participated in this race to the bottom. As circus critic David Hammarstrom notes, Barbette (né Vander Clyde), who early in his career performed as a transvestite trapezist, directed a single-ring show that toured America to critical acclaim in the 1940s. Another innovator was Jérôme Medrano. At his little circus in Montmartre, he welcomed children while continuing to produce entertainment for adults. In 1950, he recruited Rhum (Enrico Sprocani), considered by many the best auguste in history, for whom he devised full pantomimes, including *Rhum à Rome*. In 1952, he assembled clowns and circus experts from around Europe to discuss the future of clowning and possible ways to rehabilitate its image.

The preceding years had not been easy for Medrano. He had found himself embroiled in a crosstown rivalry with a family of former animal trainers, the Bougliones. Born of the fairgrounds, with roots in the business dating back centuries, the family had purchased the Cirque d'Hiver and were staging increasingly elaborate shows based on the American model, full of animals and pomp. Medrano had fought the family tooth and nail, but during World War II, they managed to gain the upper hand: with Medrano abroad as a naval officer, the Bougliones purchased his circus from the family of tentmakers who owned the lease. (Circus historian Dominique Jando told me that the Bougliones arrived at the auction with a trunk full of gold.) Upon his return, Medrano filed suit. He was able to delay the sale for almost twenty years.

Eventually, however, the courts ruled against him, and on January 10, 1964, after Medrano produced a final performance with clowns from around Europe, the Bougliones took control of the building. (Witnesses say the family stood in the hall during the show, waiting to seize the keys.) But, faced with running two circuses simultaneously and a no longer sympathetic audience, they closed the Medrano. For several years they rented the building out, first to theater companies and later to a barman who converted it into a beer hall. Then, shortly before Christmas of 1973, they had the building razed.

It was a highly controversial decision. One historian refers to the event as an "assassination." The Paris circus community received no warning of the destruction. The whole building was brought down intact—seats, railings, ring, and all—and just a week before the building's hundredth anniversary, which would have qualified it for review as a historical monument. When news of what was happening leaked, Annie Fratellini, granddaughter of Paul Fratellini, rushed to the scene to stop the wrecking balls. But it was too late. Paris's "temple of clowns" was gone.

In the bookshop, the shopkeeper and I studied the image of Fratellini sitting on the rubble. We talked about the building. I asked her if she had ever visited the circus itself.

"In fact, I grew up not too far away," she said with a smile, as she replaced the book on the shelf. "My mother would take me to special Christmas shows they put on. The circus used to parade the animals in the streets. It really was a part of the neighborhood, of *la vie du quartier.* It was a blow when it was destroyed."

Today the Bougliones are one of the great dynasties of circus, the Ringlings of France. Their legacy, however, is mixed. Traditionalists praise them for their stewardship of the Cirque d'Hiver, which they still own, and which remains the only hard circus in Paris and perhaps the most important circus monument in the world. Modernists, or those with a sentimental attachment to the Medrano, paint them as spoiled and clannish—a "mafia," even. The truth is probably somewhere in between. That said, on the day of my trip to the former site of the Medrano, I found myself resenting the family tremendously.

Crossing the street from the bookshop, I made my way over to the apartment building the family had constructed on the spot of the Medrano. I noticed for the first time the inscription above the doorway, bolted in big bronze letters: LE BOUGLIONE.

It's one thing to destroy a piece of history. It's another to gloat about it. I tried the door. It was locked, but a moment later I managed to slip inside behind a woman with a grocery bag.

The lobby was empty and dark. Small sheets of light angled through the front windows. When my eyes adjusted, I was confronted by a striking image: Built into the wall across from the elevators was a vast and colorful circus mosaic. It was strangely chilling. Most of the disciplines were represented—a wire-walker, a contortionist, a clown—but there was no movement to the work. The characters, who had black dots for eyes and black shards for mouths, appeared frozen. In the dim light, the wall looked hauntingly primitive, like a cave drawing left behind by a lost society.

THE CLOWN BAR WAS PACKED. At the front of the restaurant, the maître d' spun like a figure skater, ran his gaze over the crowd, and pointed to a table where three men sat huddled. As I shuffled back to meet the men, I reveled in the bar's décor. Near the front was a display case filled with circus memorabilia, including porcelain figures and painted plates. Framed posters lined the walls. On the ceiling, more posters were pressed into a kind of papier-mâché, their images dimmed under shellac of nicotine. Though I couldn't make out any dates, the posters looked old. They must have been there for decades.

The Clown Bar occupies a special place in Parisian circus lore. Founded in 1919, located next door to the Cirque d'Hiver, the bar had served for almost a century as the Parisian circus gathering ground, the place where producers, performers, and fans assembled to talk shop before, after, and sometimes even during the shows. (According to the owner, Joey, a secret door used to connect the kitchen to the circus, and clowns would sprint over during intermission for a drink.)

With the decline of the industry, business had sagged. The Internet changed how performers related to each other and booked gigs. The Bougliones still hosted shows next door, but the audiences weren't ideal ("kids and old people," Joey complained). Still, there were occasional highlights. During the eighties, Cirque du Soleil had rented out the building for several nights and, to hear Joey tell the story, made bedlam of the block. Annually, too, the circus hosted the Festival Mondial du Cirque de Demain (World Festival of the Circus of Tomorrow), which was the circus's equivalent to the Sundance Film Festival. Over four nights, the best international circus prospects (or at least the best prospects with a traditional seven-minute act) competed for a host of medals. Circus-lovers—including the three men I had come to meet—flocked to the festival from around the world.

At the table, I greeted Albrecht, who introduced me to Hovey Burgess and Dominique Jando. As a juggler in the seventies, Burgess had helped bring the modern circus to America from Europe and had later written a seminal book on circus skills, a subject he taught at New York University. Jando was a jack-of-all-trades—historian, teacher, clown, writer. As a boy in Paris, he had attended the Medrano with his father, a circus-obsessed movie producer, and in the five decades since, Jando had observed a number of critical modern circus moments: he was working at the Medrano the day the Bougliones seized the keys in 1964; in 1974, he helped found the first circus school in Paris; in 2002, he joined Lu Yi, a Chinese acrobatics coach, in developing a professional training ground at the Circus Center in San Francisco. Jando was something of a traditionalist, and I had barely sat down before he was impugning the state of the circus in France.

"It's very bad, what they've done here," he proclaimed, in heavily accented but grammatically flawless English. He wore thick glasses and leaned over the table so far that I thought he was going to knock over the saltshaker with his chin. "The circus here is at a low point. The technical ability is terrible! And, my God, they're so pompous!" He nudged Burgess. "I can say that because I'm French. They had this whole idea that they were reinventing circus, that they were making it art, but that is bullshit. The circus has always been art. When it started to die everywhere else, the Russians took it on."

This was true. During the fifties and sixties, while the critics were lamenting the death of the circus in the West, the Soviet circus was soaring. After nationalizing the circus in 1919, the government continued to pour money into the art, as a populist entertainment and a form of propaganda. In 1927, Russia created the first national school to assure themselves of a stable crop of circus prospects. Twenty years later, they developed what was known as "the Studio," a sort of circus production house, in which artists from all disciplines (directors, choreographers, composers) teamed up to devise original circus material. The work coming out of such institutions was unparalleled in artistry and professional polish. Unfortunately, few people knew it, thanks to the Iron Curtain. "Even the Russians were in the dark," Jando said. "They didn't know how good they were."

In 1956, the proverbial lights came on. After successfully touring Europe with its now famous ballet and opera companies, the Soviet state decided to do the same thing with the circus. For three months, the Moscow Circus visited Paris, London, Brussels. At every stop, pandemonium reigned. In Brussels, hordes of frustrated ticket-seekers gathered outside the tents, and thousands more were turned away. According to *The New Yorker*, the circus had "the most disarming effect on Paris of anything Muscovite since the October Revolution."

The Soviets scheduled more tours. In 1958, their circus returned to Europe, with similar results. In 1963, the company flew to America, where *The Wall Street Journal* called them "the most lively, talented, and attractive troupe in the history of the great circus." Audiences everywhere celebrated the artists, but the clowns proved especially popular. In contrast to the white clowns and augustes the Soviet clowns pursued a more naturalistic ideal. Many took Chaplin as their model. Mikhail Rumyantsev (a.k.a. Karandash, Russian for "pencil"), the first big star under the new regime, wore a black top hat and a black mustache. Like Chaplin, he created satirical routines, including a parody of Hitler during World War II, in which Rumyantsev wore a tin-pot helmet and screamed *"Nach Moskau!"* ("To Moscow!") at his dog, Pushek.

In the post-Stalinist period, clowns remained realistic but took on a softer, more "poetic" edge. Oleg Popov is the most famous example. A student of Karandash and a 1949 graduate of the national school, he developed an act based more in mime than in slapstick. There was something wistful and childlike about him. He had a round face and big eyes. His humor was gentle. The act could seem playfully naïve but was in fact the product of an almost philosophical approach to his craft. "The old clown routines are not good for us," he once told an interviewer. "We want some thought in our routines—laughter without the slaps and humiliation." The chief object for every circus artist, he believed, "is the high dignity of man which must be shown in the ring." In Russia, Popov became a national hero. On tour in Europe, he was a revelation. Josephine Baker made a special trip to see him in Paris. (Popov honored her visit by presenting her with a big red cloth heart.) Chaplin trailed the Russian genius through the city, "as a man follows a torch bearer down dark streets." (Popov himself was "politely unimpressed" by the clowns of the West.)

After the tours abroad, the Soviet circus spread. The state injected even more money into training programs and engaged in a building spree:

in 1956, Russia had twenty circus buildings; by 1976, they had eighty (the vast majority still exist). During this period, as many as a hundred circus programs played daily across the USSR, with five thousand artists performing twelve hundred acts. A hundred million circus tickets were sold every year. Young people dreamed of becoming circus stars, for the prestige but also for the luxurious perks: a cash per diem, the opportunity to travel, access to Western goods—all rare privileges at the time. And it wasn't just in Russia! As communism spread, the Soviet circus ideal spread with it—to Mongolia, Korea, Cuba, Cambodia, Egypt, Hungary, Romania, Bulgaria. "The Soviets created an empire of circus," Pascal once said.

In the Clown Bar, we discussed these developments and debated their influence on the West. Jando argued that the movements were intimately related. "If you're looking for the beginning of the modern circus, you have to look in Russia," he said. "If you talk to [juggler] Sergei Ignatov, he's an artist. If you talk to Popov, he is an artist. They were making art for fifty years."

While he spoke, I noticed that Burgess and Albrecht were both smiling and deliberately peering into their glasses, the way old friends might if they knew better than to contradict. Yes, the Russians had developed the art while it was languishing elsewhere. But both in their training methods and in their performances, they celebrated (and continue to celebrate) a kind of classical purity, an emphasis on form and line borrowed from the ballet. Like the Chinese, the Russians are technical virtuosos—which is why Cirque du Soleil loves them—but they have yet to embrace the modern age.

But why quibble? What unites the Russians and other European artists—and what separates them from the Chinese—is a kind of passionate personal spirit that imbues their work. (The Chinese are more practical, more self-effacing.) This was illustrated by a story that Burgess told as we were getting ready to leave.

We were talking about clowning, and specifically about what made a clown. Almost two decades ago, Burgess said, he had been brought in as a judge for the Festival Mondial. Among the obvious future stars that year was a young David Shiner, who is today an icon in the clown world. Since launching his career as the lead clown in Cirque du Soleil's *Nouvelle Expérience,* he has created and appeared in numerous internationally acclaimed shows, including, as I mentioned earlier, *Fool Moon* with Bill Irwin.

Back in 1984, however, he was just starting out, and the judges didn't know quite what to make of his act. Dressed in a blue suit and a battered derby, he was surly and aggressive, almost mean. He harangued the audience and pretended to take pictures of them with a little plastic camera that sprayed water. He stole a real camera from a professional photographer and hurled it into the air, ten, twenty feet, as if it were a toy. The crowd laughed uproariously throughout, but when it came time to award the medals, the judges balked. Several felt that Shiner was missing the spirit of clowning, that he was too nasty. They were on the verge of omitting his name from the winners when a voice rose from the back of the room: "Can I talk?"

"Everyone turned," Burgess recounted. "And there was Youri Nikouline, the famous Russian clown, alone in the corner." Burgess switched into a thick Russian accent. "For forty years I am clown," he said. "After forty years, I think I know what is clown. Today I am sitting in this circus when this young man perform. I am laughing. I am listening to the people. They are laughing. Everybody is laughing." He looked sternly at the room of circus-lovers. "This young man will be great clown one day. If you do not give him medal, you do not understand what is clown."

Burgess paused for a sip of wine. " 'Well,' somebody said, 'I guess we could give him the bronze.' "

17

The Inner Clown

ONSTAGE AT LE SAMOVAR, André Riot-Sarcey stood in the middle of a circle of clowns, a resplendent ring of plaid.

"That's right," he was saying, "shake it out! Shake the energy out of your hand!"

The clowns were warming up. A moment before, they had been mewling like animals; before that, impersonating opera singers. Now they were flapping their hands like dead fish.

"Okay, now feel the energy move up your arm." André flapped along with the rest of them, his porkpie derby jostling on his head. "Now feel it in your whole body."

The jiggling increased to a fever pitch. At the back of the stage, a man in a purple zoot suit emitted a jittery moan, like a kid riding his bicycle over cobblestones: "Uh-uh-uh-uh-uh . . ."

Observing this from the back of the theater, I had the sense all over again of knowing nothing about clowns. Nominally, André had told me, the purpose of the workshop was to help the clowns work on their *entrées*, which they had prepared in advance. But this was just a means to an end, and the real goal was to get at something deeper: their "inner clowns."

The idea, as I've said, dates back to Lecoq. As described in his book, *The Moving Body*, the "discovery" of one's inner clown is like tapping into your inner child, less a creation of character than a kind of stripping away. But how did this process work? How did interior exploration lead to laughs? André had confessed that it was an elusive process: "There are no rules to this sort of work."

On the stage, André called the shaking to a halt. An electricity ran through the group. The clowns were panting, twiddling their fingers, rocking on their toes. No two looked alike. Some were in their early twenties. Others looked to be as old as fifty. There were roughly equal numbers of men and women. Every clown had a red nose. Beyond that their clothes reflected varying degrees of eccentricity, from simple black suits to striped high-waters held up by suspenders. They were of all shapes and sizes—tall, short, skinny, fat. They did have one thing in common, though: they all seemed excited to be present. The man in the zoot suit was bouncing from foot to foot like someone looking to start a fight.

I heard the theater door wheeze open. A heavyset woman walked into the room: another clown reporting. She wore a gray zip-up hoodie and a tutu made of peacock feathers, with a rainbow of plumage spilling off her hips. Nervously she headed toward the stage, stopping at the front row, where she shrugged the canvas gym bag off her shoulder and underwent a curious transformation. First she unclasped her necklace and removed her earrings. Then she hiked up the waistline of her skirt until it was halfway up her belly. She took off her hoodie and, with her thumbs, popped the high-pointed collar on her blouse and unfastened and refastened each of its buttons incorrectly, so that its two panels failed to line up. Stooping again to the bag, she pulled out a red ball on an elastic string. Like a surgeon donning a mask, she pulled the ball over her face and settled it on her nose with a wiggle of her cheeks. The change complete, she took a breath and moved toward the stage, where, jovially, the other clowns parted their circle to welcome her.

SO HOW *do* you build a clown? Unlike in acrobatics, there is no clear progression. In any art, the greats succeed through a combination of talent and experience, leading some to suggest that clown education isn't possible at all—that either you have it or you don't, that it requires an innate comedic timing, an eye for absurdity, a taste for offbeat actions and personalities. Pierre Étaix, the great French *clown blanc*, once quipped, "Clowns are born, not made," but this is an exaggeration. Most clowns—my friend at the Place Pompidou aside—undergo some sort of training. "All too often I have seen actors trying to imitate clowns by doing no more than sticking a red ball on the end of their nose, putting on an outsized pair of shoes and squeaking in a funny voice," Dario Fo wrote. "At best this is an exercise in sheer naïveté, and the result is invariably cloying and irritating." "The only way to become a real clown is by long, energetic and dedicated work, and, yet again, by years of practice."

Historically, as we have seen, there have been various classes of clowns, though they could generally be grouped into three types: the *auguste de soirée*, the *auguste de reprise*, and the *clown d'entrée* (including white clowns). The first two comprise the traditional clowns. They wander around arenas, performing sight gags, filling time, and distracting the crowd. Often these clowns were hired as amateurs and learned on the job. They had little or no training.

That said, there have been recent efforts to train these sorts of clowns formally. The most notable example was the Ringling Clown College, operated by Ringling Bros. and Barnum & Bailey Circus in Venice, Florida, from 1968 to 1997. Part publicity stunt (the school advertised auditions wherever the circus toured), part genuine educational facility, the school attempted to train ring clowns in an effort to fill the circus's ranks, which had been dwindling. The course was short but rigorous. For nine weeks, students mastered the skills necessary to entertain children: how to pratfall, how to walk on stilts, how to design an elaborately painted face, how to take a "nap" and react to the sound of a simulated slap. In its twenty-nine years, the school had a massive, if mixed effect. On the upside, it provided a skill base for more than fourteen hundred clowns, some of whom—including Bill Irwin and Penn Jillette—went on to impressive careers. On the downside, the majority of graduates took their skills, which were intended for massive arenas, and employed them in backyard birthday parties, which didn't help the reputation of their craft.

The third type of clown, the *entrée* clown, requires more serious training. An *entrée* originally referred to a performance involving at least two clowns (e.g., Footit and Chocolat), but the definition expanded to mean any clown performance that takes up a unit of a show or "holds the ring." Often the *entrée* clown is the star of the circus. He has to be able to capture the attention of an audience even while surrounded by Russian acrobats performing triple flips. *Entrée* clowns also often serve as a unifying force, stitching together the different pieces of a show and providing the narrative backbone for the audience.

Historically, even these top clowns lacked formal training. Most learned the craft from a parent at a young age or migrated from other disciplines, often after an injury. Footit, as I've said, "took up the whites" after losing his horse in a card game. Chocolat started as the assistant to Tony Grice, one of Footit's comrades at the Nouveau Cirque. Emmett Kelly began as a trapezist. Otto Griebling, another famous American tramp, was an equestrian, as was William Wallett. Usually such clowns started at the bottom, beginning first as an *auguste de soirée*, then working their way up.

This system had several advantages. Practically, it gave circus performers a way to elongate their careers. Those who came from other disciplines were equipped with basic physical and performance skills, especially tumbling. Their first routine would often involve a burlesque of their previous specialty—a "clown to the wire," for example, or a "clown to the horse." (Such parodies are technically difficult, bringing together mastery and controlled failure. In his *Book of Clowns*, British historian George Speaight calls this combination the "golden rule" for clowning: for example, Grock sits down to play the piano, smashes his fingers under the piano lid, then proceeds to play a marvelous sonata; Buster Keaton trips clumsily out of a window into a bush two stories below, and manages to somersault unharmed out of his landing.)

But older clowns also brought an emotional and aesthetic resonance to their work, a sense of maturity, humanity, and tragedy. This is important, because a clown isn't an acrobat. Clowns are like actors. At their best, they offer nuanced dramatic portrayal. To be a clown you have to be attuned to suffering, to how it feels to attempt and fail. In this respect, age helps. "One of the things about clowning is that you're calling on a bag of tricks that has to be put together over the course of a life," Bill Irwin once said.

A clown can be a circus unto himself. He may be an expert in any skill the art can include—music, juggling, tumbling, acting, comedy, drama. Clowns at the Moscow Circus School studied a single discipline for four years, and then learned additional skills in the next four years. The quintessential example is Grock (born Adrien Wettach), the Swiss clown, a European star for over forty years at the beginning of the twentieth century. Actor, mime, acrobat, author, musician, Grock spoke six languages, produced two films, wrote three books, and played twenty-four instruments, several of which he constructed himself. He also built watches and a card-shuffling machine. A good clown, as the great Russian-Armenian clown Leonid Yengibarov once said, is "an artist who can do everything."

Today clown training is widespread. Many theater programs integrate clowning into a wider curriculum, often labeled as "physical" or "movement" theater. There are a few professional programs. In 1975, for example, Dimitri, a nationally renowned Swiss clown and mime, created the Scuola Teatro Dimitri, a physical-theater academy that is now part of the University of Applied Sciences and Arts of Southern Switzerland. Also notable is Lecoq's program in Paris,* as well as the dozens of spinoffs created by his disciples around the world, including the Pig Iron School for Advanced Performance Training in Philadelphia; the La Mancha in Santiago, Chile; and clown expert Philippe Gaulier's school in London.

Most clowns, however, cobble together their skills from a variety of sources, especially workshops such as the one André was teaching. These workshops last anywhere from a few days to a few weeks and, like the amateur juggling clubs, are open to the public. Also like juggling clubs, they are ubiquitous. Online I found them advertised in Argentina, Japan, Australia, the United States, Chile, China, Canada, Spain, and Norway. In Paris, I stumbled on their advertisements regularly in circus venues, grocery stores, and even the restaurant below my apartment. ("Everybody wants to be a clown, apparently," the Harley-driving proprietor told me when I asked where the poster had come from.)

The workshops most frequently offer the sort of training André

* Lecoq passed away in 1999. His widow directs the school now.

adhered to. One poster claimed clown training allowed a person "to get in touch with the naïveté of your inner spirit." Another promised "a new and overwhelming sense of enlightened laughter." It was as if clowning had superseded not just the circus, but all of performance, and had become a means of personal development. *The New York Times* once commented on this phenomenon: "Forget comedy class. This is more like philosophy, religion, psychoanalysis," April Dembosky wrote. "In the face of uncertainty, some people go to church. Others dive onto their analyst's couch. The next time life gets confusing, how about a clown workshop?"

AFTER THE WARM-UP, André clapped his hands and sent the clowns scuttling. The pudgy woman in the peacock skirt set up a boom box and lingered on the stage, picking at her feathers, while André settled himself in the front row.

"All right," André said, taking a notebook onto his knee, "let's see what you've got."

Each clown had prepared an *entrée* on the theme André had designated for this particular workshop: the "clown in love." This woman's *entrée* was a dance. At André's signal, she marched over to the stereo, hit "play," and moved back to center stage.

As a line of opera unspooled into the room, she threw herself around the stage with mounting aggression, lip-synching poorly. She was not graceful. Her peacock fronds crinkling and crunching, she heaved herself to the floor, crawled several feet, hauled herself up, lunged again, rolled onto her back, and then pushed herself across the stage as if she'd been shot in the leg. Within a minute she was sweating profusely. I tried to read André's reaction, but he sat stone-faced. Personally, I had a hard time seeing how the skit related to love. It was more sad than funny, even a bit pathetic, and when she finished, my overriding emotion was pity.

The boom box fell mercifully quiet. There was a pause while André reviewed his notes. The woman lay in a pile on the stage, breathing heavily.

"Here's the thing," he began, pushing himself up from his seat. "You've developed a wonderful beginning. Really. I mean it's all very . . . exuberant." As he was speaking, the woman struggled to her feet, all the while watching him intently.

"There are some nice things here," he said, "but there are also some things we need to work on."

He reached down and drew up the feathers of her skirt.

"Let's start with your look. Tell me about this. What were you thinking here?"

The woman looked sheepishly at the skirt. "To be honest, I don't know exactly."

"I see."

"No, but, I mean, it feels like me," she corrected herself quickly. "The colors, the way it moves." She shook her hips. The skirt rustled like a palm tree. "I do like how it moves."

André was skeptical. "I think we can do better."

Putting together a costume, he explained, a clown shouldn't just pick elements at random. Lecoq called the process a "personal transposition." A clown should look to express certain elements about herself and then exaggerate them. As Annie Fratellini puts it in *Destin de clown*, "I do not know of a single clown whose make-up does not correspond to his deepest being" (*son être profond*).

There are two ways of approaching this. First, a clown might call attention to a physical quality that's already a bit unusual. For example, Rosaline Guinet always called attention to her arms, which were long and pale. More classically, a costume might emphasize a personality trait or characteristic. Enormous clown shoes are a good example. Clowns were historically known for acting clumsy. (The word "clown" is etymologically related to the Icelandic *klunni*, a cognate of the Swedish *kluns*, or "clumsy.") In the nineteenth century, Billy Hayden, a clown at the Cirque des Champs-Élysées, decided to create a signifier for the trait: he adopted a pair of oversized shoes that caused him to trip. In his films, Chaplin made the shoes even bigger.

The point, André explained, is to make the clown's issues immediately recognizable and render interior dilemmas exterior.

He repeated what he'd told me previously: Like animals, he explained, clowns are physical beings. They represent their emotional states in their bodies. For that reason, clowns often develop telltale gestures, like Chaplin's nervous mustache twitch or Groucho Marx's lecherous cigar waggle. "The moment you walk onstage, we should know something about you."

In this spirit, he and the woman spent a few minutes discussing costume ideas and explored possible gestures. He told her to jump up and down. She did, and the skirt shook on her hips. He told her to try jiggling. Then he told her to make a motion, any motion. "Just make it big."

With surprising flexibility and force, the woman kicked her leg up to her face and nearly knocked her nose with her knee.

André perked up. "Okay! A big kick!" This was a starting place. He told her to do the move again and this time add another, small gesture with her head or her mouth.

Again the woman responded enthusiastically, with her big kick followed by a sloppy Bronx cheer. "Pfthhhhhh!!!" I had the impression I was watching a football drill gone terribly awry, but André was obviously into it. He had started bouncing on his toes and was nodding vigorously.

"Great, great, great. Now we need to reduce it. Watch."

He took a step back and launched into his own version of the sequence. There was a raging quality to the movement, almost like an unconscious tic. Whereas the woman's gestures had been loose and exaggerated, André's were tight and controlled. His foot barely left the ground. His tongue turtled between his lips. I thought of his rooster impersonation.

"You see that?" he coached, when he had repeated the series several times. "When the actions are big, they look absurd and out of place. Smaller, they become something else. *Il faut serrer, serrer,*" he said. Make them tighter, tighter.

The woman gave it a shot, repeating the steps several times, kicking and licking with adequate precision until the motion had assumed the appropriate spastic quality, whereupon André told her to run the whole act again. Only this time, he instructed, she was to use the gesture as a kind of tic: anytime she felt excited or energized, she should express that feeling with the move, "like a dog wagging its tail."

The simple change made a drastic difference. With the new tic, the act was more compelling. There was a manic quality to it. It was like watching somebody trying to express herself but failing—like observing someone with only a tenuous grasp on her emotions. In the audience, I now felt I knew more about her than she knew about herself.

When she finished, the woman gathered up her boom box and bounced in a satisfied way out the stage door, the sweat glistening on her cheeks. André deflated back into the front row of seats.

"It's hard," he said. "She can get a laugh just coming onstage. But you have to know how to use it. You can talk until you're blue in the face, but ultimately it's something you have to feel.

"This isn't the Comédie-Française. If she tries to base the routine on acting skills she doesn't have, the audience will know right away. We have to emphasize what we're given."

Next an Eva Braun look-alike performed a fantasy with a stuffed animal; then a shabby auguste in a navy suit juggled eggs with minimal success. André's advice developed along distinct themes. Most of it opposed what might be considered conventional clown wisdom. For example, Steve Smith, the former director of the Ringling Clown College, once told me that a clown's movements had to be legible "from the back of Madison Square Garden," and as a result encouraged broad gestures and broad comedy. But André encouraged his students to work smaller and aim for subtlety. Often he used the same gesture exercise he'd done with the woman in the peacock skirt: begin big and then pull back. The effectiveness of the movement, he said, came not from being legible but from being *"juste,"* true or real. "In theater, or even in a little one-ring show, the audience is close. Don't overdo it."

Similarly, he told them not to force the jokes. *"Pas de gag!"*—no gags! The comedy was in the details, in the honest response of the character to a given situation, not the punch line. I saw this come up while he was working with a man and a woman both in their twenties. They were dressed like nerds, he in taped glasses and high-water khakis, she in knee socks and a short plaid skirt. Their skit followed a simple sexual line. The woman, having trouble adjusting her skirt, asks the man for help; he agrees and stands behind, but his assistance quickly derails; she ends up doubled over in front of him as he bounces his crotch against her backside.

Clowns have a distinguished history of dirty jokes, of course. In Rome, the clown character Stupidus wore obscenely sized phalluses, the equivalent of leather eggplants that dangled between his legs and peeked out from under his skirt or loincloth. Commedia dell'arte, as a genre, was obsessed with sex, and most of its plot lines can be summed up as an accelerated skirt chase. Here, though, the act struck me as juvenile and facile—it wasn't performed well, and it was too aggressively realistic. I thought André would take issue with the *entrée,* but instead he objected only to the presentation.

"The joke here isn't in the sex," he said, pacing in front of the stage. "We've all had sex. We've seen sex." He encouraged them to find the comedy in the characters. How do they feel about each other in the beginning? Is she coquettish? Or maybe she's pursuing him? Don't rush the action, he said. What if he realizes where he's standing? Let us see that. Or what if he's pulled into the situation against his will? Maybe she bends over and he finds her bumping against him? Maybe he runs his hand along her back, catches himself, and pulls it away. "All this can be a starting point. You can go anywhere from here. Don't be afraid to sit on a moment and let it run. Let your frustration build. Follow your instinct. Go where it takes you." The clowns performed the act again, allowing the situation to build more slowly. What had been a sight gag developed into a small dramatic sketch about a quirky couple and the push and pull of courtship.

It was a lesson about exploring the nuances of characters, but it also related to what André called "presence"—the clown's ability to respond to the situation as it develops. First, a clown has to be "present" in the scene. Though some clowns, like Footit and Chocolat, refined their acts to exactitude, most clown *entrées* aren't fixed. Clowns adopt the model of the commedia and the Fratellinis, improvising around a simple script, or *"à la can."* It is close to improv comedy, with insertions of physical business, banter, and whatever else comes to mind. (Even the famous film clowns worked this way; Buster Keaton used to draw up a rough outline of his bits and improvise the details—the looks, trips, and twitches—on the set.)

Just as important, clowns have to stay present with the audience. This isn't unique to clowning. In the theater, there is usually an imaginary divide between audience and performers, a "fourth wall"; in the circus, performers and audience always share the same space. The audience is responsive: they applaud performers throughout the show, they get up and walk around; for a hundred years, producers left the lights on during the circus so people could talk. As Pascal likes to point out, the circus ring is the only entertainment venue in which spectators can see each other. ("The other faces are part of the décor.") Performers speak directly to the audience, saluting them and bowing. Often a ringmaster welcomes you at the beginning of the show ("Ladies and gentlemen . . ."). Paul Binder, the director and the ringmaster of the Big Apple Circus, has noted that he often has the sense of an audience entering his living room.

In his book *La Planète des clowns,* Alfred Simon called this direct relationship the circus's "great law." Clowns in particular live by it. In the Place Dauphine, Mondor and Tabarin teased and sold potions to their audience. Dan Rice, nineteenth-century America's most famous clown, scanned the headlines of the local newspaper every morning and improvised that night's material around what he had read. In Shakespeare, the clowns often step outside the play and comment on the action. For a clown, few restrictions apply. I have seen clowns rubbing their backsides in people's faces, giving viewers kisses, dousing the audience in water. A clown can literally come to your seat and drag you onstage. David Shiner was notorious for walking on his audience, literally crawling across their backs. ("He's got this special technique," Hovey Burgess told me. "It feels like he's barely touching you.")

At the workshop, this relationship between audience and performer was discussed most explicitly during an afternoon session with a pair of young clowns who stood out even among this eccentric crowd. The auguste, Mattieu Pillard, was tall and lamppost-thin. He wore a plaid suit and a beret and had a face like that of a drowsy field mouse. His partner, Patrick de Valette, was significantly shorter, but clearly the boss of the duo. In a white velour *Midnight Cowboy*–style pimp suit, he strutted around, his lips pouting under a prickly mustache, his hips thrust out in front of him.

"Whenever you're ready," André called from the front row, as the clowns huddled backstage.

SKETCHES OF AN ENTRÉE

(CLOWN enters at a jog, arms open.)

CLOWN: Heeeeeyyyyyy!

(CLOWN circles the stage, smiling, settling near the audience. Beat. AUGUSTE tramps on unenthusiastically. He jogs the same path as CLOWN, arrives at the same spot, bumping CLOWN in the back. CLOWN turns, scolds AUGUSTE with his eyes. He returns his attention to the audience.)

CLOWN: Heeeeeyyyyyy!!!!

(CLOWN strides to a new spot. After a pause, AUGUSTE again shuffles behind. CLOWN turns and glares.)

CLOWN *(whispering)*: What are you doing?

AUGUSTE: What?

CLOWN: You're supposed to stay over there. Remember? I'm here. You're there.

(AUGUSTE looks at him blankly.)

CLOWN: Jesus.

(He grabs AUGUSTE and stalks him offstage. A quiet moment. Then—)

CLOWN: Heeyyyy!

(CLOWN enters. He jogs the same circle as before, settling again downstage. A few seconds later, AUGUSTE enters, trudges up behind him.)

CLOWN: Heeyyyy!

(CLOWN crosses to his new spot. Again AUGUSTE treads after him absentmindedly. This time CLOWN is irate. He whips around and glares at AUGUSTE, who immediately realizes his mistake.)

AUGUSTE: Shit . . .

(AUGUSTE scurries back to his new position, but it's too late—CLOWN is upset.)

CLOWN: Is this complicated?

AUGUSTE: Sorry, I . . .

CLOWN: No! It's not complicated. I come here. You stay there. This isn't brain surgery. What's the freaking problem?

(AUGUSTE's bottom lip begins to quiver.)

CLOWN: Oh God.

(AUGUSTE buries his face in his hands and begins to sob. CLOWN watches him, disgusted.)

CLOWN: Really?

(AUGUSTE sobs. CLOWN waits as the sobbing continues. He begins to sympathize.)

CLOWN: C'mon. Please. Stop it.

(AUGUSTE wails on.)

CLOWN: Seriously. How long can this go on? I'm sorry. Okay? I apologize.

(AUGUSTE tries to pull himself together.)

AUGUSTE: You . . .

(CLOWN waits.)

AUGUSTE: You . . .
CLOWN: I . . . ?
AUGUSTE: You . . .
CLOWN: Say it!
AUGUSTE: *You don't love me!*

(The wailing resumes. CLOWN sighs heavily.)

CLOWN: I don't love you?
AUGUSTE: See!

(CLOWN watches AUGUSTE sob. He doesn't know how to respond.)

AUGUSTE *(through sobs)*: I want you to say it.
CLOWN: Say what?

(AUGUSTE regards CLOWN plaintively—he knows what.)

CLOWN *(turning away)*: No.
AUGUSTE *(heartbroken)*: I knew it.

(He goes back to crying pitifully. For a long beat, CLOWN tries to ignore him. He taps his foot. Gives the audience a "How's it going" nod. But he can't keep it up forever. Eventually his sympathy wins out—)

CLOWN: Fine.

(AUGUSTE falls instantly quiet. He pivots to face CLOWN, who adjusts his feet, twitches, stalls. Then, in a painful whisper—)

CLOWN: I love you.

(AUGUSTE erupts. Charging over to CLOWN, he seizes him in his long arms, hauling him off the ground, hugging him. CLOWN tolerates this for a moment, then raps AUGUSTE sharply on the back. AUGUSTE sets him down.)

A silence ensued. The clown smoothed his suit. The auguste looked blankly to André.

André: "Is that the ending?"

The clown shrugged. "Umm, yeah, I guess."

André nodded and slowly rose from his seat. "First of all, you have to do something about that ending. This isn't a movie. Even after you've delivered your punch line, you have to make an exit."

The clowns listened, still juiced with adrenaline. Both had pulled off their noses, so the balls hung around their necks like round red amulets.

The larger issue, André went on, was what he called "complicity." A clown had to make an audience feel as if it was part of the action. "You're not performing a play. Everything that happened in the space is part of our shared experience. We need to know that you see us, that you're with us." As an example, he referred to a moment during their *entrée* when another clown poked his head through the theater's rear door, as if looking for someone. "We all saw him. We knew he was there. That's a golden opportunity. Something changed in the space. So use that!" The reaction didn't have to be much, he went on—a look, a gesture. "Are you startled by him? Are you upset that he's interrupting your show? It might not go anywhere, or it might turn into something interesting or hilarious."

By acknowledging the reality of the situation and responding to it, a clown created a collaborative relationship. "You're not creating something *for* us. We're creating something together." This is what André meant by complicity, and it's what makes real clowning so difficult. (As turn-of-the-century French circus sage Georges Strehly says, "Only in watching him work with the audience can you see if a clown is good or not.") I saw this relationship approached vividly in New York City, years later, and the moment involved Pillard and de Valette.

The duo had formed a trio (with the nerd from the sexual sketch). They called themselves Chiche Capon, and by then they had become possibly the best-known clown trio in France. They had flown to America as featured performers in a theater festival.

I have never seen a crowd conquered so quickly. Within ten minutes, the room was laughing joyously. By the midpoint, audience members were yelling at the stage, addressing the clowns by name. As a climax, the clowns induced the crowd to pass Patrick over their heads. It felt like a rock concert. Afterward, the whole audience spontaneously assembled in the lobby and paraded to a bar up the street, the clowns leading the way.

BY MIDAFTERNOON in André's workshop, I felt I had a rough idea of what clown training entailed. But the psychological mind-set was still difficult to grasp. On the way to find some clowns willing to talk about their experience, I stopped by the bathroom, where I found a red clown nose resting in the soap basin.

It felt like a windfall. Like the oversized shoes, the famous red nose originated in a character trait and grew over time. Back in the English pantomime shows, when the "clown" often represented a rustic peasant with a fondness for alcohol, a few performers added a spot of red paint to their noses to indicate drunkenness. With the passage of time, the feature grew more prominent. Historically, few of the great clowns wore red noses: not Tabarin, Grimaldi, Footit and Chocolat, Grock, two out of the three Fratellini brothers, Chaplin, Keaton, Laurel and Hardy, the Three Stooges, or Jacques Tati. But the nose became a cultural signifier nonetheless, and among modern clowns it was nearly sacrosanct. The clowns at the workshop treated their noses with almost talismanic power. They put on their noses when they were about to inhabit their clowns, and took them off when the exercises were finished. "I think of the nose as the dividing line between myself and my clown," one said to me.

For all the noses I had seen, I had never worn one or even touched one. The nose in the bathroom was squishier than I had imagined, like a dog's chew toy. There were a pair of small holes in the bottom to breathe out of, and a string of elastic dangling off the back. Whether modern clowns performed in a nose or not, many of them liked training in noses—what Lecoq called "the smallest mask in the world"—because they felt less inhibited, more free.

Drawing back the elastic band, I slipped the nose over my head and looked at myself in the mirror. Something about the nose's roundness softened my features. It eliminated the angles on my face and made my eyes look bigger and gentler, more childlike. Picturing André and his deranged-rooster impersonation, I pushed my shoulders back and waggled my head. I looked less like a rooster than a pigeon.

But I strutted around anyway, winging my arms, jutting my head forward and back. My pigeon lacked André's dynamism, but it was goofy and playful and pleasing. A smile stretched from beneath my red nose.

In the lobby, I asked a few clowns how much this playfulness was part of the appeal for them.

"Oh, absolutely," said Franky, the egg-juggling clown. He had the shaggy look of an aging surfer. Dark ringlets fell over his temples, and silver hoops hung from his ears. Until his early thirties, Franky had worked as a mime, mostly in the streets of France, Spain, and the Balkans. He had made the jump to clowning six months ago and was feeling good about it.

"I'm just beginning to learn, but so far being a clown is great," he said. "You can do things you never thought possible. Scream, laugh, jump, cry. Being a clown is all about following your instincts."

Another clown added, "I'm hungry, so I want a sandwich. I'm thirsty, so I want something to drink. I want to have sex, so I have sex."

Franky was smiling and nodding. "That's right. As kids we behave this way normally—we're open to the world and to ourselves. Then, as we get older, we adopt roles and responsibilities. You have to be a good husband. You have to be nice to your boss. Be strong, be sociable, be a success." Being a clown, he said, lets a person shed all those roles, what Lecoq called the "social masks." "A clown is *supposed* to be ridiculous. He's *supposed* to be nasty and selfish and incompetent."

"It sounds cathartic," I suggested.

Franky mulled over the word. Yes, he agreed, it was cathartic. But there was something else going on, too, something deeper and possibly related to the unique kind of laughter a clown evokes. A clown, he explained, is supposed to fail. This was a golden rule of the craft, what Lecoq calls *le bide*, or "the flop." By failing, a clown makes the audience feel superior.

But a clown can't just fail senselessly. "You can't fake anything," Franky said. "The relationship with the audience is too close. They can tell." Or as the famous Swiss clown Dimitri has written, "The clown is the most naked of all artists because he risks all of himself, without the possibility of cheating. To avoid deceiving the public, he must be authentic, to sense always the impression that he is not offering enough."

Which is where the training comes in. "Our whole lives, we're basically trained not to be vulnerable, not to expose ourselves, to avoid looking foolish," Franky said. Getting in touch with your "inner clown" is all about tearing that artifice away, about becoming open to failure and in the process also more open to yourself.

This feels good on a personal level, but it's also essential for triggering a response in the audience. According to Lecoq, a clown doesn't evoke laughter through sheer failure. Failure alone is tragic, a dramatic experience that, as Aristotle says, evokes pity and fear. A clown converts the tragic into comedy by showing the audience that he is aware of his failure and that he *accepts* it. This triggers empathy.

Chaplin was a master at this. However bizarre or unfortunate his character's situation, he accepted it as the way of the world and did what he could to resolve it. (Think of him playfully eating a shoelace while starving.) Because his suffering didn't seem permanent or hurtful, the audience had permission to laugh.

As a clown, Franky said, he wasn't so much reveling in childishness as cultivating this same sense of equanimity. "It's intensely scary to embrace your failure, but it's also kind of freeing." Like a lot of clowns, he felt that he was experiencing himself in a new and potentially more authentic way. "It's nice to be yourself."

The aim of modern clowning isn't so different from that of other modern forms, like Jérôme Thomas's juggling, or Les Arts Sauts on the trapeze. In all of these cases, performers took pleasure in the circus's possibilities for expression and exploration. They found a chance to gain access to something in themselves. The only difference was the medium. Whereas some send balls or their own bodies into the air, clowns traffic in raw emotion.

Franky nodded. "Yeah, that's probably right." Around us, the other clowns were drifting back to the theater for their final lesson. "But, you know, there's a big difference, too," he added. Acrobatics, he pointed out, takes a certain physical agility. "A guy who's three hundred pounds—he's going to have a hard time doing a back flip." But clowning is open to everyone, from the youngest to the oldest, the fattest to the thinnest. "Everybody has a clown inside him," Franky said with a smile. "It just takes a little work to find it."

18

Circus City

FOR SPRING BREAK most of my fellow circus students headed home—to elsewhere in France, to Brazil, Sweden, Holland. I settled for Montreal. Outside of France, no city had succumbed to the modern circus fever so completely. Most notably, Montreal housed the headquarters of Cirque du Soleil, the biggest, most influential modern circus in the world. Additionally, the city claimed several internationally acclaimed troupes (the Cirque Éloize, Les 7 Doigts de la Main), Canada's only official "national" school (L'École Nationale de Cirque, founded in 1981), and one of the world's largest contemporary circus festivals (Montréal

Complètement Cirque). In 2004, in an effort to become "one of the circus capitals of the world," the city helped finance a $73-million "Cité des Arts du Cirque," an immense circus campus in a 119-acre former quarry and garbage dump. As well as new facilities for Cirque du Soleil and the national school, the site featured the Tohu, a one-ring building constructed purposely to host modern circus shows. It was the first such building in the world.

I went because of Pascal. As I've said, in addition to being one of the foremost circus historians in the world, Pascal is also one of the art's most dedicated fans, and an avid collector of circus memorabilia. For years, one portion of the collection filled Pascal's closets. Another was housed in a meeting room at HorsLesMurs, a circus advocacy organization in Paris. Then, in 2004, the Tohu offered to display part of Pascal's collection. They also offered to house the collection in its entirety in a vault in Montreal. And so, with the help of the official packer for the Louvre, Pascal spent a week parceling his collection into forty-five wooden crates, each the size of a piano, and then watched them depart across the Atlantic.

Pascal was melancholy that his collection was so far away. But he thought it was worth it, a first step toward exhibition. Montreal had agreed to fly him over annually to tend to the items. Joining him on this trip, I would have a rare opportunity to observe firsthand the crown jewels of the art.

THE RÉSERVE DES MUSÉES MONTRÉALAIS, the repository for Montreal's most prestigious art collections as well as Pascal's trove, is a nondescript warehouse in the city's Old Port district. I met Pascal there on the icy morning after our arrival. The historian was typically dapper: he wore a crimson velvet tie under a black silk dinner jacket, a black belt over black slacks. To the click of his leather shoes on the cement floor, we entered the building and progressed into a massive hallway. Pascal outlined the plan for the weekend.

We would spend the morning, he said, in the vault, organizing his collection and selecting objects for the next exhibition. Tomorrow, we would install them. I had also arranged an afternoon tour at the Soleil headquarters, a gigantic glass-and-steel building that looked like a space station from the highway. I expressed surprise at the building to Pascal. He shrugged. "Cirque doesn't deal with people anymore. They deal with governments."

We arrived at a pair of tall steel doors. Pascal rapped, and we entered a room of startling enormity, with twenty-foot-high ceilings. There were wooden packing cases and bubble-wrapped frames everywhere, on the ground and piled onto sturdy metal shelves. I followed Pascal to the center of the room, where Sophie, the director of collections at the Tohu, stood near a flotilla of crates branded with the silhouette of a lion and the name of Pascal's company, Panem and Circenses.

After a quick discussion, the pair began to haul objects from the shelves and unpack them on the table. Earlier, Pascal had proudly noted that his collection covered a wide swath of circus history—of subjects, types, and time periods—and the items appearing quickly verified his claim. There was a black top hat made of brushed horsehair. There was a diatonic Wheatstone concertina. Pascal brought out a brass statuette of a clown, then a poster from Fellini's 1954 masterpiece, *La Strada*. "Most collectors wouldn't collect something like this," he said, removing the poster from the bubble. "But Fellini liked the circus. He knew people from the circus—he knew the families."

As the duo worked, I raced around the room like a kid on Christmas morning. Most artifacts were sheathed in bubble wrap and labeled with a few tantalizing words. "Clown Medrano," said one box. "Boulevard pantomime," read a frame. Unable to resist, I found myself stretching the plastic wrapping for glimpses of the wonders within. And what wonders! In a stack of framed posters I found a woodcut broadside for Astley's Royal Amphitheatre. Then I stumbled onto an official portrait of Jules Léotard, taken in his early twenties, when he was at the height of his fame.

It's hard to describe how the objects made me feel. It was as if all the history I had read and heard about, all the names, all the stories, were here collected in a single room. Individually, the objects had a power that was almost talismanic: connecting each person's name to a physical presence made all their lives seem more real. It occurred to me how much my interest in the past had been an exercise in imagination. Even my ghost-hunting trips, my attempts to root out the past, had failed. Now I felt like some foreign scholar of Renaissance painting, who—after never seeing a Leonardo or Botticelli—one day finds himself in the basement of the Louvre.

Reflecting on the experience, I came to appreciate Pascal's passion more fully than I ever had. He claimed that the drive to collect was a natural impulse. "Even before the circus I liked collecting," he once told me. "Fossils. Shells. Whatever I could find." But there was a deeper motivation as well. The world couldn't be bothered with circus history. This had been proved to me time and again. Pascal's passion was a response to this destruction of the past. He was on a mission to gather together what had survived and keep it safe.

ACROSS THE STREET from the Tohu, the lobby of Soleil's headquarters exploded in light, the resplendent sun pouring through the high glass walls. Behind a high counter, a receptionist clamped a phone to her ear. "Cirque du Soleil, *bonjour.*" There was a pause. *"D'accord."* She hung up and peered at me. "Chantal's on her way."

Chantal was Chantal Côté, Soleil's head of public relations. With the items safely delivered to the Tohu, I had slipped across the street for a tour. By any practical measure, Soleil was the biggest, most profitable, most influential circus that had ever existed. It had catapulted itself from humble beginnings as a troupe of circus radicals to become one of Canada's biggest companies, with a four-thousand-person staff and annual revenues approaching $1 billion. In more than twenty-five years of existence, Soleil had played to over seventy million people on every continent but Antarctica, and in the process utterly changed the understanding of circus around the world. "They legitimized the circus," Ed LeClair, the executive director of Cirkus Smirkus, an American youth circus, told me. "They got it out of the carny attitude and helped people understand it could be a beautiful art form."

In the early days, when Soleil was just a bunch of longhairs from Montreal, the company received a torrent of criticism for its novelty. "For many tradition-bound fans perplexed by the theatricality and outraged by its lack of animals, Cirque du Soleil is nothing more than an upstart hybrid," Ernest Albrecht wrote in his 1995 book, *The New American Circus.* Today the criticism comes from the other side, from "the moderns," especially in France, where the prevailing opinion of the company hovers between suspicion and outright scorn. Specific complaints vary. The pay, some say, is low for the work. Others claim the performers are treated like disposable cogs: worked, worn down, and then cast off in favor of younger, trimmer recruits. More generally, the company is chided for its "American" (read: commercial) approach to the craft. I heard it called a "circus factory," a "circus machine," and the "Hollywood circus."

By the time of my visit, I knew enough about both the circus and the French to take such opinions with a mound of salt. The company is hardly a sweatshop. On the road, performers travel with amenities that would have made an elite acrobat weep for joy just twenty years ago: high-end caterers and masseuses at your beck and call, comprehensive health insurance, superb hotel rooms, personalized coaches recruited from the Olympian echelons of sport and fitness. The money is good, and sometimes great. A juggler can make six figures and retire to Switzerland.

And yet, lingering in the lobby, I found myself feeling cynical. The building, as I said, looked industrial. Everything was too perfectly polished. Waiting for Chantal, I watched a line of hale corporate types and a few acrobats swipe their badges with efficient aplomb through turnstiles at the entrance. Clearly, the company represented a vastly different model from any that had come before. But had the model betrayed its roots? Were these headquarters the base from which Soleil stalked and destroyed the poor, artful circuses of Paris and the rest of the world?

"You must be here for the tour!"

I looked up. Chantal, a small, pert woman in casual Friday attire, stood on the other side of the turnstiles. Her hands were open in a gesture of generosity.

"Welcome to Cirque!" She was smiling.

I beamed back. "It's great to be here!"

And away we went.

IN THE HOLLYWOOD VERSION of the modern circus story, the birth of Soleil in 1984 is often considered the moment when the circus as an art form rushes headlong into modernity and the present boom. In fact, the shift started almost twenty years before.

By the mid-sixties, the circus was mostly in the doldrums. In Paris, the Medrano was slipping into financial insolvency under the Bougliones. Across Europe, troupes were packing up their tents and selling their animals at auction (and, in a few egregious cases, abandoning them by the side of the road). The few shows that survived were relegated to cultural irrelevance. "The blindness of critics and the media to the art of the Circus fills me with despair," circus writer George Speaight complained. Even the most die-hard circus lovers were skeptical. How long could the circus survive?

Unbeknownst to these doubters, big changes were afoot. As part of the social upheaval sparked by boycotts and brick-heaving students, boundaries between high and low cultural forms were crashing down. Andy Warhol painted soup cans and pop icons. Rock and roll had won out. In the theater, directors such as Peter Brook and Joseph Chaikin staged shows in abandoned factories and warehouses, in public squares and swimming pools. In Vermont, the Bread and Puppet Theater company performed politically charged parades with human-sized puppets. In England, the Footsbarn Travelling Theatre began touring in a tent.

Many of these artists were drawn to circus. In 1970, Peter Brook staged a circus-arts-inspired *Midsummer Night's Dream* with the Royal Shakespeare Company, with fairies swooping in on trapezes and Bottom transitioning into a clown rather than an ass. Some theater companies integrated so much physicality and circus into their performances that those skills came to define their shows. The San Francisco Mime Troupe leaned on juggling and the clownish techniques of commedia dell'arte to make political criticisms.

Soon, full "new circus" companies began to emerge, troupes interested in remaking the circus itself. There was no official first such company, but the Cirque Bonjour, founded in 1971 by Jean-Baptiste Thiérrée and Victoria Chaplin, daughter of Charlie Chaplin, is often cited as seminal. Accompanied by their pet rabbit, the duo toured France in a little tent, performing a simple, poetic mix of circus skills, puppetry, theater, and magic—"a circus of lightness," as one critic said.* In Belgium, the Cirque du Trottoir took to the road in 1972. A year later, Christian Taguet, a young Parisian with a background in theater, acrobatics, and music, assembled a group of eclectic performers under the name Puits aux Images.

Once the movement took hold, foreign artists observed the phenom-

* The pair make a brief, magical appearance in Fellini's *The Clowns*: Chaplin runs the bubble machine; Thiérrée, who wears a magician's cape, seizes a bubble between two fingers and taps it with a ball-peen hammer.

enon while traveling in Europe and carried the flame back home. In 1975, a pair of married acrobats, Peggy Snider and Larry Pisoni, created the Pickle Family Circus in San Francisco. In Australia, the Soapbox Circus combined with the New Circus to create Circus Oz in 1977. By the late seventies, critics had come up with a name for the genre: the *nouveau cirque*, or "new circus." The term is something of a misnomer. For starters, referring to the movement as "new" discounts the advances that had already been made in Russia. But the term also implies a false universality. Among the groups emerging during the period, there were of course similarities: most were small, usually fewer than a dozen people; most eschewed the use of animals, for moral as well as economic reasons. But there were vast differences, too: some performed for children, others for adults; some worked in tents, others in theaters.

Most striking were the differences in ambition. The "new circuses" were a reaction to the codes that the circus had followed in the previous decades, but they had very different ideas about how to react. On one end of the spectrum were the "neoclassical" or "nostalgic" circuses, such as the Big Apple Circus in New York or the German Circus Roncalli, created by Bernhard Paul and André Heller in 1976. These companies attempted to develop not a circus of the future but an idealized circus of the past, classical one-ring "European-style" shows with ringmasters in red jackets and riding boots, complete with trained horses and dogs.*

On the other end of the spectrum were the true "modern" circuses, troupes hoping to create shows that expressed the challenges and thrills of their time. One example is Archaos, the French "circus of character." Founded as Cirque Bidon in 1975 by Paul Rouleau and Pierrot Bidon, the company began as an archly traditional outfit, with twenty-five horses and caravans that toured the villages of France and Italy. By the eighties, however, the troupe had reversed course completely and looked like something out of a dystopic future. Clowns stomped around in leather armor and corrugated metal helmets. Acrobats roared in on motorcycles and in Mack trucks. Many of their shows were politically or socially provocative. One celebrated piece was entitled *Beau comme la guerre* (*Beautiful as War*). Another, *Metal Clown*, told the history of Brazil, including its slave rebellion, through Capoeira dancing set to heavy metal. When

* Some shows, like the Big Apple Circus, use only domesticated animals, such as horses and dogs.

Archaos played Paris, tickets sold out months in advance. In 1990, when the company squatted at Cirque d'Hiver, their event threw the neighborhood into bedlam. It wasn't kid stuff. (One Archaos program, with tongue firmly in cheek, advised pregnant women to sit near the exits: the show's unpredictability could induce labor.) The company aspired to create a circus for adults—especially young, cool, urban adults—and by all accounts they succeeded spectacularly.

As Archaos was budding in France, a group of scraggly street performers gathered across the ocean in a bar in Baie-Saint-Paul, a little town near Montreal, hatching plans for a circus of their own. Several of the performers, including Guy Caron and Guy Laliberté, had seen the burgeoning action in Europe. Their tastes fell between the new and the classical. They liked the modern troupes, but also the refined one-ring shows like Switzerland's traditional Circus Knie. They longed to create a local company that captured the best of both worlds: the whimsy of the past coupled with the theatrical techniques of the future.

In 1983 they got their chance. To celebrate the 450th anniversary of Jacques Cartier's "voyage of discovery," Quebec announced a series of cultural events across the province. The young crew approached the government with a plan. Laliberté, the spokesperson for the group, was all of twenty-three. His primary professional qualification was the ability to blow a mouthful of kerosene over a raging torch. He wore a ponytail so long it knocked against his backside when he walked. Fortunately, Montreal is known for its lovable eccentricity, and Laliberté is nothing if not persuasive. And so the government agreed to fund a thirteen-city tour to the tune of $1.7 million. The group adopted a moniker that Laliberté had devised while staring at the sun on a beach in Hawaii: Cirque du Soleil.

The first year went well enough. According to plan, the company trouped across Canada with their classically modern show—mostly traditional acts embellished with touches of futuristic fantasy and a loose story. Audiences responded well to the combination: carried by solid reviews, the company rolled into Montreal in the black.

But the venture wasn't all sunshine. In preparation for another tour, Laliberté, by now the de facto business leader of the group, jetted off to Europe, where he plunked down a $10,000 down payment on a new fifteen-hundred-seat tent (twice as big as he was advised to buy), plus

$2 million in contracts. To cover costs, the circus expanded its tour, adding stops in Toronto and Niagara Falls. But this time, the crowds failed to materialize, despite positive reviews. The company limped back to Montreal $750,000 in the hole.

In the United States, where cultural ventures live and die by their ledgers, this would have ended Soleil. But the circus lived under a sheltering Francophone sky, and at a crucial juncture in Quebec history: French Canadian identity was a hot topic; a critically acclaimed local circus led by French-speakers appealed to the powers that be. Moved by the company's plight, the provincial government refinanced the troupe and retired the debt.

But the circus couldn't keep relying on government largesse. What it needed was sustained commercial appeal. As luck would have it, the troupe lived across the border from the richest market in the world, the United States, still largely untapped by the circus frenzy that had seized Europe. Based on its strong reviews, Soleil finagled an invitation to the 1987 Los Angeles Arts Festival. The gig was potentially lucrative, but there were no guarantees; to appear, the company would have to spend its entire budget traveling to Los Angeles and paying for marketing. If Soleil had flopped then, it might have disappeared forever.

As it turned out, the appearance of Soleil in Los Angeles created a sensation unprecedented in circus history, potentially rivaled only by the arrival of Barnum in New York a hundred years before. Within days, the city was abuzz with word of the strange new circus. Steve Martin, Elton John, Francis Ford Coppola, and other celebrities flocked to see it. Tickets—fifty-five thousand in total—sold out weeks in advance. "It was beyond our wildest expectations," a musician from that first American tour told me. "It was like *we* were the stars."

Every circus needs a hook. For neoclassical circuses, the appeal lay in nostalgia and nebulous "warmth." Modern shows like Archaos offered energy, shock, and politics. Soleil produced something else, which it learned from Hollywood: glamour. A circus, its directors realized, could be swanky and fine, with VIP rooms and valet parking. Soleil was a throwback to the extravagant circodramas of the Belle Époque, where audience members wore fur and pearls, elephants slid down waterslides, and acrobats lacking "irreproachable freshness" could be fired on the spot.

NOBODY AT SOLEIL HEADQUARTERS looked older than forty. Everyone I saw carried a bottle of water or a clipboard. The vibe was equal parts Hollywood movie studio and Olympic qualifying trials. Passing through a narrow hallway, we emerged into one of the company's training facilities, Studio E, a vast gymnasium at least twice as big as the Great Hall back in Paris. "Wow," said Chantal, tipping her chin back to take in the space. "We're a little busy today!"

And indeed they were. High and low, the hall crackled with acrobatic action. Directly in front of us, a group of women, either tumblers or contortionists, stretched on the floor, their limber legs splayed. Above, a brood of broad-shouldered men hung from a trapeze rigging; I determined from their pythonic arms that they were catchers.

Chantal let me admire the scene for a second and then got down to business. We talked about how the company created its one-of-a-kind shows. After its initial triumph in Los Angeles and the successful subsequent tour, the troupe found itself at a crossroads. Typically, circuses developed new shows according to one of two models. Most traditional circuses followed what you might call a piecemeal approach: each season, the producer purchased complete acts, which he cobbled together in a few weeks, adding lights, sound, and some minimal choreography. Modern troupes took a more theatrical approach. Rather than temporarily hiring performers for individual acts, a resident ensemble created its own shows from scratch, which it toured for as long as possible. When the market lost interest, or when the company grew bored, it started over, developing a new show for the same performers. This was the model of the majority of the companies in France. The emphasis was on artistry and collective experience.

Initially, Soleil was torn about which way to go. Guy Caron, the first artistic director, wanted to follow the modern European circuses. Guy Laliberté, more business-minded, argued for a hybrid: Every season, Soleil would create an original show, and hire performers as needed. He thought profits should be reinvested in the business, allowing the company to create new shows, which could tour simultaneously with the first.

After much discussion, Laliberté won out, and his model is in use to this day. As Chantal explained in Studio E, each new show begins as an idea of one of the company founders. With the assistance of a director, usually imported from theater or the film industry, the idea is fleshed out with themes, characters, and costumes. When the concept is complete, a few pre-existing acts are purchased and added, whole-hog. Most acts, however, are created in-house by the company's team of directors and coaches, and taught to Soleil's on-staff performers.

The system isn't totally original: the Russians did something similar at the Studio. But Soleil brought the system west and reproduced it on a massive scale. Performing in Los Angeles, the circus started pumping out shows. In 1985, it hired Franco Dragone, a former commedia actor and professor at the National Circus School in Montreal. In 1990, he directed *Nouvelle Expérience,* a Jules Verne–inspired fantasy. Two years later, the company premiered *Saltimbanco,* a darker fantasy, also directed by Dragone, starring artists from fifteen countries.

From a business perspective, the decision to tour multiple productions at once was the best move the company ever made. Each new show solidified Soleil financially by dispersing risk through an additional revenue stream. (Archaos, by contrast, was crippled when a storm destroyed its tent in Dublin.) And because Soleil owned the rights to their material, they avoided paying hefty royalties. In the event of an injury, advanced age, or a nasty contractual dispute, one performer could be dropped for another. Shows could tour ad infinitum.

As you might imagine, however, the system also provoked much disparagement. Keith Nelson, co-founder of the Bindlestiff Family Cirkus, once referred to Soleil as the "Walmart of circuses." The performers weren't real artists, other critics complained, just painted gymnasts culled from abroad, from Russia and China. "They go to Russia and say, Hello, we're from Cirque du Soleil! Wouldn't it be wonderful to work for Cirque du Soleil?" Dominique Jando said in the Clown Bar. "They pay them a few hundred dollars a week, use them for a couple of years, and then toss them out."

Obviously, some of these complaints are misinformed. The average Soleil performer isn't any more an automaton than any actor working in a play, or any singer in an opera. Still, observing the scene in Studio E, I wondered if some of the criticisms had merit. The energy of the hall was unlike anything I had experienced in France. The bodies were bigger; the equipment was shinier. The hum in the air was unmistakably one of efficiency. There was also something notably Slavic about the performers—the blond hair, the light eyes set behind attractive mantel cheekbones. In front of us, a group of men were huddled around a coach who spoke to them in Russian while gesticulating forcefully at a television. A Russian bar lay on the floor next to them. At the back of the group a wiry man in a blue-and-white tank top stood with his hands on his hips; RUSSIA, the shirt said.

I asked Chantal: how did the company turn foreign gymnasts into first-rate performers?

"You know, that's a real issue for us," she replied, squinting to indicate her seriousness. "A lot of the training is mental. When recruits come to us from sports, they arrive with a competitive mind-set. They try to impress each other, dueling to see who can jump the highest or be the strongest, that sort of thing. We encourage them to take a more collaborative approach, an approach more focused on the audience."

I asked her for an example.

"Oh, there are all sorts of little ways," she replied. "We're very conscious of environment, for example. Like this . . ." She reached up behind us and tugged at a black curtain hanging over the doorway. "This was a recent addition."

I reached up and stroked the curtain. It was velvet.

"It's a curtain," I said.

Chantal nodded. "That's right. It communicates they've entered a theatrical environment."

I felt my eyes move between the curtain and the hall of burly gymnasts.

"Of course, that's just an example," Chantal added quickly.

"Okay."

"Most of our work is centered on helping them develop the tools necessary to connect to an audience—their voices, their sense of rhythm, how they use their eyes. In a performance, the goal is communication as an instrument; we teach them how to reach off the stage and really grab somebody."

It wasn't hard to imagine the French response: *Bof!* You can teach a bear to dance but it is still, *hélas,* just a bear! Where is the art? *La créativité?* But I opted not to press Chantal on the issue. It was beside the point. Soleil was trying to make performers, not artists.

The Russians in front of us were on the move. The little fellow in the RUSSIA tank top led the charge. Behind him, his beefy compatriots marched in pairs. One of the men held a Russian bar, a flexible balance beam, like a spear. From somewhere in the ceiling, a line of classical music, vaguely Wagnerian, drifted into the space.

"But of course it's not entirely up to us," Chantal remarked, apparently oblivious to the gathering action. "The performers have to take creative responsibility for themselves, and we try to leave room for that."

I watched the Russians. The little one had stepped onto the bar, which the bigger men were hoisting onto their shoulders.

"Dancers, for example, can become dance captains. At that point they are in charge of an entire team and can suggest changes in the choreography."

The little Russian started to bounce, low at first, then higher, landing on the bar each time.

"Or take Viktor Kee, the juggler. He was a relentless artist, always tweaking his routine. And we encouraged that! Whenever he proposed changes, we said, Sure, go ahead."

The Russian was really going at it now, rocketing himself skyward. He flew ten, maybe twenty feet in the air, his tank top rippling.

"Of course, it's in our best interest to help our performers stay interested. If you're willing to grow, we'll help you. But, let's also be honest, the circus is a job. And like any job . . ."

Now the little Russian had launched into the meat of his routine, a series of impossibly difficult flips and twists. His lean body sliced the air. Each time he landed, the big men bent at the knees to receive him, then launched him skyward again.

I had never witnessed anything like it. In the circus smorgasbord, the Russian bar is a standard *entrée*. But in height, difficulty, and execution, the little Russian was an order of magnitude better than anybody else I'd seen. His form was flawless: his body was perfectly arched, his toes were tightly pointed. With each trick, I felt my eyes widen and my breath shorten.

Soleil is a throwback to the Belle Époque in more ways than one. In addition to glamour, what Soleil offers is what the circus has always offered: refined demonstrations of human mastery, exquisite bodies engaged in beautiful achievement, what French writer and dramatist

Théophile Gautier called "an opera for the eye." For decades the circus had lost sight of this appeal, had buried it in cliché. Building on the legacy of Soviet circus, itself inspired by ballet, Soleil resurrected virtuosity and proved that people still responded strongly to it. And if they went to Russia or China to find performers to do this—well, that's because the Russians and Chinese did it best.

BACK IN THE HALLWAY, our tour picked up speed. In the makeup room, where another Slavic beauty was marking black spears on her forehead, Chantal informed me about Soleil's official policy regarding facial design: performers get step-by-step instructions and precise visual patterns to follow; the pre-show prep can take upward of ninety minutes. From there it was on to the costume shop, where Chantal told me that, on any given night, the company employs more than forty-five hundred costumes. Every costume is made at headquarters by a team of more than four hundred lace-makers, milliners, and wigmakers. No other circus troupe comes close to Soleil in terms of size and production capacity. With forty members, including performers, cooks, musicians, administrative staff, and children, Les Arts Sauts is considered a sizable company in France. Soleil's costume shop alone is ten times larger.

Chantal stopped in front of a glass display case in the hallway. "Here," she said chipperly, "you'll appreciate this." On the shelves of the case were a curly black wig, a pinstriped jail uniform, and a pair of blue suede shoes. "It's the Elvis team," Chantal said.

Ah yes, Las Vegas. Hollywood had made the company famous, but Vegas made them ludicrously, bombastically rich.

Soleil's relationship with the city dates from 1993. After almost a decade of touring, the company announced that a new show, *Mystère*, would premiere in Sin City. That Soleil would play Las Vegas wasn't unusual. Jugglers and acrobats had long been featured in casino variety shows. In 1968, Jay Sarno, creator of Caesar's Palace, opened Circus Circus, a popular hotel and casino, featuring indoor circus acts and carnival games. (Writing in 1980, at the pit of the circus doldrums, Speaight observed in *A History of the Circus*, "It is an eloquent indictment of our civilization that this beautiful display of choreographed skill has found it most profitable to appear as a kind of aerial sideshow at Las Vegas, coaxing a passing glance from the gamblers on the floor below.") What was startling, however, was Soleil's plan: not only would the show premiere in Vegas, it would *never leave*. As part of a ten-year deal with Steve Wynn, the casino magnate remaking the city, the company would install *Mystère* as a "resident show" in a custom-renovated theater at the Treasure Island hotel. It would be, in essence, a stable circus, like the Medrano in Paris or the circuses dotting Russia, except the acts wouldn't change.

"They said we were crazy," noted Chantal, referring to the circus community. The show, which was directed by Dragone, was darker and moodier than any of the previous shows. On seeing the first dress rehearsals, Wynn was apparently irate. "You guys have made a German opera here," he told Laliberté. (Dragone took it as a compliment.)

The skeptics failed to take into account the city's burgeoning transition from Mafia-run casino den to America's Shangri-la. Every week, millions of visitors flocked to the city from all over the world with money to burn. What better show to attract these tourists than a circus, the universal spectacle? Put another way, Vegas was for Soleil as New York was for Barnum. It was the opposite of the touring tented circus. Instead of traveling to the people, Soleil would let the crowds come to them.

And they did. From the premiere on December 25, 1993, *Mystère* did gangbusters business. The first season, the show played to 98 percent capacity. Today, the show continues to run after more than eight thousand performances, a Vegas record.

Quickly, the company moved to duplicate the "resident" model. In 1998, it installed *La Nouba,* from the French *faire la nouba* ("to live it up"), at the Walt Disney World Resort in Orlando. The same year, in another throwback to the glory days of the Belle Époque, they returned to Las Vegas with their first water circus, *O,* again directed by Dragone, now officially the company's muse.

By 2009, the circus was operating ten resident shows, more than they were touring, including seven in Las Vegas. Some, like *Zed,* the Tokyo-based show directed by film director François Girard, were pure circuses. Others, like *Viva Elvis,* the spectacle commemorated in the hallway display, are better described as "acrobatic theater," physical and visual phantasmagorias set to music. Collectively, they earn the lion's share of the company's profits, and the numbers are staggering. Sixty percent of Soleil's revenue comes from Vegas. The company's nightly takings there are greater than all of Broadway's nightly income combined. At one point, Soleil was netting over $1 million a night in Vegas alone.

Most of the circuses in France are essentially theater troupes, and sometimes "artistic circuses," nonprofit enterprises. But just as there are "art films" and commercial films, circuses exist in different registers. Soleil is a "commercial circus"—it is a business, or, as Chantal put it near the end of our tour, "an entertainment company." Like all businesses, it has the goal of making money, and it is transparent in its aim. Critics, especially in Europe, condemn Soleil for this approach. "It became this unstoppable commercial entity," said Chris Lashua, the director of Cirque Mechanics, an American modern circus company. "People started treating it like it was a job instead of a creative endeavor." And it's true there have been sacrifices. To justify the enormous costs of its productions, the Soleil shows have to be accessible to what the French call *"le grand public."* They can't be too challenging or disturbing, lest they risk alienating the public. "Cirque doesn't have a choice," Roger Le Roux, the director of the French Cirque-Théâtre d'Elbeuf, said. "It has to sell!"

Yet none of this diminishes Soleil's importance to the art or the legacy the company will leave. After all, the circus has always been a business, dating back to the merchants on the fairgrounds. Sometimes business worked against artistry; sometimes it worked in art's favor. Soleil's grow-or-die mentality is responsible for its influence, which has been huge and, thus far, for the good. In Europe, proactive governments enabled the new circus movement. The French state established the National School and subsidized experimental companies, as did governments in Belgium, England, Sweden, and a dozen other countries. Going forward, not all countries will have the ability or the will to support the circus like that. If the circus hopes to spread, it will have to pay its own way, fueled as much by entrepreneurs as by artists. Soleil proved that the circus is a viable economic enterprise.

What's curious for now is that Soleil is the only modern circus to achieve such financial success. Partly this is cultural. In Europe, there is a suspicion of commerce, especially among artists, and *especially* among circus artists, who often see themselves as countercultural. "There's a perception among a lot of the companies that money is dirty, is vulgar," Le Roux told me. Certain troupes avoid marketing themselves properly so as not to be perceived as shallow. In a few cases, troupes rejected growth altogether. According to several sources, Les Arts Sauts was approached by an important producer during their American tour. "He wanted us to stay a year," Laurence told me. He would leave the company creative control, but reproduce the existing show into multiple companies, to tour simultaneously. But Les Arts Sauts refused. "We told him to fuck off" was how Frank, the catcher, put it. "We're not going to sell out to the Anglo-Saxon system."

The creators of Soleil had a different attitude. Being Québecois, Chantal said, they were in a way able to straddle the divide between Europe and America. "They had the artistic sense of being Francophone, and North American marketing skills. That turned out to be a winning formula."

This confluence of values is epitomized in Laliberté. In skill and spirit, he is a circus genius of the oldest, rarest sort. Like Barnum, Laliberté was a born entrepreneur who skipped college to work the streets of Europe, stilt-walking and breathing fire.* Like Barnum, he has a mania for marketing and reputation: when the company first opened in Los Angeles, Laliberté insisted on spending an obscene amount of money plastering posters across the city. And his life, too, is one of Barnumesque proportions. As 95 percent shareholder of the company, he has a net worth, according to *Forbes* magazine, of approximately $2.5 billion, making him the eleventh-richest person in Canada and 459th-richest person in the world. He has houses in Montreal, Cancún, Moscow, and the French Riviera, which he circulates between by private jet. His bonhomie is legendary. Rumors abound of wild bacchanals populated by corporate scions, supermodels, Arab princes, Russian oligarchs, and the stars of sport and entertainment—parties that purportedly culminate in the host's blowing fire over the crowd. Bono, the lead singer of the rock band U2, once called Laliberté the "most alive" person he had ever met.

"Guy doesn't live on this planet," Pascal said. We were discussing Laliberté outside the company's headquarters. Pascal's words were ironic: as we spoke, Laliberté was in Moscow, training to become Canada's first space tourist, a privilege for which he had paid $35 million.

* Laliberté supposedly left his parents a note with a quote from Kahlil Gibran: "Your children are not your children. They are the sons and daughters of Life's longing for itself."

I brought up Barnum, how similar the two titans seemed. Pascal chuckled. Yes, he said, they had a lot in common. But in terms of circus history they don't compare—and it's Barnum who doesn't measure up.

Barnum & Bailey, he explained, came to England for the first time in 1889, then returned to Europe just eight years later to tour Austria, Germany, Belgium, France, and Italy. But the troupe never played South America or Australia. Nor did Ringling. In this context, Laliberté's achievements were all the more impressive. In his early fifties, the Canadian has already installed himself at the top of the art's pantheon.

"There's only one person who compares," Pascal said. By the sparkle in his eye, I could tell he was talking about Astley.

"Astley built nineteen circuses across Europe." He smiled wryly. "Guess how many shows Cirque will have next year?"

I didn't need to guess. It was nineteen.

THE FOLLOWING MORNING, I met Pascal in the large, sunlit lobby of the Tohu. Even more than Soleil's "resident" theaters, the Tohu is symbolic of the circus's return. A throwback to the hard circuses of yore, the building was round, with seventeen hundred seats wrapped around a single ring, and built exclusively for traveling circus shows, almost all of which are modern. Pascal's exhibit was housed in a curved passageway under the seats, also known as the *vomitoires*. (The word comes from the Roman Colosseum, the passages of which "vomited" the spectators out into the streets.) By the time I arrived, Sophie and a trio of assistants in white cotton gloves were already hard at work, unwrapping items from their bubble cocoons and mounting them in glass cases set into the hallway's interior wall.

As Pascal chatted with them, I roamed around, mooning over each item, taking pictures and notes, basking in the details. The exhibition was organized chronologically. Walking the length of it, I had the sense of traversing time. The highbrow splendor of the nineteenth century was represented by a poster of Footit and Chocolat at the Nouveau Cirque. From the Soviet period, there was a rubber doll of the famous clown Yuri Nikulin, who was awarded the title of People's Artist of USSR in 1973. Behind me, the voices of Pascal and the young women formed a sweet circus chorus.

"The Japanese juggler?"

"Over here."

"What about the Fratellini plate?"

"I'm not sure."

"You might check near Madame Saqui."

At the end of the exhibit, I came to a section labeled "Modern Era." The section began with a poster for Cirque du Soleil's *Nouvelle Expérience* and told the story of the spread of the modern circus through the nineties and into the new millennium. Soleil was an important part of the tale, but it wasn't the only game in town. A legion of other companies and artists had spread the gospel of the modern circus to heretofore unconquered lands. During the nineties, Pierrot Bidon, one of Archaos's founders, left France for Brazil, where he established Circo da Madrugada; he later went to Guinea, in West Africa, and created Circus Baobab, often considered the first modern circus on that continent. Around the turn of the millennium, jugglers began appearing on the streets of Buenos Aires, performing for change at stoplights, and during my year at France's National School, a group of students visited from Escuela Circo Para Todos, a circus school in Santiago de Cali, Colombia. "A few years ago, people in our little town had never even heard of circuses before," a tall, dreadlocked juggler told me. "If they did, it was something kind of dirty, low-class." But one day a group of French performers had shown up and started offering circus classes. "It wasn't like the circus we knew," the juggler said. "It was cooler, more interesting." The Colombian students had come to France to take a workshop, to bring even more of the modern circus spirit back home. "Next year some of us hope to create a company of our own."

In Australia, new troupes continued to form through the nineties, including Bizircus, a collective of acrobats and artists based near Perth. In 2001, the government helped create the National Institute of Circus Arts (NICA), a full-time university circus training school in Melbourne that offers a three-year bachelor's degree. Today the Australian circus scene is one of the most dynamic and vibrant in the world and, according to Pascal, the most innovative after France. The country has more than thirty-five circus companies. Circa, one of the most renowned troupes, has toured internationally, including to New York and London. *The Guardian* called its shows "knee-tremblingly sexy, beautiful and moving."

Several factors made these places fertile ground. In countries where governments provided funds for circus companies and schools, the circus thrived. In the best cases, the government established a professional training program, which generated a steady stream of elite performers who served as models for young people. Canada, Belgium, and Australia, for example, all have national schools—and strong circus.

It also helps if an impassioned individual decides to make the spread of the circus his life project, especially in countries where cultural funding is poor. In Croatia, for example, Ivan Kralj, a journalist turned circophile, paid for Zagreb's first contemporary circus festival out of pocket. In Prague, I watched local impresario Ondrej Cihlar perform in a contemporary circus festival that he helped found. At his apartment afterward, I flipped through a book he had written about the art while he described his vision for a contemporary circus institute (the Institut Nového Cirkusu). "It was slow at first," Cihlar said, rolling up his sleeves, "but people are starting to come around."

Oddly, though, with very few exceptions, the countries with the strongest modern circus scenes are countries with little circus legacy. Finland, for example, is doing quite well. In 2004, Parliament allocated part of the federal budget to circus support. According to critics, Finnish companies, including Circo Aereo, do some of the most sophisticated work in Europe. Some people credit the success, or a good chunk of it, to the work of a single man: Tomi Purovaara, director of the Finnish Circus Information Center, unofficially known as "Mr. Contemporary Circus." Purovaara himself attributes the progress to history—or lack thereof.

"We were blessed with a tabula rasa here," Purovaara said when I met him at the Helsinki headquarters of Cirko, an organization dedicated to spreading the circus in Finland. After the Finnish Civil War of 1918, he explained, the victorious conservatives levied a 40 percent "recreational tax" on venues where the working classes were likely to converge, including the circus, essentially eradicating the form for almost fifty years. "We had to build everything from scratch," he said, "but we also didn't have to tear anything down. We had no reputation to deal with. We could define the circus however we wanted."

Purovaara's comment came to mind as I examined the objects of Pascal's exhibit. Like Finland, Quebec had had a limited circus history. John Bill Ricketts, the father of American circus, established a building on the banks of the Saint Lawrence River in 1797, but he left after six months, and for centuries the province had never hosted a native company. When the modern circuses, including Soleil, emerged in the eighties, the lack of negative stereotypes around their work allowed them to convince authorities to give them funding and space.

But at some point Montreal's circus caretakers must have realized that practicing an art without understanding its history was a mistake. For a movement to continue to grow, for it to sustain itself and develop its own culture, it has to examine its tradition. Lacking a history of its own, Montreal bought one in the form of Pascal's collection. And it wasn't just any past. On display here in the hallway was the circus at its best. "I want them to see the cultural dimension," Pascal had said in the vault. He'd stooped and picked up a poster drawn by Jean Cocteau for the Medrano. "I want people to know that the circus could have produced something like this."

The circus of today is serious business—but so was it always. The mission of the exhibit was to ensure the link between the present and the past. This was made particularly clear to me as we were preparing to leave.

Waiting for Pascal in the lobby, I happened to notice a lantern dangling above the doors that led to the performance space. The lantern was old and antique-looking in a way that was at odds with the building's modern, nondescript décor. The glass bulb was cloudy, white, and tulip-shaped. Thin vines wrapped around it and connected to a brass chain that ran to the ceiling. When Pascal arrived, he cheerily told me that the lantern came from "Amiens," circus-lover's shorthand for the Cirque Municipal d'Amiens, one of the few remaining circus buildings in France and a totem in the circus world. Built in 1889, Amiens had been the passion project of Jules Verne, who fought to construct it and then delivered the inaugural address. ("The new circus is a work of art endowed by your municipal administration with every improvement of modern industry!")

"We liked the idea of a tangible connection between the old buildings and the new," Pascal said, gazing up at the lamp. "This building"—the Tohu—"is actually based on the old circuses in France. I was on the design committee. We wanted the building to be reminiscent of the old circuses of before, but also to be unique, to be alive." Stéphane Lavoie, the director of the Tohu, had told me that ten cities had sent emissaries to study the Tohu in the hopes of constructing hard circuses of their own.* "I like to think of it less as a copy than an echo," Pascal said. "The voice changes as it recedes, but there's always the essence of what came before."

* In 2007, Madrid converted an old cookie factory into the nineteen-hundred-seat Teatro Circo Price, named for the city's old circus.

19

Popular Art

AFTER SPRING BREAK, I returned to Paris to find an enormous circus tent in the school's courtyard. Henceforth, we were told, classes would be there instead of at the Great Hall. We spent the following Monday hauling over equipment—the mats, the trampolines—the big freshman Baptiste carrying the weight bench all by himself. There was no official explanation for the move. When I asked Anny, she said, "A circus school should take place in a tent." Personally, I thought the tent lacked the Great Hall's shabby warmth. Big and echoey, it was lit by a few harsh bulbs dangling from steel tensile chords.

Within a week, however, my opinion had altered. There was something energizing about the tent. Approaching the school through the suburbs, I was struck by the tent's incongruence and specialness. Training in it felt more authentic, somehow. You had a more direct connection to the elements. In between the mats you could feel the ground pressing against your feet. When it rained, you could hear the drops before you saw them. A tent wasn't just a space, it was a symbol, and as such it reinforced our collective purpose and imbued every activity with a kind of circus spirit: This handstand isn't just a handstand; it's a circus handstand.

It even felt like a promotion of sorts, another step in our acculturation. Participating in the circus, I'd concluded during my visit to Les Arts Sauts, was as much cultural as physical. It was as much what you wore and how you behaved as the particular tricks you learned. But I'd increasingly seen this in the students as well: I saw them dress more eccentrically, speak more philosophically. I grew less critical of the school's culture than I'd been, and even participated in it myself: I bought a colorful scarf and started rolling up the cuffs of my jeans; I walked around my apartment with my shirt off.

I never thought of this process as an "acculturation" at the time. I was participating, absorbing whatever attracted me or seemed to express part of me. It didn't occur to me that I was adopting a "style," and only rarely did I glimpse how my participation had affected my personality or the way I was perceived.

One such moment, however, came a week or so after we moved into the tent. We were visited by a group of neighborhood boys I had never seen before. They were intrigued by the sudden appearance of the tent over the school's ramparts. The boys were middle-school-aged, mostly of North African descent, sons of the immigrants who populated the apartment towers around us. The first day, they drifted as close as the courtyard. The next day, their numbers had swelled, and a few ventured to talk with some students juggling by the mouth of the tent. The third day, they came all the way inside. They sat on mats near the doorway, awestruck by the tent's volume.

It felt like a collision of worlds. To the boys, the students were exotic and extreme. They could manipulate their bodies in hard-to-fathom ways. They dressed in ratty, colorful garb, spoke in unfamiliar accents. I say "they" because I didn't count myself among them until one of the smaller boys approached me, his hair in a high Afro, walking with a swagger. He peppered me with questions: Could I do a back handspring? Could I do a back flip? Could I juggle? Had I flown on a trapeze? As I continued to answer yes, his eyes grew wider, until he finally, simply said, "Cool."

I still saw a huge difference between myself and the other students, the "real" acrobats. But to that boy I was part of the circus: an ordinary acrobat.

THIS SMALL ACKNOWLEDGMENT of my place in the circus world came at a pivotal time: the *concours*, the school's placement test, was less than a month away. Among our prep group, only Maud and Fanny were scheduled to take the exam. As Luc had predicted early in the year, pursuing degrees in philosophy and circus concurrently had distracted Boris, and so he had withdrawn his name. (He had also found another calling: during spring break, he flew to Vietnam, where he volunteered at a circus school run by his former coach, and now he wanted to go back. "They have a completely different sense of space over there," he said after his return. "You could build a show around it.")

My own plans for the test were less clear. Early in the year, I had surrendered any hopes of passing and accepted my role as what anthropologists call an observer-participant: I had come to study the circus, not to be in it. I presumed once more that I would return to the "normal world" and "normal life."

Yet now I found myself more seriously entertaining the thought of taking the test. A circus life seemed more attainable than it had. Meeting so many performers and students had shown me that the circus was always open, even to someone only ready to pursue it as an adult. The test had grown less intimidating to me as well. In the early spring, I noticed that the gap between myself and the other students had narrowed. By April, I had pulled even with Boris at tumbling and with Fanny on the trampoline. (I was putting in extra hours with Ryszard, who thought I was more dogged and ambitious than my French partners.) My odds of passing were low, but what if I got lucky?

With two weeks to go, this question came to a head of sorts when I hosted a little soirée at my apartment. I invited my cohorts in the prep program—Boris, Maud, and Fanny—as well as most of the freshmen and some friends from the city. By midnight, my third-story walk-up was rocking with the sort of party I had come to associate with the circus over the year. There was loud singing fueled by cheap red wine and hand-rolled cigarettes. There was ecstatic dancing punctuated with paroxysms of skillful acrobatics—handstands on the kitchen tile, break-dancing on the living-room rug.

In the mêlée, Maud, Fanny, and I found ourselves together on a couch and reminisced about the year. We talked about the professors and their quirks, about the girls' hopes for the upcoming test. Then, as the night was winding down, Fanny turned the question on me.

"So what about you?" she asked. She had paused next to Maud in the doorway to wrap her scarf around her neck, a buttress against the damp spring chill. Outside, dawn was breaking.

I asked her what she was talking about.

"The test," she said matter-of-factly. "Why aren't you taking it?"

I fidgeted. I didn't know how to respond. I asked her if she believed I had a shot. She shrugged a casual shoulder in reply.

"I don't see why not. We've all seen you improve. And you obviously care about it."

I was flattered. Only later did I realize that her words were an uncanny echo of what the beautiful trapezist had said to me years before, the words that launched me on this whole escapade: "I don't see why not."

And so I spent the next week thinking about it. I could have taken the test merely for the experience. But that seemed wrong somehow. The exam was a genuinely important moment for the applicants, and it felt selfish to diminish the process or risk distracting them. If I was going to take the test, I would have to take it for real. But what would happen if I passed? Was I willing to dedicate the next four years to training, and years after to performing? Did I want to be a circus performer?

After several late nights, I had my answer: I did not. I enjoyed imagining a circus version of myself, ten years down the road, buff and bare-chested, dangling from a trapeze with my buxom Ukrainian wife in my arms. But in truth I wasn't a performer, not in the way I needed to be. I did not like the idea of appearing publicly. Even executing a move in class felt pressurized. I couldn't imagine reproducing the move in a ring in front of a scrutinizing public. And training felt like a chore. I liked acrobatics, the trampoline especially, but I was too lacking in abandon to really excel at it. After a few months, my juggling obsession had faded as well.

Being a strong circus professional requires a special dedication, a commitment bordering on faith. Becoming a circus artist isn't like becoming a dentist or a real-estate agent. It's not a practical decision. You have to burn to do it. You have to risk losing yourself—to risk losing your life, even. Without this passion, it *is* possible to work as a professional: you can make a healthy, exciting, engaging living, with four-star hotels and international travel and, rumor has it, lots of very good sex. But you can't make art.

What I liked were the aesthetic and critical possibilities of the circus. I liked examining the form historically and understanding how it had evolved through time. I liked the sense of mission, the feeling that the history and the form itself were underrepresented and misunderstood—and the idea that I could change that. I even liked considering the business of the circus, and occasionally entertained visions of producing or directing. In short, I had intellectualized the art. I wasn't an artist.

Therefore, I decided to abstain from the test. I would attend instead as an observer, to cheer on Maud and Fanny and witness the selection of the next generation of circus stars. That was the right decision. Nevertheless, in the days after officially withdrawing from the test, I found myself feeling disappointed. My classes seemed suddenly arbitrary. Watching Maud and Fanny tumble in preparation, I again felt outside their world, as at the beginning of the year. I walked around with the suspicion that I had truncated my future in some horrible way. I believe Ryszard picked up on this, because in our last class he decided to offer me some consolation.

By now I had essentially adopted Ryszard as a surrogate uncle. Since the rough winter months, his life had perked up considerably. He had decamped from the janitor's closet into an apartment within biking distance of the school, while somehow managing to retain the house in Normandy. The cost of the house was still an issue, but the garden was in bloom, which made him happy. One weekend in April, he even took me out to see its progress. "Look at the spring lettuce and daffodils," he said, pointing with a tuft of weeds he'd just pulled. "A garden is like a mystery. You put in all this work and you never know what will come up." In happiness, I threw a few awkward back flips in his potato patch.

In the tent, we were still working on my back flips. The move consisted of two parts—jumping into the air and tucking my knees. I threw one flip after another, each sharper than the last. My knees pumped toward my chest. My rotation was tight with barely a touch from Ryszard. Without the pressure of the impending test, I found that I was able to release into the moves more freely, and so was performing them better.

At a certain point, my stomach muscles were wailing and my feet were stinging from the impact, so I paused to drink from my water bottle. When I returned, Ryszard was watching me with a peculiar, hard-to-fathom look, something between a smile and a smirk. I asked him what he was grinning about.

"I am thinking . . ." he began, before his smile widened. "I am thinking that if I have modern circus I take you. Maybe not if I have traditional circus. But for modern circus, yes."

He was impugning the technical quality of the modern circus, but I didn't care. For years to come I would cling to those words. I would remember that I had once been so close that a future in the circus could have been mine.

I bounded over and gave Ryszard a hug.

WITH A WEEK to go before the test, there was one last person that I wanted to meet, Bernard Turin, the director of the Centre National des Arts du Cirque (CNAC), the big-brother institution to my school in Rosny-sous-Bois.

I wanted to talk to Turin about the return of the circus in France, and about the role of the government in that return specifically. Although France's modern movement started of its own accord—with independent troupes and schools in the seventies—the government had been instrumental in recognizing and helping the movement to grow. "It's not a coincidence that we have so much circus," Jean-Michel Guy, a government representative himself, had told me early in the year. "We made this happen."

As director of the National School, Turin was in a special position to observe this government effort. In a certain sense, he was even a product of the effort himself. Before taking the reins at the school, he had worked as a professional sculptor, and the state had intentionally recruited him to supply the school with a more progressive vision, which he had done. According to some circus thinkers, including Jean-Michel Guy, Turin had even been responsible for launching the circus into another stage of development, its most recent stage, what has come to be known as "the contemporary circus." "Bernard was a *visionnaire*," Pascal told me. "All these questions, 'Is the circus art? Is it not art?' Bernard showed what an artful circus would look like. At the school, he created a lighthouse."

I met Turin in his work studio in Paris, a high-ceilinged room in a building of government-subsidized artist studios. In his sixties, he was round as a marshmallow, with a considerate, warm grandfatherly air. His beard was dusty white, and he wore a pair of wire-rim glasses, and, to my surprise, limped on a metal cane.

"It's only temporary," he explained, as we entered the space. "For my knee." He drifted over to a makeshift kitchen to prepare a pot of tea. I lingered in the entryway. Around me, framed articles and photos speckled the walls. Artistic debris littered the floor, fluorescent tubes and rolls of paper, soaked in a bright wash of sun that poured through skylights.

I asked him what happened.

At the end of the year, he said, he would be retiring. In preparation, he was readying his studio, so that he could take up sculpting again. "My first project was to redo the floor. All the kneeling put a weird pressure on my knee, and something popped. It's actually kind of funny, when you think about it. Ten years as circus director and I never get hurt." He smiled from the kitchen. "Turns out it's the art that's dangerous."

BY THE SEVENTIES, the traditional circus in France had reached its breaking point. Wracked by the 1973 oil embargo, which sent gas prices skyrocketing, the industry saw a rash of closings. The Cirque Medrano was demolished in 1973. In 1978, Cirque Jean Richard, one of France's biggest and best-known operations, threatened bankruptcy, an event of national magnitude. Rénée Sasso-Cuinat was special assistant to the minister of cultural affairs at the time. "You can't imagine how bad it had become," she told me. "Shows were literally abandoned, hordes of people and animals sitting by the side of the road in protest." In 1977, beset by rising debts and wary of the future, Alexis Gruss, Jr., head of one of the most venerated circus families in France, brought the suffering to the government's attention. The circus needed help.

In 1978, inspired by Gruss's plea, the government took action. Led by France's then president, Valéry Giscard d'Estaing, the state sanctioned the creation of an "inter-ministerial commission," a sort of circus think tank, composed of representatives of the ministries involved in the crisis (finance, education, culture, and agriculture). Charged with determining why the circus, once a mainstay of French popular culture, had degenerated to the point of near extinction, the commission ordered a series of studies, the results of which were clear: to survive, the industry would have to modernize. The commission ordered the creation of a fund, aptly titled "The Fund for the Modernization of the Circus." More symbolically, the commission transferred custody of the art from the Ministry of Agriculture, where it had wallowed because of the animals, to the Ministry of Culture.

That was in 1979. For two years the effort stalled. In 1981, François Mitterrand, a socialist, was elected president; overnight, cultural funding doubled. With the increased funding came a shift in emphasis. The state would now support all cultural output, not just high culture but popular forms as well, including jazz, rock music, graffiti, comic books, and fashion. Christian du Pavillon, author of a book on circus architecture and adviser to Jack Lang, the new minister of culture, was given responsibility for the circus. He proposed a three-pronged attack.

Part One: Promotion. To shine a light on the circus's importance to France's patrimony, the government would designate an official "National Circus of France." (For the first year they selected Alexis Gruss's Cirque à l'Ancienne, a "classical" equestrian circus.)

Part Two: Education. Like the other arts, du Pavillon argued, the circus needed an institute of higher education, a space to provide performer training of the highest caliber and serve as an incubator for theorizing the circus of tomorrow. As Jack Lang told an interviewer, "We knew there could be no future without education." The result was the National School.

Part Three: Support. Going forward, the government would subsidize the circus as it subsidized other arts. Some of the money would go to the traditional companies for equipment and touring support. The rest would aid the new work being produced by the *nouveaux cirques,* such as Archaos.

This last point was particularly important. In deciding to accept the circus as an art rather than a business, the government changed fundamentally and forever the landscape of the circus in France. With state support, companies had time to rehearse and create new material. They could risk making work that might not succeed financially, that was difficult or dark. "I make the work I make because of state support," Jérôme Thomas told me bluntly.

Interestingly, it wasn't the first time the French state had rallied to haul an art into the present. In the sixties, recognizing that its modern-dance movement lagged behind other countries, especially America, the state injected money into the scene—for new companies, for national choreography centers, for a robust audience-development program. But the case of the circus was somewhat distinct. Though not always contemporary, dance in France has long been esteemed. In subsidizing the circus, the government was elevating it. It was asserting, for the first time, the importance of the art.

IN THE MIDST OF ALL THIS, Bernard Turin was thinking about ice. Born in 1940, he trained in painting and sculpture at Ateliers d'Art Sacré, and after graduation specialized in installations. His sculpture was often big ("monumental," according to one critic) and ephemeral. His most famous piece consisted of three thousand enormous fluorescent ice blocks, each one eight feet tall and bigger than a telephone booth, arranged on a beach like dominoes.

"It was for the Festival of American Film at Deauville in 1990," Turin said. We admired a newspaper article about the exhibit that was pinned to his wall. The picture of the piece was shot from at least a hundred yards away, but even at that distance the ice blocks looked enormous and Stonehengian. "I had been working for a decade, but my career was really taking off then."

It was also his final piece. Concurrent with his rise in sculpting, Turin had developed a conflicting passion: the flying trapeze. He had discovered the discipline as a sixteen-year-old, and by thirty was an accomplished amateur. In 1980, he purchased a rig and founded a part-time amateur school of his own, first in Bobigny, then in Rosny-sous-Bois. His timing was good. Government attention had jump-started interest in the circus as an amateur practice. Enrollment rose quickly. Within a matter of years, Turin had a tent and more than 350 students, several of whom departed regularly for competitions abroad and sometimes came home with medals. In 1988, in recognition of his success, he was elected the first president of the French Federation of Circus Schools (Fédération Française des Écoles de Cirque). The work there was part-time, but Turin was pleased with his schedule—sculpting by day, flying at night. "I was happy," he said. "I thought I had found life."

Then, in 1989, he received a call from Bernard Faivre d'Arcier, the director of theater and spectacles for the Ministry of Culture. He wanted to talk about the National School. It had become the government's one glaring failure in an otherwise successful plan to save the circus. Five years after its inception, the school was a mess. Students complained of dropped classes and a constantly changing curriculum. There was conflict among the faculty. "The school was split in half," Anny told me. "Teachers weren't even talking to each other."

The problem was a clash of cultures. In creating the school, the state had hoped to unify two worlds: the traditional circus and the modern circus. It intended for the skills of the former to be joined with the ideas of the latter. This proved difficult. The two camps were too far apart and could not unite around a common purpose. The traditionalists saw the modernists as hippies and upstarts who lacked respect for the customs and commitment of the art. The modernists thought the traditionalists were too stuck in their ways, unappreciative of the changes bubbling up in the form. The government cycled through a series of directors, four in five years, including Guy Caron (one of Soleil's founders). Each proved less effective than the last. Now the government was running out of patience. The squabbling was unbecoming of a national institution. The school was hemorrhaging money.

At their meeting, Faivre d'Arcier solicited Turin's opinion on the issue. Turin said the school's real problem was a lack of ambition. In creating the National School, the government relied on conventional models, largely drawn from the communist world. The first director, Richard Kubiak, was the former director of Polish circuses; his curriculum centered on the "master-pupil" relationship, wherein teachers spoke and students listened. The course load revolved around technical prowess, and each student graduated with a "number," a five-to-seven-minute act, to begin their careers. To Turin, the model was potentially effective but "artistically reductive." What was needed, he felt, was a more forward-thinking approach. Instead of technique, the school should emphasize creativity. It should be, he said, an art school that lived up to its name.

Prior to their meeting, Faivre d'Arcier had assured Turin that their talks would be purely informational. But at the door, as they prepared to part, he offered Turin the job of director.

"It was one of the great shocks of my life," Turin said in the studio. "My first instinct was to refuse." Although he considered himself a capable amateur coach, he had never performed or even worked in a circus. Besides, he had his sculpting career to think of. To walk away now would be professional suicide.

But Faivre d'Arcier responded with an offer Turin couldn't refuse: carte blanche. He would have the full backing of the government to remake the school however he chose. "It was an artist's dream," Turin told me. "I wasn't just making art. I was helping define an entire art form." This liberty was in fact a last-ditch attempt by the authorities to save their initiative. "We didn't know it then," Anny told me later, "but if it didn't work under Bernard they were going to close the school."

In the autumn of 1990, Turin assumed control of the Centre National des Arts du Cirque. As a first order of business, he split the school in half: in order to remove incoming students from the "poisoned" environment of Châlons, the first two years of study would take place at Rosny-sous-Bois, where he installed Anny, his former assistant, as a director and his proxy. Next, he overhauled the curriculum. Following up on his comments to Faivre d'Arcier, he scrapped the technical model and replaced it with a course of study based on his experience in the *beaux arts,* with an emphasis on innovation and interdisciplinarity (*polyvalence*), as expressed through "a kind of artistic osmosis." Drawing on his contacts in the art world, Turin invited a fleet of "contemporary creators" to teach workshops at the school. More than a hundred artists from all manner of disciplines—theater, painting, sculpting, composing, dance, writing, and filmmaking—would "nourish" the circus with lessons from their disciplines, while supplying the students with "a sense of the thinking and the conditions of the creator," so that they could eventually design their own shows.

In the circus world, especially among traditionalists, the policy changes were met with skepticism. People complained that the school lacked technical rigor. They said it was too intellectualized, too artistically driven. The school's "final exam" was particularly controversial. Instead of encouraging the students to develop a "number," Turin added a year of what he called "professional invention," during which the students would stay at the school and create a full-length modern circus show under the guidance of a professional theater director or choreographer.

To critics, the model was ridiculous: how would the students find jobs? Turin disagreed. He felt the new system would provide the students experience in creating original work and exposure to boot: each new show would premiere in Paris, where producers, critics, and government ministers would be watching.

In 1995, Turin's method was put to the test. After four years, his first complete class was graduating and would be performing its final show in Paris. As director, Turin had selected Joseph Nadj, a young Yugoslavian-born choreographer. It was a risky choice. Today Nadj is a bellwether of the French dance scene, but in 1995 he was still very much an upstart, known among modern-dance specialists for a dark, almost dystopian style that they liked to label "Kafkaesque." But Turin felt that Nadj "had something to offer the circus," an intense playfulness that would translate, and he offered the choreographer the same vote of confidence that Faivre d'Arcier had given Turin: carte blanche.

Nadj's show, entitled *Le Cri du caméléon* (*The Cry of the Chameleon*), premiered at the Parc de la Villette on January 12, 1996. The crowds who made the trek that night encountered a startling phenomenon. The show, based on a novel by Alfred Jarry, felt less like a circus than a piece of surrealist dance. The theme was metamorphosis, the tone abstract and unabashedly avant-garde. The performers dressed like Magritte characters, in tattered brown trench coats, baggy pants, and bowler hats. The music was discordant: trombones, snare drums, and xylophones battled messily. The circus skills were presented not as displays of prowess but as the work of bodies in motion, theatrical elements creating a world that was at times deliberately disturbing. For one handstand routine, an acrobat wore a white plaster-of-Paris mask. At the culmination of the show, the performers arranged themselves into a kind of giant slug and slithered across the stage. *Le Cri du caméléon* was, quite simply, the strangest circus France had ever seen.

It was also a smash hit. After several weeks of sellout crowds, La Villette was forced to install televisions outside the tent to accommodate the audience. The show toured for almost three years with the same cast, playing over three hundred performances in France and abroad. At every stop, critics hailed its originality and creativity.

Today, *Le Cri du caméléon* is considered one of the most important shows in modern circus history, in France and, by extension, the world. Previously, even the so-called new circuses adhered to fairly traditional structures; shows mostly consisted of unrelated acts, or "numbers," knit together by music or a loose story. In *Le Cri du caméléon*, Nadj aspired to create a more unified whole, a true mix of dance, theater, and circus. There was no boundry between the genres. Performers were actors as much as gymnasts. As a choreographer, Nadj brought a choreographer's ambition, with an attention to theme, rhythm, pace, unity of action, shape, energy, and time. The show had a clear and distinct voice, the way a painting can feel uniquely Degas, or a work of music uniquely Satie. "Never was a circus so clearly authored," Jean-Michel Guy noted.

Le Cri du caméléon was the first truly *modernist* circus: skeptical, self-referential, symbolist. But since the "modern circus" had already emerged, critics found another category to describe it. In *Libération*, Marc Laumonier wrote, "After the traditional circuses, then the *nouveaux cirques*, we should add henceforth the contemporary circus."

IT HAD BEEN SEVEN YEARS since the Parisian premiere of *Le Cri du caméléon*, but Turin was obviously still proud. "I was totally satisfied," he said animatedly. "It was a complete validation of the school and of our method. Joseph told me that the work was only possible because of the unique training of the students." After graduation, every student in the class found a job.

Since then, the school has continued to premiere a new show every year. Each stars a different batch of students working under a different director. Because the directors are encouraged to experiment and challenge prevailing notions of what a circus contains, each show is a case study of sorts. The year I was in France, for example, the show—*Bye Bye Prospero*, directed by theater director Christophe Lidon—explored circus and speech, with trapezists whispering breathily into wireless microphones.

Invariably, the reactions to the shows are mixed. Some are huge successes that tour widely, like *Le Cri du caméléon*. Many play once in Paris, travel a little, and die quietly. Traditionalists especially tend to find the shows aggravating. In the Clown Bar, Dominique Jando called Turin "a sculptor who makes circus like a sculptor." Later, he said the French circus was "dominated by intellectuals, by theater and dance people, with no sense of what the real circus is."

Nevertheless, the effect of Turin's vision—intellectualized, interdisciplinary, and culturally relevant circus—is undeniable. In France, the echoes are everywhere. Circus artists hoping for state support must submit stacks of information about their artistic intentions and their intended contribution to the aesthetic landscape. At French schools, the circus is taught as an inherently open and creative endeavor. At the National School, this openness can even be an issue. At the beginning of the second semester, when it came time for the students to choose a specialty, some of them refused, hoping to study "acrobatics in a general sense." (Frédéric's reply: "It doesn't work like that.")

Abroad, Turin's philosophy has spread, and more companies are making work according to the "contemporary circus." Circa, an Australian company, has become globally famous for their stripped-down mix of dance and acrobatics. "With a bare stage and some minimally thrumming music, the company creates moments of exemplary and sometimes astounding skill," circus critic John Ellingsworth has written. "Cutting out the chaff of imposed narrative or imagined character, they replace structure with rhythm." In Helsinki, Finland, where the contemporary circus scene is strong, the shows are minimalist and abstract. As Tomi Purovaara, director of the Finnish Circus Information Center, told me, "We learned a lot by studying what they did in France."

In Turin's studio, our cups were empty. He stood and escorted me to the door. On the way, we chatted about his regrets, the missed opportunities during his tenure as head of the school. He told me that he had always hoped to bring one of the great European directors in to direct a circus show, somebody like Peter Brook or Pina Bausch, the seminal German choreographer. "Pina and I actually discussed it once," he said, leaning into his cane. He had taken the students to see her show at Avignon, the important European theater festival, and, afterward, she had joined them for dinner. As they were eating, Turin pitched her on the idea of doing a show at the school. "She liked the idea, but of course it was only a fantasy. The circus is young yet. I never could have afforded her."

While Turin was talking, I happened to notice a pair of star-shaped silver medals on the shelf behind him. They were resting in a pair of velvet-lined jewelry boxes amid a sea of bric-a-brac. One was inlaid with blue, the other with green.

I asked Turin where they came from. He smiled. They had been given to him by the Minister of Culture. One proclaimed him a Chevalier dans l'Ordre Nationale du Mérite. The other the Chevalier des Arts et des Lettres. Both were orders created by de Gaulle after World War II, to celebrate contributions to French society, a bit like knighthood in Britain.

The medals struck me as indicative. Even if the circus was still young, even if it did have a long way to go, it had come even further. Just over thirty years before, the art had been a part of the Ministry of Agriculture. Now the Minister of Culture was awarding medals for its development. I was reminded of a question that had been on my mind for some time. It was obvious, but it also struck me as complex: Why? As in, why had the French government cared enough about the circus to undertake the enormous effort of renovation?

"Bah, c'était nécessaire," Turin said, when I put the question to him. "For a long time, the circus was the popular art *par excellence*. Everybody came to the circus. You can see this in old pictures. You had the king in his box, and the aristocrats in their loge, and then the working class up top. It was a mix of every social and economic class."

Over the twentieth century, the circus declined. A new popular art rose to take its place: television.

"But television is different," Turin continued. "A popular art should bring people together. It should unify them and pull them upward." It should engender civic discussion, aid in intellectual and moral development, inspire and enliven. "Unfortunately, television doesn't do this," Turin said. "Instead of pulling the people upward, it pulls them downward. Instead of bringing them together, it isolates them."

And so the state turned to the circus, which, despite its suffering, remained a place where people of all classes, races, and viewpoints could gather.

"I truly understood this for the first time at *Le Cri du caméléon*," Turin said. On the surface, the show was a moody avant-garde theater piece. "But when I looked at the audience in the tent, I saw all sorts of people you'd never see at a regular theater show. There were people from every rung of society—intellectuals and children, the bourgeoisie and the working class—all taking pleasure together."

Listening to Turin talk about the role of art in the world, I fully appreciated, for the first time, how unmitigatedly *French* the whole thing was. The French hold a belief in the power of art to influence society, in the benefits of creativity and personal refinement. De Gaulle's and Malraux's post–World War II offering of *"élitisme pour tous,"* or elitism for everyone, was an extension of this belief. In the eighties, the idea further flourished as part of Jack Lang's larger effort to cultivate popular arts, from jazz (with the creation of a National Jazz Orchestra) to the circus.

Today in France art is everywhere. In Paris alone there are 120 festivals every year and 130 theaters. "You have the sense that theater is a part of their culture, and not in a superficial way," my American friend Tina said during our trip to the Boulevard du Crime. "It's part of their cultural conversation." Artists I spoke with took for granted that their society supported them and expected them to participate in the public sphere. "The artist gives to life, as to the world, flavor, sense, and beauty," former French president Jacques Chirac once said. "Mirror to mankind, he decodes his soul."

How you feel about the government's including circus in this effort depends on your feelings about the circus in general and about government intervention. If you're a purist who appreciated the old circus, then you probably don't like it at all. If you're laissez-faire, or given to cynicism, then you might consider it manipulative, a way of seducing the masses into art appreciation the way you con children into eating vegetables by putting them on pizza.

In any case, it will be interesting to see how long the French attitude survives. During my stay, there were indications that the nation might be changing. Economic forces and conservative politicians were threatening the financial support that the state offered to performers between engagements. This *"intermittent du spectacle"* statute is critical to the work of all performing artists, and circus artists especially, since they often rely on it during periods of training and creation. According to Fred Cardon, a circus producer, shows would immediately grow smaller without that support. Prices would rise. The work would have to be less risky, since artists would need to survive on their performance revenues longer, lest they be forced to take slightly demeaning work (which Jérôme, in his inimitable way, calls "playing Santa at the mall").

During my time in France, artists and technicians rallied against the measures, signing petitions, writing stinging articles, gathering en masse. One night I joined an immense crowd of artists and supporters of the arts—a million strong, the papers later said—who had gathered at the Bastille to march toward Place de la République. Street protests in Paris are nothing novel—there seems to be one a week—but this one was especially large and had an air of adventure. Many cultural venues had gone on strike in solidarity with the artists. The cinemas canceled their film showings, and enormous banners hung from cultural institutions, such as *"Opéra Bastille en grève."* "You will not turn our country into a cultural desert!" someone shouted. A moment later, a woman appeared next to me in a clown wig and a red nose. The next thing I knew, we were moving together down the Boulevard du Crime.

20

Cirque de Demain

THIS TRAIN IS a goddamn circus," the stranger muttered as he moved down the crowded aisle. Fanny watched him pass, her head propped against the window, then returned her gaze to the lush countryside racing by. She released a small but noticeable sigh. "I'm not sure how I feel about that expression."

It was the audition day, and we were on the move, to the branch of the National School in Châlons-en-Champagne. For the young women, the day marked the culmination of years of work, and their nervousness showed. Maud couldn't stop commenting on the passing scenery, on the appealing shape of the houses and the lazy looks on the faces of cows chewing grass in the fields. Fanny popped her gum incessantly and had the music on her headphones cranked up loud enough for me to hear it over the noise of the train. Personally, I was thrilled. With the easy end to the year, I had found my thoughts drifting less to the past and more into the future: Where was the circus going? What would the next generation contribute to this evolving art? The day would provide the chance to investigate.

In Châlons-en-Champagne, we piled off the train and hiked through the center of town, which was cute, vine-strewn, and cobblestoned, yet stained by hints of industry in decline. Over a muddy brown river, sooty buildings loomed ominously. It was barely noon, and already the park benches were packed with men drinking from plastic bottles of beer. The school, I was disappointed to find, was in similarly rough shape. The red paint on the front doors was blistered and marred by several wide pink swaths, failed attempts to camouflage graffiti. The plaster façade of the building appeared to have been laid into by a machete. Cracks slithered toward its cupola.

Fanny and Maud disappeared through a pair of glass doors to check in. I lingered on a wooden fence outside, basking in the buzz of the crowd. Nervous kids stood clustered together in a parking lot nearby. Around the periphery, solitary parents hovered anxiously, eyeing each other over steaming cups of coffee.

According to Turin, during the school's early years it had struggled to recruit students from diverse backgrounds. The new circus had been around for twenty years and state-supported for ten, but the general public still regarded the circus with suspicion, and so parents—especially middle-class parents—had trouble accepting their children's interest in the school. "They thought their kids were running off to become chicken thieves," Turin said. Accordingly, the kids who had enrolled tended to be those who struggled in traditional academic settings. Rebels themselves, they were attracted to the circus's outsider reputation.

Today this has changed. As the circus penetrated the mainstream, it became less of a professional risk. Parents understood the circus: they had attended shows like Cirque Plume and Cirque du Soleil and seen circus performers in hotel and car advertisements. There was an infrastructure to support their children, a network of schools, venues, and resources. "Parents today have a better understanding of the life their kids are choosing,"

Turin said. "It's a viable professional field, something between sports and performance." Accordingly, the school's demographic had shifted. The kids today are working-class, bourgeois, high-school graduates, some college graduates. "It's easier now for a kid with other options to choose the circus," Turin said.

In the parking lot, I couldn't help noticing traces of this shift in the kids' behavior (lots of amiable chatting) and the parents' dress (khakis, windbreakers, fitted leather gloves). Later, I tracked down one of the parents, a dowdy dad named Pierre. In a neon-green jacket with a logo on the pocket that looked vaguely molecular, he was pacing circles around a tree, puffing Gauloise after Gauloise, trying to distract himself from what the fate of his son, Guillaume, would be. I asked Pierre if Turin was right, if parents were more open to the circus than they used to be.

"It depends," he said. "I'm all for it. His mother still has some issues."

I asked him what the problem was—safety?

"No, it's nothing like that. It's more the conversations. You know, 'What does your son do?' 'Well, actually he's training to be a contortionist.' " Pierre paused. "It's not something you expect yourself to be saying as a parent."

BEFORE DEPARTING FOR CHÂLONS, I had sat down with Frédéric. As director of programming, he could give me the best sense of the selection process. It is cringe-inducingly tough.

The test unfurled in three phases. In the early spring, the school received over three hundred applications from around the world, including dossiers describing each applicant's training and goals, plus a video sample. Working with a team of administrators, Anny and Frédéric trimmed the group to 120, all of whom received an invitation to the "pre-selection." This test, which I would be observing, lasted two days (sixty students per day) and consisted of classes in the school's major disciplines: acting, dancing, and acrobatics.

"In the pre-selection it's mathematical," Frédéric explained. Judges—mostly professors from the National School—graded the students on the same scale that Luc had used at the beginning of the year: 0 for hapless, 7 for breathtaking. At the end of the day, the judges met together and tallied their marks. The candidates with the top forty scores moved on to the final round. The only exception, Frédéric noted, came when a student failed to score at least the median in acrobatics. "If you're not at least an average acrobat, you don't belong in a professional circus school."

In France, most of the top universities—in engineering, politics, law—select their students through rigorous exams called *concours*. For the circus, the *concours*, the third round, is like a cross between a bar exam and an NBA training camp, complete with cafeteria-style meals and dormitory beds. The whole process, which is meant to determine the fifteen best circus prospects, lasts ten days and covers most physical disciplines (juggling, jumping, the splits), plus a battery of artistic workshops. The judges pay attention not only to a candidate's achievement but also to her responsiveness to teaching and guidance. "We want to get a sense of how they might develop," Frédéric said. Do they seem eager to improve? Can they integrate criticism into their work?

There's also a social component. Attending the National School is an intense experience: classes are small, quarters close. Trust is obviously a big issue, both in the training room and outside. ("It starts to feel like you're alone in this little circus world," Tiriac, a freshman, once said to me.) Given this, the school watches how the students relate, how they chat and bond in between classes.

The goal, Frédéric said, was to pick a cohort as much as individuals. "We want a balance of skills," he said, "but we really want team players, people who can listen and share. The circus is an inherently collaborative endeavor. We think the same qualities that allow students to excel at the school would also allow them to excel in a company: teamwork, a certain humility, an interest in placing the company over yourself."

To this end, the school is willing to make sacrifices. I discovered this one wintry night when I accompanied a dozen freshmen to one of Paris's famous cabarets. We sat front row, thanks to a student named Jonas, who went to prep school with a juggler in the show, Vincent. The night is mostly a fuzzy memory, a wash of bright plumage and bare breasts, but I remember Vincent's entrance distinctly. About twenty minutes in, he came bounding on, with thick pectorals and biceps bulging under a stretchy shirt. He sprang into the air in a *grand écart*, landing in full splits. He could juggle seven balls, upright or inverted. He could back-flip high and tight.

Unfortunately, he was also as cloying as a cell-phone salesman. In the lobby, where we met him after the show, he greeted us with high-fives and winks. When I told him I was American, he asked me if I was carrying a gun and then pretended to shoot me with his fingers. ("Bang! Bang!")

As we were leaving, Étienne, another student, mentioned that Vincent had applied for the National School the year before and had been rejected. I asked him why. He shrugged. "I think he's just not what they're looking for."

THROUGH THE SCHOOL'S narrow interior hallway, packed now with circus hopefuls, Maud and Fanny moved toward a list of classes taped to the wall. On the bus, there had been some vague hopes expressed that the school might pair the girls together, but this was not to be: Maud would start with dance, Fanny with acrobatics.

I opted to follow Maud first, and we made our way into a mirror-lined studio where a group of jittery candidates had formed a line of spandex against the wall. It was a noticeably young group. The school's official entrance age is sixteen to twenty-three, and many kids apply as early as possible, to have multiple opportunities to pass the test. Surprisingly, the group was also mostly female—surprising because the majority of the graduating classes at the National School had been disproportionately male. (The only explanation for that I ever heard came from Luc. "Men are generally better acrobats than women," he told me in a moment of candor. "They're more willing to take risks.")

The test passed quickly and frantically. A parade of clipboard-wielding judges entered and arranged themselves silently near the door. Carine, a dance teacher at the school, emerged from the group and led the candidates through a brief warm-up followed by a rigorous series of dance combinations choreographed to Dave Brubeck's "Take Five." (If France's National School had a sound track, Dave Brubeck would occupy half the tracks, Jacques Brel another third.) Normally meek and encouraging, Carine put on a drill sergeant's growl for show. "Push the sky!" she barked. "Push the ground! Don't just link the moves. Move *through* them! *Soyez dynamique!*"

The students lurched around the room with frightened looks. I watched Maud. Dancing wasn't her strong suit—she's too tentative—but she held up well, and this despite some stiff competition. The school makes no secret about the contents of the test; most applicants arrive with at least a little dance training. (For guys this can be an issue, though less than it used to be since forms like hip-hop and Capoeira have become more popular.)

After fifty minutes or so, a bell rang in the hallway. The students flooded into the hall, energized. I spotted Fanny on the other side of the hall. I plowed my way toward her, and together we slipped into her next test: acting.

Unlike dance, which is stressed in the curriculum, acting occupied a peculiar position at the National School. For freshmen and sophomores, it was a core yet secondary skill, a bit like music lessons, with less frequent classes than in acrobatics or dance. I thought it was an odd arrangement, given the prominence and importance of acting in professional shows, not to mention the relevance of the training. Acting teaches a performer how to understand the conceptual core of a piece; it determines her ability to source and channel her emotions, to re-create an interior state that transcends not only however she happens to be feeling in that moment but whatever *specific physical act* she happens to be performing.

The test seemed to confirm the necessity of acting training. The applicants were dreadful. One little bruiser, a floppy-haired man built like a linebacker, played every scene with a sneer and a low growl, as if impersonating Robert De Niro. Before the improvisation portion of the test, the teacher had to explain to several others how improvisation worked. ("It's like make-believe. Whatever comes from your imagination is valid.") The scene reminded me of watching athletes in television commercials, and what a rare thing it was for a person to be both physically and expressively gifted.

Fortunately, Fanny was the exception to the rule. As the daughter of actors, she was easily the best in the room, and it was largely her acting ability that carried her through to the next round. Later, after I had returned to America, I would hear that she had been cut in the last round, just like the year before. I was sad at the news, but I knew she would be all right. There are worse places to be an actress than Paris.

BEFORE COMING TO FRANCE I had never heard of, much less been to, a circus library. Now they were a fetish of mine. The library at CNAC was supposed to be exemplary. I had been hearing about it since the beginning of the year. "Oh, wait until you get to Châlons," Anny had told me during our tour of her own collection, a few shelves in a trailer. "That's serious."

During lunch break, I made my way up to the library, which was tucked off a narrow hallway on the second floor. The place immediately struck me as almost pitifully small, the size of a modest classroom. Half-empty shelves lined three of the walls.

Near the door, a woman in orange glasses sat behind an impressively messy desk. This was the head librarian, Miriam. We soon embarked on what she generously called a "tour." She pointed out what was on the various shelves while rotating like a weathervane. She showed me a metal cabinet containing the boxed archives of Tristan Rémy, the influential circus historian. "The lock on the cabinet is broken," she said as she jiggled the handle. I asked what exactly the boxes contained. "You know, we've never really had the time to go through them," she replied.

Just as I was about to leave, the librarian produced something that changed my mind not only about the library, but also about the future of circus.

"Can you tell what it is?" she asked.

I was looking at a book she had presented to me. It was spiral-bound and as thick as a dictionary. Flipping through it, I judged it to be some kind of catalogue. Every page outlined a different show, with a list of acts and names next to each. The old-time circuses kept what were known in the business as "route books," thorough logs of their activities—expense reports, towns visited, miles traveled, plus descriptions of special events. But this wasn't detailed enough to be a route book. And the shows listed were too new; the majority seemed to be from the last decade. Stumped, I asked what the book was.

"They're films!" the librarian announced proudly. She tapped a number in the corner of each page—the running time.

I ran my thumb through the book. There had to be hundreds of them.

"A lot of the films we took ourselves," she went on cheerily. "We have a videographer on staff. I mean, he's based here, but he travels all over, filming. And not just shows. He records workshops, rehearsals, lectures, events—anything related to the circus. We want to record the history as it's being made."

I had thought before about the role of technology in contemporary circus. Circus artists are increasingly incorporating video and digital effects in their shows. The Internet revolutionized how performers book gigs, how they find inspiration, even how they learn—in the modern world, anybody with a decent Internet connection can tutor herself on everything from a back handspring to a pratfall. Stupidly, though, I had never reflected on the effect of technology on circus history, and it excited me to think about it now. Video makes it economically feasible for the art to have a lasting legacy. In the future, a circus historian will be able to read about Les Arts Sauts and watch them fly, to observe Jérôme Thomas for himself. The art's history will play a greater role in the present. Every historian must view this change as important—what would a Civil War historian give for a live recording of the Battle of Gettysburg? And for the circus, the difference is particularly seminal. For the first time, the skills of an artist can live on after she is gone.

DOWNSTAIRS, the hallway was empty. The tests were rolling again. I could hear the murmur of commands and vocal warm-ups and, from somewhere, Brubeck's "Take Five" again. At the end of the hallway, a pair of glass doors led to the parking lot. Through them, I could see the parents milling around. In a few hours the kids would come streaming out, hopeful and spent.

I checked the schedule on the wall. Maud's acrobatics section was all that remained. But there was something else I wanted to look into first. Following a hunch, I pushed through a set of double doors along the interior wall of the hallway, which led to a set of cement stairs. I climbed them and, sure enough, found they opened onto a landing surrounded by a railing, overlooking the old ring.

I knew of the space from my reading. Built in 1889, the building had witnessed a century of highs and lows. According to Charles Degeldère and Dominique Denis, who write about the building in *Cirques en bois, cirque en pierre de France*, its inaugural show was *Cuba*, a three-act pantomime "celebrating a glorious episode of the Spanish-American War." Not long after, with the circus at its apex, a telepath named Lucile made an appearance, followed by Barnum & Bailey, which passed through on the westward leg of its great European tour.

The high times lasted for decades. Then, during World War II, the building took several direct hits, and it fell into disuse. For several years, the circus lay dormant. That it survived at all was mere good fortune. With the decline of manufacturing, workers migrated to bigger cities, and factories in Châlons had closed. There was such a glut of property that nobody felt the need to tear the old circus down.

The space was quiet now, empty and small, almost quaint compared with other rings I had seen. Eight rows of wooden benches encircled a simple floor littered with the sort of detritus I had come to associate with circus training grounds: a plastic water bottle, a juggler's club. There was nothing showy or even decorative about the space. Hairline fissures wriggled through the plaster ceiling. The benches, once bright red, had faded to dull pink, with ghostly white splotches marking the spots of heavy traffic. The only real ornament was the cupola in the ceiling, a circular crown of dirty windows. Hazy sheets of sunshine poured down into the ring.

I felt unexpectedly moved by it all. There was something comforting about the simplicity of a ring surrounded only by benches. I walked down and took a seat.

According to the librarian, the building was scheduled for renovation that summer. The classrooms, the library, the ring—the whole thing would be given a $7-million face lift, as part of France's developing interest in circus patrimony. Of course, I was happy to hear it. A few of France's other circus buildings had been renovated, and the results were impressive. In Elbeuf, Normandy, the *"cirque-théâtre,"* constructed in 1892, with a stage overlooking the ring, had been redone. During the spring, I had paid a visit. On walking into the space, I nearly fell over. The enormous proscenium had been re-created with the original staff—a gypsum compound resembling plaster of Paris—and then painted a glowing baby blue. "The companies are excited to perform here," Roger Le Roux, the director of the space, told me. "They feel as though they are connecting to something."

Even so, I was thankful I had come to Châlons before the repairs. The building would look magnificent all dressed up, but something authentic would be lost. In the space now, there was a raggedness that testified to the building's resilience. In the dim, dusty light, I felt as though I was seeing the circus in its original state. For once I didn't have to imagine the history.

DURING MY TRIP to Montreal with Pascal, as we left the Tohu one evening, we had spoken about where the circus was going, about how the form would evolve. There were reasons for optimism. The possibilities for professional growth look good. According to rumors, Soleil has its gargantuan eye trained on Asia, specifically China and India, where a rising economic tide is lifting millions of people into the middle class, affording them the opportunity to travel to cities like Macao, the Vegas of China, where nightly receipts already quintuple those of the American gambling capital. If Soleil can convince these tourists to spend their yuan on circus instead of gambling, the circus stands to profit handily.

But for the first time it might have real competition. In 2000, Franco Dragone, Soleil's old artistic muse, returned to his boyhood town of La Louvière, Belgium, where he established the Franco Dragone Entertainment Group, a company bent on creating shows to rival Soleil. One of Dragone's first productions, *Le Rêve,* was a $110-million spectacle at the Wynn Resort in Vegas. More recently, he created *The House of Dancing Water,* a $250-million water extravaganza for Macao. Not long after, Soleil was forced to close its own $150-million Macao show, *Zaia,* due to poor attendance. A spokesman for the company claimed that China wasn't ready for circus, that that entertainment sector was underdeveloped. This is hard to believe: across the street, Dragone was doing 95 percent capacity.

Behemoths aside, the circus is poised to grow in other ways. Circus schools have continued to emerge around the world. In Rabat, Morocco, the Minister of Professional Training had recently sanctioned the first circus school, L'École Nationale de Cirque Shems'y. In Puebla, Mexico, the Universidad Mesoamericana recently added a Center for the Development of Circus Arts, a four-year professional training program with an emphasis on "the creative body language specific to the aesthetic of contemporary circus."

Meanwhile, modern companies continue to appear in places previously untouched by the form as well. One such company is Sapana in Nepal. Every year, dozens of Nepalese young people are sold into Indian circuses against their will. A nonprofit organization, the Esther Benjamins Trust, works to rescue them. Sapana is the result of a collaboration between the trust and a group of British circus artists who wanted to give the children hope and work after they returned to their homeland.

America is another place that has seen a recent resurgence, especially at the amateur level. Around the country, community circuses have sprouted up, such as the Stone Soup Circus, based in Princeton, New Jersey, the mission of which is to "build community through sharing the fun of circus." The States has also seen an uptick in circus education. The American Youth Circus Organization, America's network of youth circuses and circus educators, currently includes more than two hundred programs, with 350 total members. Most major cities have at least one school, and the biggest of them are major operations. The Minneapolis-based Circus Juventas, founded by Dan and Betty Butler in 1994, has an annual budget that tops $2 million and a tent that cost another $2.1 million. At any given time, over eight hundred students are enrolled in their classes, with another 250 waiting to join. When I met Betty at their facility in Minneapolis, she was exhausted but ecstatic. "It's like a runaway train down a mountain!" she told me.

That said, America also faces a particular problem. Though the boom in amateur interest had led to the same renewed interest in circus as in Europe, it hasn't necessarily translated into professional artistic work. Currently, there are few working circus artists in America and almost no full-fledged companies. There's no professional group to advocate for the sector, no major festival where performers can meet, and, most critically, no professional training ground. What makes this especially frustrating is that America was an early adapter of the form: during the late sixties and early seventies, the country produced some of the first circus schools, and many of the early modern vanguards, such as the aforementioned Michael Moschen, Bill Irwin, and the Pickle Family Circus.

What happened? Two factors contributed heavily: reputation and economics. As elsewhere, traditional notions of circus have proved a burden, and arguably more so than in Europe. Even during the down days, the European circus retained a certain artistic dignity. The most traditional European shows, like the Circus Knie in Switzerland, are still performed in a single ring. Groomed horses feature prominently, and their riders often wear cravats.

In America, by contrast, the traditional circus is louder and wilder. It's bigger and more overtly popular—the three-ring extravaganzas of Barnum & Bailey, and the hundred-car trains of Ringling Brothers. Moreover, the American circus history was rougher, filled with freaks and con men, which taints our modern conception of the form. As Jay Gilligan once told me, when he was touring with his first company he and his partner had struggled to find a label for their work that wouldn't stigmatize them. "We couldn't say 'juggler,' because that had a negative 'clown' sense in America," he said. "We couldn't say 'artist,' because that sounded too pretentious. We certainly couldn't say 'performance artist'—that's like shooting yourself in the head." Eventually, they chose to describe their work as "postmodern juggling," a phrase they appropriated from a review. The moniker was potentially esoteric, but it served their purpose. "It mostly left them confused, but in a way that we could explain ourselves. It would start a conversation."

But even the historical challenges facing American artists pale when compared with the economic woes. America has no Ministry of Culture, and little public funding for the arts. (The entire National Endowment for the Arts, America's cultural fund, hovers around $150 million, roughly equal to what the French government spends annually to support the Paris Opera.) Of course there's private money—foundational grants, corporate sponsorship, donations from deep pockets—but donors like local causes, and foundations tend to favor established institutions, not arts trying to reinvent themselves. To make matters worse, most grant applications don't include a section for the circus, and certain arts bodies—including the New York State Council for the Arts—explicitly ban funding for circuses, since they associate the form with carnivals. "With a lot of description, you can get beyond their prejudices and show that there are theatrical merits to your work," Keith Nelson of the Bindlestiff Family Cirkus in New York told me. Often he applies the category of "performance art." "It is a joke, but it's also the reality. They understand classical theater as being important to the history of art, whereas circus is not."

For the time being, some Americans circumvent these problems by teaching. Many more work day jobs and channel their passion into nights and weekends. For serious performers, the most popular route is commercial or corporate work. They flip in rap videos, twirl on trapezes at car conventions, lead workshops for hundreds of employees with ladder-balancing acts that symbolize the climb to the top. The gigs can be lavish (one juggling duo purportedly makes $20,000 per show). They can travel the world, sleep at the best hotels; one performer, Christine Van Loo, at the Hermitage in Saint Petersburg, soared above the stage at a Paul McCartney concert before a crowd including Vladimir Putin, a squadron of military leaders, and a hundred thousand Russians with tears streaming down their cheeks.

Over time, however, such work cuts with the proverbial double edge. It employs circus skills divorced from circus context, and devoid of much of what makes the circus special: culture, community, collaboration. "It's basically a commercial transaction," Aloysia Gavre, a Los Angeles–based circus director, told me. "You arrive at three p.m. Do your light check, check your rigging. Okay, here's a little dance number we're going to do at the top of the show. Great. Do your act. Here's your paycheck."

Many performers are of course happy to have this paycheck, and some take great satisfaction and pride in the gigs. Over time, though, they've had a detrimental effect on the circus as an art form in America. "Performers lost intention," Gavre said. "They lost integrity—really, the ethics of what it means to be part of a troupe." Today this challenge endures. After years on the commercial cycle, a performer might find herself less willing and possibly less able to suffer the pangs of real art-making, to endure whatever misery or failure it takes to create work of her own in an unwelcoming climate. "The next generation hasn't come around yet," Gypsy Snider said. "When you're young and doing circus, you don't want to be bothered to invest and take on the responsibility of a company." She added, "Dedicating your life to a circus company here is almost suicidal."

How American artists respond to and evolve under these circumstances, especially now that interest is rising, will dictate their future. Many believe the circus could thrive here. "The market is there," LeClair said, after pointing out that his troupe sells 94 percent of the tickets for every show. Demographics also seem to be working in favor of the circus. Americans are redeveloping downtowns, leading to a rising interest in urban live entertainment. "What's missing are the producers," LeClair said. "If a few capable people decided to get involved, the whole thing could explode."

....

IN A CAB IN MONTREAL, Pascal and I chatted about all this. His most impassioned moment came not in reference to the modern circus, but to the traditional circus, the old animal shows. When I asked him what he thought would happen to such shows, he grew quiet for a long moment, his eyes panned out the window at the cityscape of this new circus capital.

"I really don't know what will happen," he said finally. "Will Cirque du Soleil continue to grow, with four, six, eight, ten, twelve, twenty, forty, fifty more shows touring in the world? Yes, I'd say that's possible. And if that happened, it would truly be a *bouleversement*." It would be an upheaval, because, wherever Soleil appears, it imposes a new definition on the local landscape, a new image of the circus, which the traditional shows are often unable to survive. "It could kill the conventional circus entirely. In a sense, it might *become* the new traditional circus. And that would be sad."

I thought about this while overlooking the ring in Châlons.

Pascal is a modern, an intellectual in the purest sense, but the idea of losing the traditional circus hit him hard. He had grown up leaning his elbows on the ring at Cirque d'Hiver, feeling his heart soar to brass-band marches, admiring the turn of the tigers, smelling their musk in the sawdust. The traditional circus was a wonderful world for him.

I had no such associations, especially now. After nine months, the modern circus had come to dominate my perspective, to define the art in my head as much as or more than the old clichés. Yet, just as I was glad to have visited this building before its renovation, I was happy to have discovered the circus now, before it changed completely. Over the year, I had come to appreciate the old form, historically but also aesthetically. I attended traditional shows whenever I could. I found even the worst shows endearing; the best, like the Cirque National Alexis Gruss, exemplars of a kind of quaint, classical form of skill. I had a respect for their discipline, grit, and resilience. Ironically, I had now come to love the circus that had bored me as a boy.

I heard a rising commotion in the hallway, the sound of the students flooding between sessions, laughing, chatting. Maud's acrobatics test was next. I would go watch her rip her way through the routines. Three months later, on the final test, she would score just as well, and cruise into the school, part of the next generation.

I stood and walked down to the ring. In the modern circus, performers are moving away from the ring. The majority of the shows I see occur on theatrical stages, or in nontraditional spaces like the dome of Les Arts Sauts. And yet performers look to the ring with an unexpected romanticism and affection. They like to talk about the strange power of standing in the middle of a ring, the eyes of a crowd converging on you from all sides. "The public is close to you, but there's no sense of opposition," Hélène Cadiou, the *secrétaire générale* at the Cirque-Théâtre d'Elbeuf, told me. "They surround you, almost like they're protecting you." There are even those who feel that the ring defines the circus, that the art, in its purest sense, should rely on a space more than an assembly of forms. During the planning stages for the Tohu, Lavoie told me, the architects originally proposed a square building. "But then we attended the Festival Mondial de Cirque du Demain at Cirque d'Hiver, the famous hard circus in Paris, and everything changed," Lavoie said. "We sat down in the building and we understood right away what a circus is. When the lights came up, we all agreed that the building had to be round."

I descended the cement stairs and stepped over the metal railing and hopped down into the ring. It was the first time I had been in one. The floor was made of hard rubber. A narrow entrance led into a hallway. I staked out the center of the ring and stood there. Even without an audience, I understood immediately what the performers had been talking about. I had the sensation of imaginary eyes on my back and the instinct to turn—and keep turning. It occurred to me how rarely—if ever at all—I was completely surrounded.

When Philip Astley created his first circus ring in 1768, he chose the shape to aid the riding master: he stood in the middle of the ring with his whip and kept the horses turning around him. But the ring predated Astley. It went back to the riding masters who innovated equestrian theater—to Johnson, Bates, and Sampson. It went back to the itinerant performers who gathered crowds on dusty crossroads and cobblestone town plazas. It went back to the earliest memories of man. "The circus isn't just a show," Pascal had said in Montreal, surrounded by his relics from the circus past. "It's a link through time. At the risk of being dramatic, it's the closest thing we have to the origins of human spectacle, to men sitting around a fire in a cave, casting fantastical shadows on the walls, larger-than-life impressions of themselves. That was the original *mise en jeu*, the point of departure for everything theatrical that followed. There were no words, no drama, just the presence of the body. The body expresses the story, and its impact is as strong as words."

For a period, I thought, this connection had been in danger of being lost. But to judge by the joyous, anxious din in the hallway—the excited chatter of the circus's next generation—that danger had now passed.

Acknowledgments

Hundreds of people have contributed their time and energy to see this book through to completion. I couldn't name them all, but a few deserve particular mention. First, my family—Mark, Claudia, Erin, and Bryan—supported me throughout. My editor at Knopf, Jonathan Segal, took a chance on the book and was endlessly patient with me, a rarity in publishing, and under especially trying circumstances. Thank you, Jon. Also, a special thanks to Jane Chelius, my agent, for helping the book find a home and guiding a rookie writer through the complexities of publishing, and to Joey McGarvey, Lena Khidritskaya, Meghan Houser, and the whole team at Knopf, who made the book a reality. Tim Bradley and Judith Muster suffered through some particularly late nights to help see the book out the door. Dominique Jando, Andrew Winchur, Sarah Fishbein, Amy Cohen, Martha Gribbins, Karen Lange, Joran Elias, Audrey Elias, Hollie Sexton, Rosemary Wells, Megan Hyslop, Cata Ratiu, and Andrew Middleton all read portions and offered helpful suggestions. The experience upon which the book is based would not have been possible without the generous support of the Fulbright Commission, who facilitated the journey, and without the openness of Anny Goyer and the entire staff at the L'École des Arts du Cirque de Rosny-sous-Bois, for letting me into their world for a year. During my time in France and for years afterward, Pascal Jacob, a circophile if there ever was one, patiently tolerated my ceaseless questions. Anna-Karyna Barlati, Rainie Themer, Maureen Brunsdale, Cirque du Soleil, and Steve Gossard assisted with the research. Fréderic Thevenet, Mose Hayward, and Tina Sherwood played along. And a special thanks to all the circus performers, advocates, and thinkers who took the time to speak with me, especially Fred Dahlinger, Jr., Jay Gilligan, Jérôme Thomas, Les Arts Sauts, André Riot-Sarcey, Collectif AOC, Gulko, and Steve Smith. The book is meant to be the record of a community, and these people are the exemplars of it. Circus history is notoriously sketchy. I've done my best to find the facts, but I'm sure there are mistakes. They are my responsibility. A few events have been shifted in time to help the narrative, but every person and action is real. Please go see them perform. Nothing I can write could do justice to their abilities.

Index

Page numbers in *italics* refer to illustrations.

ILLUSTRATION CREDITS

3, 13, 19, 54, 76, 93, 123, 181, 205, 218, 276; insert pages 1 (top right), 3 (top left), 4 (bottom left): Used with permission from Illinois State University's Special Collections, Milner Library

41, 108, 134, 169, 237, 293; insert pages 1 (top left), 1 (bottom), 2 (top), 2 (bottom left), 3 (top right), 3 (bottom), 4 (top left), 5 (bottom), 6 (bottom): Courtesy Collection Jacob-William, Tohu Cité des Arts du Cirque, Montreal, Canada

151, 254; insert pages 4–5 (top), 5 (center), 6 (top): Courtesy of Timothy Noel Tegge—Tegge Circus Archives, Baraboo, Wisconsin

Insert page 2 (bottom right): Courtesy of Steve Gossard

Insert page 4 (bottom right): James McAllister Collection, Alexander Turnbull Library, Wellington, New Zealand

Insert pages 6 (center), 7 (top), 7 (center), 8 (bottom left): Christophe Raynaud de Lage

Insert page 7 (bottom): Michael Meske

Insert page 8 (top): Martin Gallone

Insert page 8 (bottom right): Cirque du Soleil